The Stories They Told Me

The Stories They Told Me

The Life of My Deaf Parents

Maria Wallisfurth

Translated by Cornelia Wallisfurth

Gallaudet University Press
Washington, DC

In memory of Peter Jankowsky, a sensitive artist and a friend

Gallaudet University Press
Washington, DC 20002
http://gupress.gallaudet.edu

Printed in the United States of America

Library of Congress Cataloging-in-Publication Data

Names: Wallisfurth, Maria, 1927– author.
Title: The stories they told me : the life of my deaf parents / Maria Wallisfurth ; translated by Cornelia Wallisfurth.
Other titles: Sie hat es mir erzählt. German
Description: Washington, DC : Gallaudet University Press, [2017]
Identifiers: LCCN 2017004996 | ISBN 9781944838027 (pbk. : alk. paper) | ISBN 9781944838034 (e-book)
Subjects: LCSH: Giefer, Maria, 1897– | Deaf—Germany—Biography.
Classification: LCC HV2747.G53 W3413 2017 | DDC 362.4/2092243—dc23
LC record available at https://lccn.loc.gov/2017004996

First published in 1979 in Germany by Verlag Herder under the title *Sie hat es mir erzählt* (*She Told Me*).

∞ This paper meets the requirements of ANSI/NISO Z39.48-1992 (Permanence of Paper).

Preface

Alexandrine is a beautiful name.

It was the name of my godmother, my father's mother. As was the custom then in Catholic Rhineland, I should have been named after her. But my parents, Wilhelm and Maria, who were born deaf, found it difficult to say and lipread *Alexandrine*, and so my father gave me the same name as my mother.

My parents subscribed to a daily paper. Every morning, my father put me on his knee, and in his incomprehensible, but to me so familiar, voice he taught me the letters of the alphabet from the paper. When I started school at the age of six, I was already able to read.

The exceptional situation of my parents, and of myself, caused me to ask early for the why and how. I wanted to know the story of their lives—where they had been before I was born, and who they had been without me. And, I wanted to write it all down.

I read about "deaf-mutes," as deaf people were called in their time. People without speech and hearing have always been seen as strange and mysterious. In so called primitive as well as in advanced cultures they were regarded as condemned by the Gods, as creatures living under the curse of invisible, demonic forces. Sometimes they were killed, but in some cultures, they were revered as beings with magical powers.

In European antiquity, Greek philosophers discussed the phenomenon of deaf-and-dumbness and assumed that a person without hearing could not think. Plato granted deaf people a certain amount of intelligence because they were able to communicate with gestures, but Aristotle decided that people without hearing could not be educated. The Church Fathers of the Christian Middle Ages saw deaf people as monstrosities from Hell. To teach them speech, they thought, was impossible and, worse, presumptuous to divine intention. St. Augustine proclaimed that "the deaf-and-dumb from birth can never receive the gift of Faith, as Faith arises from the spoken word, from sermons, from what is heard." When my parents went to school, attendance was not compulsory for deaf children; it did not become so until 1911. Despite this, there were several schools for them around the country. The first school was founded in 1778, in Leipzig, by Samuel Heinicke, who was a strong advocate of the oral method. The school in Aachen opened in the 1830s. Without the help of their teachers, my parents would have remained speechless all their lives. They talked to me in their laboriously acquired speech, which I had no problem understanding. They, in turn, read from my lips what I told them soundlessly, while also reading my signs and facial expressions. We always signed and "spoke" with each other. My parents could never do without these.

I grew up among deaf people because my parents had deaf siblings and many deaf friends. They were part of my family; I felt at home among them, but also lonely. I found release and happiness in reading and writing, in the great gift of language.

Again and again I pleaded with my mother. "Mama, please, you tell me about your life! I want to write down!" I placed paper and pencil in her reach, so that she could jot down bits of memories as they came to her. Initially, she was reluctant. "Why write down? For whom?" she would tell me. "I poor, deaf-and-dumb, Papa too. People not interested!" The notebooks and readers from her years at the Institute for the Deaf in the town of Aachen, which she had kept diligently over the years, now turned out to be of great help in my undertaking.

I also asked my father to tell me about his childhood and adolescent years. How had they lived without me, without the daughter who, from early on, had been their interpreter? My parents would be amazed today if they could see with how much interest my readers follow the story of their lives!

Over the years, they did tell me about their lives, and I have written their stories here, in the way that they told me. Direct quotes are transcribed in the language they used; in other words, the way they signed to me. For this reason, the translations may not appear to be grammatically correct, though they are if one saw them signed.

Finally, I would like to express my heartfelt thanks, my respect, and admiration to all the teachers of the deaf for their demanding and invaluable work.

Maria Wallisfurth, Aachen, 2017

1

Near the young Ahr River, near the source, in the village of Freilingen, Maria Giefer was born on the fourth day of August in 1897. Freilingen, near Blankenheim, belonged to the district of Schleiden, the "poorhouse of Prussia." The village is situated on a rise with a view all around of the forests and peaceful valleys of the Eifel mountain range with its extinct volcanoes the Hohe Acht, the Nürburg, the Aremberg, and the Michelsberg. The house she was born in is made from solid stone taken from the Freilingen Castle just across the road. The castle, an impressive structure with two corner towers, had been torn down around 1830.

Maria's parents kept a black trunk with iron fittings in their bedroom, on which was written in block letters,

> HUBERT GIEFER FREILINGEN KR. SCHLEIDEN REG. AACHEN RHEINLAND PREUSSEN-STEINBÜCHEL & BRO. INSURANCE LAND LOAN STEAMSHIP LINE AGENTS WICHITA KANSAS

In 1893, when the best wine of the century was ripening on the banks of the Moselle River, the Eifel was suffering famine due to a drought and a bad harvest. Hubert Giefer, Maria's father, decided to leave impoverished Freilingen for America to become a rich farmer. He worked as a farm laborer in the endless wheat fields of Kansas and Michigan. For three summers, he saw only yellow stalks reaching to all horizons. Hubert earned money and saved it so he could progress in the new land. He saw where his future lay. But he could not forget Elisabeth, his sweetheart back home in the Eifel. So he returned to take her with him back to America.

But Elisabeth's parents would not allow their daughter to move to a strange land. So far away from the village—somewhere beyond a vast ocean! Hubert had to make a choice: Elisabeth or America, and he decided

Maria's parents—Hubert and Elisabeth (née Luppertz) Giefer.

to stay. He married Elisabeth and they lived on his mother's farm. Elisabeth soon bore two daughters, Maria and Gertrud. He never forgot his dream of a wheat farm of his own in America. It only slumbered.

Hubert found it hard to stay in Freilingen. It was a place where time stood still. For centuries, the people in Freilingen and in the higher lying village of Lommersdorf had lived as diggers, coal miners, charcoal burners, or carters. The high-grade iron ore from Lommersdorf was transported by horse-drawn carts to the small steel mills in Ahrhütte, Stahlhütte, and Antweiler, where it was processed into iron bars and then sent to the arms factories in Brabant in the Netherlands and Liège in Belgium. In the forests, the charcoal burners produced charcoal for the smelting furnaces. Their kilns were ever smoking.

The people in both villages did only a little farming on the side, but by 1880 the coal pit and steel mills closed down, and poverty and need settled in. Hubert Giefer saw the narrow fields, the small gardens, and all around the forests, marshland, and moor. If he had to stay in Freilingen, he at least wanted to get out of poverty! He calculated, he planned. He also acted. Soon people were saying, *By the time Hubert Giefer gets up, he has already made money.*

2

Hubert and Elisabeth Giefer work from early in the morning until late at night. They till the fields and care for the animals. How fortunate that Grandmother is there to care for the children. When little Maria has not seen her for a while, she goes on a search. Maria knows every corner of the house. It is divided down the middle; the part with the front door facing west belongs to Aunt Barbara, Hubert's sister who, together with her husband Ernst, does a little farming and runs the only grocery and post office in Freilingen. Hubert and Elisabeth's entrance faces east. A small passage leads past the living room door and then widens out to the large kitchen, with its range with a chimney hood, the baking oven in the wall, and the door to the vaulted cellar.

Maria climbs up the wooden stairs to the bedroom facing the village street. Her little sister Gertrud is lying asleep in their parents' bed. The room next door is unoccupied, filled with sacks of grain and flour standing between old bits of furniture and junk. Grandmother is not to be found in there, nor in the bedroom at the back looking out onto the meadow with its apple and plum trees. Maria goes to the stables and the feedstore, but Grandmother is not there either. Next, she goes in the dim henhouse, with its tiny window veiled by cobwebs. Nothing moves. The barn is joined to the house at a right angle. A smaller door is set into the huge barn door, and Maria has to step up high to climb through it. She still cannot find Grandmother.

Maria would rather sit on the stone steps in front of the open house door. She pulls up her straight frock that reaches down to her laced-up shoes and with her heels, taps on the wide strip of flagstones in front of the house. Then, she sits in the shade, protected from the blazing heat and glare of midsummer. The sheepdog is stretched out sleepily in front of the pigsty. Swallows swoop across the yard with a manure heap in the middle.

In the open shed, hens perch on the wagon shaft and the plow and harrow or scratch around on the hard-trodden ground. All is peaceful. The people from the village are out harvesting. Nobody passes by on the village street that curves around the Giefers' farm.

Finally, Grandmother comes. The dog wags its tail and blinks. The hens leisurely get out of the way. Maria stands up quickly and runs toward Grandmother, arms opened wide. Her hair hangs tousled around her happy face. Her eyes are bright. Her face and hands are dirty. As she thrusts her head into Grandmother's apron, heavy muffled sounds come out of her throat. Grandmother is here again! Grandmother is something soft, something warm, something good, like fresh, fragrant bread, like sweet milk straight from the bucket, like the soft fur of the big dog and the secureness of the stables when the animals are at home, like the delicious smell in the kitchen when you are hungry. Grandmother is comfort, the nest, the home.

At first, Grandmother, Hubert and Elisabeth, the neighbors, and the children who play with Maria were puzzled, surprised; then they became concerned. They worried, they watched the child. Now, the people of Freilingen have begun to talk—"What misfortune! Hubert Giefer's firstborn cannot hear or speak. She is deaf and dumb!" Terrible suspicions have been confirmed. The nearest doctor lives in Blankenheim. He costs money. Nobody has time to take Maria to the doctor, and she is not actually ill. One just has to accept things as they are.

Little Maria is quite unaware of her misfortune. In the mornings she lies in the big bed. Grandmother smiles at her, lifts her out, and gets her dressed. Downstairs in the living room there is bread, sometimes with cream, curd, or even butter, and a cup of milk. While Grandmother peels potatoes, Maria sits beside her on the bench in front of the house in the morning sun, handing her brown potatoes from the basket, dropping the peeled ones to soak in a bucket of water. When Grandmother moves her mouth, Maria looks around. She sees people who also move their lips. They often do it for a long time. Even when men or women pass by on the street, Grandmother moves her mouth.

It's nice when the other children take her by the hand and toddle off with her. Such fun to romp around with the others, and she only needs to watch and see what they do—climb; throw things; build little houses out of stones, leaves, and twigs; pick up a stick when the two cows have to be led to pasture; and try to sweep dirt onto the manure heap with a brushwood broom.

In the evening, after milking time, Mother will bring a bucket of milk into the house. Maria only has to show her with tiny hands that she wants a drink. Then, Mother gives her the ladle of sweet milk—how good it tastes, so fresh and warm!

Maria learns she always has to watch! When Grandmother waves her hand and puts her finger to her open mouth, as if she wants to put something into it, Maria nods her head yes or no. Often, when Maria runs over to Grandmother and presses her hand on her throat, Grandmother looks at her. Maria does not know that she is making sounds. She points her finger at her mouth, and Grandmother cuts her a large slice of bread and gives it to her.

Maria watches everything around her. Her experiences form themselves into pictures and movements in her mind. She stores everything that happens repeatedly. She knows what is not allowed: getting under Father's feet, chasing the hens, following Mother all the time. Sometimes Mother picks her up and holds her little head to her face. That is what Maria really likes, and she would like to stay in Mother's arms. But Mother has to work.

3

Summer is a good time.

Mother takes Maria by the hand, and in the other hand she holds a knotted scarf filled with slices of bread, along with a jug of coffee and the sickle. Mother is wearing a long dress reaching to her ankles, a large apron, black woolen stockings, and stout lace-up shoes. Her dark hair is covered by a white cloth tied in a knot at the back. Father walks beside her, the scythe over his shoulder. A hollow cow's horn hangs from the leather strap around his waist. Within this sheath is the whetstone. He has clapped an old straw hat on top of his reddish blond hair. The wide rim casts a shadow on his face.

Men and women carrying scythes, sickles, and knotted scarf pouches walk along the village street and spread out onto their fields. Wagons are underway. The road leads down into the valley. At Grindel Creek, Father bends down and fills the horn with water. The three climb to the top of the hill called Am Zollstock, where the wayside cross stands and the view is open and wide. They walk along a rutted path that branches off from the main road and come to the field where Father wants to work that day. Mother sits down on the edge of the ditch with Maria next to her, and Father sharpens the scythe. It is just past noon. Big bushes of chamomile give off their scent. The heat crackles through the field. Father begins to reap the field with broad swings of the scythe.

Mother stands up and gestures to Maria with her hand to stay sitting. The child nods. Her eyes follow Mother who has taken the sickle and, with swift movements, gathers up and rolls out the cut stalks. She takes a handful of stalks out of the loose sheaves and winds them around each sheaf like a ribbon. Then, quick as a flash, she twists the two ends together and sticks them into the sheaf.

Maria already knows what will come next—Mother will build a shady little house. She takes six sheaves, props them up against each other and waves to the little girl. Pointing to the bundle with the bread, she makes the gesture for carrying. Maria nods. With both hands, she grasps the cloth, carries it in front of herself, and sets it down to go and fetch the jug of coffee. Mother stows the things inside the shock of sheaves. Inside the shock, in the shade, she puts two more sheaves. She lays her head on her folded hands. Maria understands: *sleep*.

Mother starts her work in the sun, her back bent deeply. Father is almost at the other end of the field. The freshly cut stubble stands up straight. Lots of little stones lie in-between. The sheaves lie across the field, all pointing in the same direction. Only in the evening, when the field has been reaped, will Father and Mother put up the shocks.

Maria feels good. Beetles scuttle around and grasshoppers leap with their long, angular legs. A flock of earth-colored partridges flies past her. Maria crawls into her little house of sheaves so that the wandering sun cannot find her. She pulls her frock right down to her high-topped shoes. That way the stubble and thistles can't scratch her legs. There is a smell of bread and coffee and straw.

Maria can't keep her eyes open. Her hands sink down her side and open. When she wakes up, there is no more to be seen of the waving field of grain. The sun is sitting low in the sky, casting long shadows. She eats the food her parents have left for her and waits until all of the sheaves have been set up. For that, the farmers put up one sheaf in the middle and four additional ones around it. That is a *Kasten* (a shock of sheaves), as the Freilingers say. In windy weather, they put up nine sheaves to form a Kasten, making it more stable.

On the way home, Maria sits on Father's shoulders and Mother carries the scythe. From all directions the people are coming home. Long clouds of dust rise up behind the swaying hay carts. Down below at Grindel Creek, children are watering the cows they have brought down from the pastures.

Maria senses a slight trembling in Father's throat around which her hands are clasped. Then she knows Father is moving his mouth now. Sometimes she can also feel him laughing. Then Father's back moves. Maria looks, and feels, and is happy.

4

Although Maria has grown quite a bit after a few years, all she can see when she looks through the living-room window is the snow on the barn roof. She would have to push a chair to one of the windows high up in the thick wall to see the snow-covered road. The sun is shining and the room is bright. Grandmother comes stamping through the door with snow still on her shoes, which quickly melts into little puddles. From her sturdy apron she tips oak and fir logs into the basket behind the big iron stove. Maria feels the floor, the bench, and the table shake. With a hook Grandmother opens the stove door and throws wood into the red glow. Maria sees the flames licking. Her sister Gertrud is playing with their little brother Willi, who is crawling on the floor and ruffling the dog's coat. In a wicker basket on the long bench lies her youngest brother. He tries again and again to raise his head. He is called Nikolaus, later nicknamed Klöss. Only Maria will call him Nikolaus later.

Maria picks up her doll from the windowsill. She has made it herself from a piece of cloth. She wrapped the cloth around her fist, tied a strip around her wrist, and then pulled her hand out. She stuffed another piece of cloth inside the pouch, pulled the strip tight, and made a doll's head. With needle and thread she sewed on eyes, a nose, and a mouth. The loose ends of the cloth are the arms and legs. She lays her doll in the wicker basket next to her baby brother.

Grandmother brings in potatoes, beans, and some bacon. Quickly Maria runs to the door to close it. The cold has to stay outside. Maria opens the largest of the small oven doors so that Grandmother can place the bowls in the small oven chamber to keep warm. All at once there is an appetizing smell in the room and Maria hurries to clear the table. Grandmother wipes it clean and Maria goes with her to the cupboard in the hallway.

Grandmother hands Maria the plates with the cutlery on top. Maria sets the table.

She is suddenly very hungry. She goes to look for her parents. In the yard a path to the barn has been shoveled clear; the manure heap has disappeared under the snow except for the dung from yesterday and this morning. The barn door is wide open and Father and Mother are standing opposite each other threshing. Rye sheaves lie spread out in two rows, the ears pointing inwards. Again and again her parents raise the smooth handle of the threshing flail and drop the swingle down on the ears rhythmically, two-strokes. Father has made the flail himself on the chopping bench. Hubert and Elisabeth's faces are red from exertion. When they glance toward Maria without interrupting their work, the child points her finger to her opened mouth: *Time to eat!* Mother nods her head. The parents turn the sheaves over and carry on threshing until the ears are empty. Then they shake the rye straw thoroughly so that all the grains fall out and gather it into a corner of the barn. Later they will use it to bind the shorter sheaves of wheat, barley, and oats.

Mother stretches herself. Her back aches. Father sweeps the grain and chaff into a pile. Dust swirls up. Hens run between his legs and peck greedily. Mother comes out into the snow, wearily takes off her headscarf and shakes it out. Father also shakes his jacket. They go into the house with Maria. They all sit down at the long table and make the sign of the cross. Willi, who is a toddler, sits on Mother's lap. Father, Mother, and Grandmother move their lips very quickly for a long time while Maria watches them attentively, then they cross themselves again and begin to eat. Father insists on order at table, as the children well know. They sit quietly without fidgeting or talking. Maria props her feet up on the dog, who is lying under the table with his head on his paws. After giving thanks, Maria helps Grandmother with the dishes and then she sees to Gertrud, who has pushed a chair up against the wall to look for her cap amongst the hanging trousers, jackets, scarves, aprons, and coats that all smell of the barn and stables. Mother swaddles little Nikolaus and feeds him. Maria likes watching her. Soon, Mother goes back to her work. Maria fetches the birch broom and sweeps the bits of straw, wood, and stable muck out of the room into the yard. She wraps herself in her woolen scarf and steps outside to lean against one of the half-round stones that protect the barn

The Giefer farm in Freilingen.

doors from being rammed by carts. Children from the neighborhood are also watching Father's new winnowing machine in the barn.

Father shovels the threshed grain into the uppermost of three sieves along with the debris, chaff, and ears. Mother, with a crank, turns an axle to which four blades are fixed. They make so much wind that everything lighter than the grain is blown away. At the same time the sieves shake and tilt forward, so the grains become cleaner and cleaner as they drop down through the sieves.

Maria runs over to Mother and wants to help, but Father sends her back with a stern look. Maria dashes back to her stone; she doesn't want to make Father cross. Maria's cousin takes her by the hand and together they run around the house to Aunt Barbara's big living room. The cat is sitting on the bench around the tiled stove, licking its coat. Maria always enjoys being at Aunt Barbara's. It's friendlier and cozier than at home. Her aunt always has a treat for Maria—raisins, dried fruit, sometimes even an egg or a slice of white bread with butter.

Aunt Barbara goes out into the passage where a barrel of sugar beet syrup stands for sale. In the barrel next to it there are salted herrings. The oozing juice has already corroded the colors of the stone floor. Maria sees that the postman has come. He comes to the village every other day and has a long walk up from Ahrhütte via Lommersdorf in the west. He lets Aunt Barbara know when goods for her shop have arrived in Blankenheim-Wald, a small, nearby village. Then Mr. Dreimüller, from Lommersdorf, picks up the goods with his horse and cart. Maria sees the postman take letters out of his shoulder bag and hand them to Aunt Barbara, who gives him other letters to take away with him. He smiles at Maria, moves his lips, and leaves. Aunt Barbara brings the mail into the shop and puts the letters on the mail table next to the rubberstamps. In the shop, shiny cow chains, ropes, and bridles hang from the walls. A sack full of salt sits on the floor. Copper kettles gleam, buckets are stacked one inside the other. Cans of petroleum stand in the corner. There are petroleum lamps with flashing mirrors, stable lanterns, striped apron cloth, thick underwear, and yellow linen. Boxes hold spools of yarn, cards of thread, needles, writing paper, and nails. Sugarloaves are piled on the windowsills. Eggs that have been brought by farmers' wives to exchange for goods they have bought, lie in willow baskets. Nobody pays with money. Once a week a carter comes from town to fetch the eggs. Aunt Barbara gets money in return.

Scales with two shiny brass trays sit on the counter. Whatever Aunt Barbara puts items she wants to weigh in the tray on one side of the scales, and on the other side she puts brass weights, large or small ones. The pointer in the middle of the ornate iron bow dances to and fro, and Aunt Barbara has to take away goods or add a bit until the pointer stands straight up. Grasping the sides of the table with both hands, Maria rests her chin on the table top and eagerly watches the wavering pointer. She is delighted when the trays balance. But Aunt Barbara hears only incomprehensible sounds. For a moment, the child sees her aunt's eyes turn sad, then Aunt Barbara puts her hand into a wooden box and passes Maria a handful of raisins. *How terrible!* thinks Aunt Barbara, *and little Gertrud can't hear either!*

5

Village life is set by the seasons and by the weather. The children build snowmen and get frosty hands. Snow melts, then spring comes with fresh green. Summer smells of hay, and harvesting is hard work. Then apples, blackberries, and hazelnuts will ripen. And finally, snow falls once more. Everything has its set order. Everyone has to work in order to eat, and the earth and the beasts are there for the people.

Life carries on around Maria in its customary rhythm. She has no idea that everything has a name. She does not know that her village is called Freilingen and that she goes to church in Lommersdorf. When the street is swept in the evening, and the shoes are cleaned, greased with oil and lined up in a row, Maria knows that the next morning Grandmother and Mother will wear a good dress and a dark, fringed headscarf. Father will put on a clean shirt, a proper pair of trousers, and a jacket. In groups and in rows the villagers of Freilingen make their way to Lommersdorf, to the white parish church there with its Romanesque steeple. They carry thick prayer books with them. In the afternoon, when they again make their way back home, they have rosaries wrapped around their hands.

Maria sees pictures and thinks in pictures. She observes all movements, sees colors, and has a nose with a sense of smell she can rely on. She trusts in everything in her small world. Everywhere is safety.

Maria's home is in the lower part of the village near the chapel, whose history dates back to the Middle Ages. Opposite the chapel is the splendid, ancient Gilles Farm, one of the largest farms in Freilingen. All along the rising village street are the little farmhouses, close to each other, separated only by the low, dark stables and open yards around manure heaps. Animal urine and sewage run down the street into the gutters. Some of the houses are so old that their doors and windows have become crooked in the half-timbered framework. Large patches of yellow loam and interlaced branches are visible beneath the plaster. The mossy roofs have sagged. The windows of the houses built during the French occupation in the early 1800s are less than two feet square in order to avoid the window tax imposed at that time. The school is in the middle of the village. It is a stone building with large windows. The schoolmaster's wife has hung homemade curtains in the windows of their rooms above the one and only classroom. Maria gazes at them in wonder because no one else in Freilingen has curtains or shades in their windows. Maria rarely goes to the upper village, only when her parents take her along on a cart to the fields in the direction of Reetz, a village to the west, beyond the woods and heath.

Maria's deaf sister Gertrud lies buried among age-old stone crosses in the old churchyard in Lommersdorf. Maria can hardly remember her anymore. Weeds are growing on the small grave, as they are on most of the graves. *Who has the time to care for them?* she wonders.

The stone parish house stands behind the tall churchyard trees. One day, Hubert and Elisabeth Giefer go to see the priest to talk about their deaf and mute child Maria. She is now seven years old. How glad Elisabeth is that her husband wants to send Maria to a school! Without his consent in this paternalistic society, this would be impossible. His will alone counts. When "paternal authority" is officially laid down, a mother has no rights at all. Hubert is not required to send his deaf child to school; there is no law forcing him. He would even save money and have more help if he kept Maria at home. The priest promises to make inquiries.

Maria is a great help to her mother and grandmother around the house. She helps five-year-old Willi into his knee breeches and buttons the flap at the back. She pulls three-year-old Klöss's frock on, which he wears because he is not yet big enough to wear trousers. She feeds her baby sister Christina who will soon be two years old. Maria carries her in her arms and, if the neighbors come, she goes up to them, nudges them, and shows them her little sister. The neighbors laugh, nod their heads, pat the little girl or clap their hands together, and move their mouths. This delights Maria. Christina is a placid child with curly chestnut brown hair. Like Maria, she cannot hear. Their brothers, however, charge round like all the village boys, scrapping, shouting, running, chasing each other, and filling the house and yard with life.

Maria has learned to look at people's mouths. Grandmother always makes the same movement with her mouth when she points to Father, as does Mother. They do it for a lot of people and things, for everything has a distinct movement of the mouth that is repeated again and again. Maria is observant, and gradually she grasps the meaning and takes exact notice of everything. Her visual mind begins to connect the persons and things with the shapes the grownups make with their lips. When she thinks of Father or Mother, she also will see in her mind the mouth movements the others make to refer to them.

When Grandmother looks at Maria and her mouth forms the word *mother*, Maria knows what she means, runs off quickly, looks for Mother, tugs at her dress and indicates with her finger that Mother is to come to Grandmother. Maria always tries to imitate the lip movements. Over time, she has learned to press in the back of her throat and breathe out at the same time. When she feels slight vibrations in her head, the people near her look at her face. Even those further away, so far that they are out of reach, notice her when she does this; one just has to push in the throat a bit harder.

More and more often, and more and more distinctly, she calls "Father" and "Mother." Strangers do not understand her when she does this, but her family does. She cannot pronounce "er" because she cannot read it on other people's mouths; instead she ends the words with "eh," because that is what she sees. Only her parents, brothers, Grandmother, and Aunt Barbara understand her two spoken words. Maria also can point with her hands, and with a nodding or shaking of her head she can tell them yes or no.

6

In winter there are days when Mother stays in the house in the afternoons, knitting thick woolen socks. Somedays, Grandmother wraps herself in her heavy woolen shawl and goes around to Aunt Barbara's side of the house. Willi and Klöss go tobogganing on the slopes opposite with the sled Father has made for them; Christina stays inside and sleeps on the bench. Maria kneels beside her and tucks her dress beneath her knees because the wooden floor is hard. She has four needles in her hand, but they seem to have a will of their own. Knitting is not so easy! Maria concentrates so hard the tip of her tongue pokes out between her lips. The thick, black, wool thread just will not pull through. But she refuses to let that make her angry, for she is much too good-natured. Mother has shown her so many times how to knit, stitch by stitch. All little girls in the village learn how to knit, and one day, if she practices ever so earnestly, she will be able to knit as fast as Grandmother or Mother. Grandmother even closes her eyes while knitting, as if she were asleep.

Mother gets up and tosses some wood into the stove. She looks at Maria's fingers, then she gives a kind nod, takes the knitting out of her hands and lays it aside. Maria looks up expectantly. *Will Mother now point at the cupboard?* she wonders. *Yes!* Maria scrambles quickly onto the arm of the bench, and from the top of the cupboard she takes down a small cardboard box that is kept out of reach of Klöss and Willi. When she stretches, she makes a gasping sound with the effort. Quickly, she kneels back down and takes a pencil and some folded sheets of paper out of the little box. Full of joy, Maria smooths out the paper. Mother turns her chair around so that Maria can look directly at her face and watch her mouth. The mouth movements of people are a great mystery to Maria.

Neatly written on the paper are two words: *Father* and *Mother*. On previous winter days, Mother has already taught her how to write these. Now

Mother slowly moves her mouth, and the girl tries to form her lips just as Mother does. Over and over. And again. Then Mother writes the word *Maria* on the paper. Mother points to each letter in turn, and each time to her mouth. "Ma-i-a" says the child in a discordant voice which she herself cannot hear. Mother listens. Maria's "i" is not a clean [i]. Mother points to each written letter and to her own mouth again. Maria understands the connection for the *M*, *a*'s, and *i*, but at the *r* she shakes her head. No, she cannot fathom what Mother means, no matter how often she tries to show her. The *r* remains beyond her grasp.

"Ma-i-a," the girl says. Mother looks pleased. *But what is that "Ma-i-a"?* Mother points to her, taps the child on the chest, and with her lips she forms the word again slowly and clearly.

"Maria."

The child thinks for a while, points her finger inward, and looks down at herself. *That which she can see when she looks at herself, is that "Ma-i-a"?* Suddenly her face lights up. Excitedly, she thumps on her chest with her extended finger, forms with her mouth, presses in her throat, and says harshly and too loudly the word "Ma-i-a." She has grasped her name.

Maria excitedly hands her mother the pencil and watches closely how Mother writes the word. Maria tries to write it herself. With much perseverance it gradually gets better. How strange that the marks on the paper mean so much. The word *Mother* starts with the same letter as *Maria*. And for both words one has to form the mouth into the same shape, pressing the lips together.

Maria senses everything she sees has a name she can write down and call with her mouth—"Fath-eh," "Moth-eh," "Ma-i-a."

Maria's mother takes a deep breath. Her child can speak even if it sounds loud, shrill, and coarse in the room. The sounds are uncommon. *Who will ever be able to understand them?* Mother wonders. She looks over at Christina, but the child is sleeping and is not wakened by the sounds because Christina is also deaf. She will never be disturbed by noise either.

Mother's heart aches. She suppresses a sudden stab of fear. Maria gives her a questioning look. Then Mother fondles Maria's hair affectionately. Suddenly Mother looks up. Mother always knows when someone is about to come in. The door flies open and with a cold gust of air the two brothers come bursting in. They look curious in their old jackets and long trousers and move clumsily. Their faces are rosy and both noses runny, they sniff or wipe them on their sleeves. Maria gathers up her treasures in a hurry. The lovely afternoon is over. She is happy. She has learned a new word—and now she knows what to say when she means herself: "Ma-i-a!"

The room is getting dark. Mother puts her knitting in the cupboard. She lights the paraffin lamp hanging on the wall that blackens the ceiling. The animals have to be fed, and the cows have yet to be milked. Mother is glad to see Grandmother coming back.

Maria runs to Grandmother in excitement. She points to herself and says "Ma-i-a." Grandmother is very astonished and it shows clearly on her face how pleased she is; how she praises the girl! When Father comes in, the child says her new word again. Everyone wants to hear that she can say "Ma-i-a," and that she means herself.

After supper, the children follow the grownups out to the warm stables. They have eaten their fill of tasty potatoes with cream. The storm lanterns are hanging in the stables, their faint light in the yard is absorbed by the falling snow.

When all the children are in bed in the cold bedrooms upstairs, Mother takes off her blue linen apron and drapes it across one of the windows; Grandmother already has hung hers over the other. All the women in Freilingen do so in the evening. The front doors remain unlocked, summer and winter. There is nothing to be afraid of in Freilingen. No one locks up their houses because there is peace in the village and in the country.

7

It is Shrove Sunday. Maria watches in amazement when Father puts on Grandmother's skirt and blouse. He ties a scarf round his head and hides his face behind a black cloth with three holes he has cut out for his eyes and mouth. Father is unrecognizable. Maria follows him downstairs into the living room. Grandmother laughs when Father prances around disguised as a very fat woman.

All that morning and into the afternoon strangely dressed figures are dropping in, chasing the children and dancing around until Mother gives them little cakes baked in lard. Only then will they go off again. Father, Willi, and Klöss go out into the cold, and all kinds of disguised figures run after them, from house to house, throughout the entire village.

Maria is alone with Mother and Christina. *What will Mother do? Is she going to get dressed up so strangely, too, and jump about and be merry?* Now she goes to the front door and slides the bolt across. She fills the stove up with wood, sits down between the high windows and starts knitting. No one can see her from outside. It is dim in the pale winter light. Maria looks at her mother, who appears to be sad and lonely. She presses up against her and plays with Mother's hair. She wants to be close to her. Mother lets her do as she pleases. Maria pulls the hairpins out of her bun and when they are all lying on the table, Mother's long plait falls down. Mother does not move, she keeps knitting. Maria undoes the plait so that Mother's hair hangs down over the back of the chair, then she picks up the comb from the windowsill. It is already missing quite a few teeth, but that doesn't matter; one can comb so finely with it.

Mother's hair is thick and, now that she is sitting down, it reaches right down to the floor. Maria stands on tiptoe and lets the comb glide through Mother's hair, but she must bend down to reach the ends. *Lovely!* Mother's hair is different from Maria's, it's much thicker, stronger, and darker.

The room gets dark, and sometimes it seems to the child that someone is rattling at the door. She can feel it through the floor. But it looks as if Mother does not want to open it. Maria lets the comb glide through the hair again and again, gently and carefully. *Does Mother enjoy it?* The child looks around the chair at Mother's face. It is lovely, and quite sad. *Is Mother crying?* Maria keeps combing softly. *Why is Mother sad when everyone else—even Father—is so merry?* Mother puts down her knitting, plaits her hair again and pins it back up. She pays no attention to the little girl, brushes the loose hairs from her shoulders, and then goes out the kitchen door, back to her work outside.

8

May starts off cool. The calendar in the living room reads May 8, 1905.

Maria is awakened by someone shaking her arm. Mother is standing in front of her bed holding a light in her hand and motioning her to get up. With a shiver, the girl crawls out of the warm straw bed. In her undershirt and barefooted, she follows Mother down the wooden stairs and hops across the cold stone floor into the living room. Grandmother has already lit the fire. A bowl of warm water is standing ready. Mother helps her daughter bathe. Fathers nods kindly to the child and puts on his heavy hobnailed boots. Slowly the day dawns, pale and misty, outside the window. Mother hands a new linen shirt to Maria. It clings cold and heavy to her skin. For the first time Maria puts on a pair of drawers with long lace-trimmed legs and buttons. The girls and women in the village do not wear drawers, not even in winter. The long woolen stockings that Maria puts on have been knitted by Mother. They are fastened to her bodice with straps. The high lace shoes have been custom made for her. The warm underskirt is long and the new dress with puffed sleeves made out of dark blue cloth, reaches down to her shoes. Mother combs the child's hair and ties it with a bow.

Puzzled, Maria lets it all happen.

Over the past few weeks, Mother has taken her to the dressmaker and to the cobbler in Lommersdorf for fittings. *Why ever is she being dressed up so nicely?* Mother is wearing her best dress. It has spherical buttons and the wide collar is embroidered with little black pearls. A small brooch is pinned to the collar.

She has made fresh butter from white cream. Now she spreads it on long slices of bread, as thickly as only Father usually gets it. There is even an egg and hot milk. Mother wraps the buttered slices of bread in a clean dishtowel and puts them with a few hardboiled eggs, sausage, bacon, a whole loaf of bread, and dried plums into the oval travel basket with its two lids opening up toward the handle.

After breakfast, Father takes down Maria's new coat from the hook. She has never worn a coat before, neither Mother nor Grandmother even own one. Mother wraps her wide woolen shawl round her shoulders. Little Maria is given a new headscarf. Father looks out of the window at the gray morning, then he puts on his jacket and goes out into the yard with the travel basket. Grandmother cries and blows her nose. She makes the sign of the cross on the girl's forehead. Maria throws her arms around the old woman's neck and gives her a kiss. "Ma-i-a," she says, and indicates with her hand that she will return. Grandmother nods tearfully.

In the yard, Father has hitched the horse to the boxcart and stands waiting. Aunt Barbara waves from the window. She hands out a bundled cloth full of sweets. Maria takes the bundle and Aunt Barbara claps her hands together in amazement at how fine Maria looks! Maria strokes her hand over her coat, sticks out her tummy, and makes loud, happy noises. Aunt Barbara shakes Maria's hand and says, "Farewell." *What is this?* she wonders. She is going away with Father and Mother, but *where? Why?* The little deaf girl cannot imagine. But she feels joy in the knowledge that something special is happening, and everyone is being particularly nice to her.

Mother has already climbed up onto the cart, which is normally used to carry potatoes, turnips, sand, stones, and even manure. Now clean boards have been fitted to the sides and a board laid across as a seat, covered with the horse blanket. Father helps Maria up into the cart, climbs up himself, takes the reins in his hands, and flips them gently on the horse's back. The cart rolls off. Grandmother and Aunt Barbara wave and Maria waves cheerfully back. The horse trots down the road toward Grindel Creek.

The day is brightening. The dew in the meadows glistens. Wisps of mist float up out of the valleys like long white strips of cloth. The blackthorn bushes bear fat buds. Soon white blossoms will appear on the bare branches, even before the leaves dare to come out. At the creek, the stiff reeds have grown tall. April was wintry. Spring still refuses to come.

The travel basket, secured to the side with a cord, slides back and forth in the empty cart. Bumping along, they ride across the Grindel Creek bridge, up to the top of the hill. From there, Maria looks back once more and sees the blackthorn shrubs along the hillside, the steeple of the chapel, and the roofs of Freilingen. White swirls of smoke curl into the sky. It is cool. Maria shivers. The fresh wind blows into her face and makes her eyes water. Mother spreads a blanket across Maria's and her own knees.

From the hilltop the rutted path leads down through hazelnut bushes into Hüngersdorf Valley. Father jumps down from the cart and pulls the brakes. The road is muddy and washed out by the thawing snow and April rain. The basket begins to bounce.

In the Ahr Valley below, the meadows are veiled in mist. Maria smells the damp earth, the water, and the young grass. Crows squat gloomily on newly plowed fields and fly over the cart with a lazy flap of their wings. The three are quite alone on the twisting road along the Ahr River. They head toward Blankenheim, where Blankenheim Castle looms high above the small town. In the early morning sun, Maria glimpses sleepy faces behind some of the windows in the little town. The cart rumbles across the cobblestone pavement and out through the old town gate. Further uphill they come to Blankenheimerdorf. There, the villagers are awake and the animals are being fed in the stables.

After another half-hour ride along the road, with its sharp gravel stones, they reach the railway station at Blankenheim-Wald. Only the train station and a sawmill are located here in the fir forest. It smells good, of freshly cut timber. One track leads northeast to Cologne on the Rhine, the other one goes south, via Geroldstein, to Trier on the Moselle River.

Maria stares in wonder at the silver rails that lie on the ground coming out of the forest and vanishing back into the trees again. Mother is very excited. When the train pulls into the station, Maria is stunned. Black, hissing, on huge wheels, it comes thundering toward the platform. Maria can feel the ground tremble. Anxiously, Maria grabs Mother's hand and shrinks back. Mother has to drag her forward and gesture for her to come along. Father lifts Maria into a compartment and waves goodbye to her. She is alone with Mother. They take seats in the middle of a wooden bench facing the engine. At first, Mother places the picnic basket between herself and Maria, but when the train jerks to a start and Maria looks at her wide-eyed with uncertainty, Mother puts it on the opposite bench. Maria slides up next to her quickly, close to her side.

The train picks up speed. The child can feel its steady rhythm. She is attentive and all eyes, feeling and smelling everything. Broad valleys unfold past the windows, trees swish by, drifting clouds and flying birds are left behind, and whenever Maria wants to look at something more closely, it has already passed. She feels rather strange, but not scared. When she looks questioningly at Mother, she gets a tender smile in return. Villages appear and disappear, as do red slagheaps from the lead pits and scarred mountains. The train stops now and then. People get off and on. Passengers take slices of bread out of their baskets and knapsacks and eat.

In Euskirchen, Mother and Maria change to another train. After a while, the ticket inspector comes along. He and Mother move their mouths for a long time. Mother becomes very agitated and jumps up. Maria is alarmed. When the train stops, they get off. They are all alone on the platform of a small station. Their train pulls away, gradually fades into the distance, and is gone. Only a puff of smoke hangs in the air. Mother points in the direction the train has taken, shakes her head, points to herself and Maria and then in the opposite direction. Maria understands. In her excitement about the long journey, Mother mistakenly took the train to Cologne when they changed in Euskirchen. Now they have to wait for another train to take them back to Euskirchen.

There, they get on the correct train, after Mother reassures herself again and again that it really is going toward Düren. Maria looks out the window at the flat countryside. She has never seen such a large plain before. Here, farmers plow with horses, not with cows as they do at home. The fields are also much larger than in Freilingen, and sometimes she catches sight of farmhouses with mighty towers, gateways, and high walls around them.

In the Düren train station they sit in the waiting room, eating their bread while Mother talks to strangers. Once more they get into a train, and this one finally takes them to their destination, to Aachen. Maria is surprised to see that they have entered a huge sea of houses. Mother stands up nervously, reties her headscarf, and straightens Maria's coat. Under the huge vaulted roof of the new train station, still in the final stages of construction, they get off the train, go down the steps and down a long passage.

Now they stand in front of the train station and shiver in the weary afternoon light, although the air seems softer and milder to them than at home. Their limbs are stiff from sitting still for such a long time. Mother has set the basket on the ground. A bit lost, they stand in this foreign place, Aachen.

Maria holds tightly on to Mother's hand. Outside the train station, houses and trees surround a wide forecourt, and at its far end there is a war memorial. Streets lead off in all directions, and there is one house next to another. Horse-drawn cabs are waiting. People come and go. A green tram on rails drives off.

Mother waves at a boy. They both move their mouths, then he points in a certain direction. While they are walking, Maria looks all around her. The streets are all made of stone, and carts pulled by horses roll by. Mother keeps to the sidewalk with the child. They pass Marschiertor, a solid watchtower with a steep roof helmet. Children are playing underneath its arch. Up Boxgraben, they come across the railway bridge at An der Schanz, and finally arrive at the Institute for the Deaf.

Inside the brick building, Mother speaks to a gentleman with a white goatee. Maria gives him her hand when Mother gestures her to do so. In the high-ceilinged room, Maria sees an elevated desk with a half-circle of little desks and chairs in front of it, a blackboard, a cabinet, and pictures. Mother, pushing her gently, asks her to slowly repeat after her the three words they have practiced, "Father, Mother, Maria." Maria repeats loudly. The gentleman is pleased and gives her a piece of chalk. He motions for her to write on the blackboard. Mother gives her a nod of encouragement. Maria looks at the chalk. Hesitantly, she goes over to the blackboard and writes in big letters *Maria Giefer, Hubert Giefer, Father, Mother, Grandmother*. Mother smiles contentedly and the gentleman looks surprised. He goes over to the cabinet and brings a new slate for the child. Then he accompanies Mother and Maria out into the hallway, disappears briefly behind one of the many doors, and returns with an older girl. The gentleman moves his mouth very slowly to this girl and points to Mother and Maria. The girl watches his mouth attentively, then nods her head with understanding and moves her lips, too.

Suddenly Maria has understood something that moves her in a strange way: This girl, unknown to her, is like herself, not like the children in Freilingen and not like all the people she knows. There is something familiar, something alike. When the girl takes Mother's basket in one hand and holds out the other to Maria, she gladly takes it.

The girl guides Mother and Maria under the railway bridge and up Vaalserstrasse to St. Jakob's church. A tram is just coming down Jakobstrasse. They wait for it to pass before crossing the street. Maria feels how the ground trembles. They walk down the street a bit and then up again into Stromgasse. At number 17, they climb up a lot of stairs. The girl knocks on a door and a small, plump, friendly lady opens it. The room inside is as spotless as the lady with her white, starched apron. At the windows are airy net curtains and drapes. In one corner stands a wide bed with lace-trimmed pillows and a quilt. The sheet is turned back and looks white and smooth. Through an open curtain Maria can see into a small kitchen. The nickel handrail of the coal-fed stove gleams like silver and the hotplate like a mirror. The floor is painted a glossy brown and is as clean as if no one has ever set foot on it.

Mother opens her basket and puts bacon, eggs, bread, and butter on the table. Then they all sit down and share coffee. The door opens and in comes a man with a chubby, cheerful looking girl. He shakes hands with Mother and Maria and gestures to the chubby girl to do the same. Maria again realizes that this child is also like herself. The girl takes Maria into the kitchen. In a niche under the window are three shelves with toys. Maria lets the girl show her everything. The child indicates with her hands, "That belongs to me, and that belongs to the big girl." Mother watches quietly. After supper the small lady, Mother, and the three children climb up the stairs to an attic room. The lady lights a candle and shines it on three neatly made little beds. She waves "good night" and leaves. On one of the beds Maria snuggles up to Mother, who puts her arm around her. Maria lies as if in a nest. A star shines through the open attic window. Maria gazes at it until her eyes close.

9

Maria no longer knows how much time has passed since she first woke up in Aachen and found that Mother had gone. Suddenly she was so alone! So forsaken! She had cried and cried.

But, that was a long time ago.

Now it is summer, and every morning is lovely. Mrs. Bunden comes to wake the children. Their laced-up boots have been polished and Mrs. Bunden ties a clean starched pinafore around each child's dress. Maria calls Mrs. Bunden "Mama." The other girls call her Mama as well. Maria can tell from their lips.

After breakfast, the three girls wait at the front door. Mama dips two fingers in the basin of holy water that sits near the door and makes the sign of the cross on each girl's forehead. Proudly, Maria carries her linen schoolbag by its wooden handles. It is embroidered with pretty flowers. Two cords hang from it, dangling a sponge and a wiping cloth for her writing slate.

Down on the Stromgasse, the children wave at the window once more. They hold hands when they walk up Mühlenberg because the path is uneven and narrow. Each morning, when they reach St. Jakob's Church, the oldest girl stops and tucks her schoolbag between her knees to free her hands. She points to the four-sided clock tower. The big hand has almost reached the top. The smaller girls look at the older girl's mouth. "Seven o'clock," her lips say soundlessly. With that, she holds seven fingers up in the air. Maria does not quite understand the meaning yet, but every morning she tips her head back to look up at the high clock tower.

The morning is warm, but they feel the air cool when they enter the church and smell the old wood, the incense, and candle smoke. They go up the Gothic nave to the seats for the deaf children from the Aachen

Institute. Maria's teacher, Master Wennekamp, and the headmaster who gave her the slate are already there.

Every morning Maria sees the priests and the altar boys repeat the same movements. She folds her hands, she kneels, stands up, taps her chest, crosses herself, bows her head—mimicking whatever the teacher and the other pupils do. After Mass, in front of the church portal, the children start chatting with gestures and exaggerated expressions. "Chatting" is what they call their conversation. They prod each other and point their fingers. Their unmodulated, excited voices shriek across the square. People always stop and stare at them with curiosity or pity.

On the way to school, Maria sees a horse-drawn cart loaded with milk churns. Women come out of the houses with their jugs and pots. Milk is measured out and poured into the waiting vessels. Maria is reminded of the gloomy stable and the cows back home in Freilingen. She can picture Mother bent over on the milking stool, a pail between her knees, and stroke by stroke a fine jet of milk squirting out of the warm udder into the pail. As she walks through the stable, the hem of her dress sweeps over the wet straw. The fresh milk has to be strained through a boiled linen cloth into a clean churn. Mother must rinse out the churns with hot water every day. Milking, feeding, pasturing, cleaning the stables, making hay to provide food for the beasts in winter . . . what an endless round of work just to get milk! But here, the women get their milk from the milkman's cart—they hand over some coins for it and take it back with them. How easy that is!

Maria sits in her classroom with twelve other children, their desks in a half-circle. Each child can see the face of the others because only in that way can they learn from each other.

Some of the deaf children come into school without manners or knowing how to behave. They don't understand what is going on around them. Their parents feel helpless and at a loss to know what to do with them, so they send them to Aachen. Others are filled with fear and only want to be left alone. And others just sit with listless, dull eyes, staring blankly into the day as if their minds are numb. But there are also others, some of the younger girls and boys, whose alert eyes dart everywhere, missing nothing, not a single movement or change in their surroundings. They are curious, restless, loud, and demanding; sometimes suspicious, wary. And then, there are children like Maria, who are cheerful, attentive, willing, and full of anticipation, but at the same time doubting, tentative, unbelieving, and shy.

Rarely do any of the children know even a few words when they arrive at the school. Most of them first have to become aware of the vibrations in their throats. They have to learn that people around them react to these vibrations and that, therefore, they must have meaning. Many tears have already been shed. Many of the children want to run away. But Master Wennekamp, has patience, lots and lots and lots of patience. By and by, the children become calmer and learn to form their lips in order to pronounce the vowels *a*, *o*, and *u*. Again and again, they do voice exercises and learn to lipread these vowels from the teacher's mouth and to write them down. Then they learn the plosive consonants *p*, *t*, and *k*, which must be said without using the voice.

Bit by bit, the children feel their vocal muscles vibrate. The teacher corrects the position of their tongues with a little wooden stick. Finally, they learn to feel the sound of *f*. Maria takes great care to place her lower lip against her upper front teeth and blow out her breath like she felt the teacher do. But, he is not satisfied until she finally realizes that there should be no vibrations in her throat or head. She need not do anything with her throat, only her breath is allowed to move. When she gets it right at last, she is allowed to cover her slate with *f*s.

Today one of the little desks has remained empty. One child, and then another, run to Master Wennekamp, tap on his arm, point out the empty desk, and wipe their hand over their forehead: *Josef is sick*. The children demonstrate the gesture to each other, pointing to the empty desk and nodding their heads in understanding. None of the children can actually say the word *sick*, but when a desk stays empty, it means that one should make the gesture for sickness: the damp cloth on a fevered brow.

Master Wennekamp bangs on his desk, taps the floor with his stick, and once more slaps the flat of his hand on the desks of those children whose attention has not been caught by the vibrations of the floor. They all have to look at him. With wide open eyes he points his finger to his mouth. They all have to look there, all of them! If a pair of eyes darts anywhere else—slap!—he bangs again on the little desk of the inattentive one. Finally, all their eyes are held firmly by his hypnotic glance.

Now the teacher points to the closed cupboard, shrugs his shoulders, spreads his arms wide and indicates with this gesture and his expression ignorance and curiosity. Then he approaches the cupboard cautiously, opens it very, very slowly, and then quickly shuts it again. The children are all eyes. Again the teacher inquisitively opens the cupboard, claps his hands together in surprise, and carefully takes out a bag. He indicates to the children that he does not know what is inside.

A few begin to wriggle on their chairs, others open their mouths wide with suspense, and two run right up to the bag and want to open it. Master Wennekamp sends them straight back to their seats and then, tentatively, fearfully, he slides his hand into the bag, opening it just a crack. Presently, he withdraws his hand with an expression of pain and shouts loud and clear, "ow!" He blows on his fingers, rubs them as if they hurt—but then again, he sticks his hand slowly into the bag. Again he cries "ow!", pulls his hand back quickly, and begins all over again.

The children watch spellbound. Now the teacher makes each one come forward, guides each child's hand carefully into the bag, pulls it out quickly, and shows the child his mouth forming "ow." The children understand and make such a sound of pain themselves. Maria has to laugh because her finger does not hurt at all, it is so funny.

Slowly, Master Wennekamp opens the bag and warily takes out a small toy monkey, an animal with red paws and a long tail. The children are astonished, let out shouts of surprise, leap from their chairs, surround the teacher, and grab for the toy. Some begin to crawl around on the floor on all fours like animals. In no time the class is in an uproar. One boy keeps tapping the teacher's arm, pointing to himself and to the monkey, and nodding his head slowly. One girl wants to drag the teacher outside to show him just such a monkey because she cannot say where she has seen a monkey before.

It takes some time before Master Wennekamp can get the children to sit down in their seats, and the monkey is sitting safely on his desk. Then he draws a big monkey on the blackboard. Again the children jump up making a lot of inarticulate sounds, running to the teacher, pointing to the toy monkey and the drawing. They have realized it is meant to be the same animal. One girl grabs the monkey from the desk and holds it up next to the drawn monkey and laughs loudly, shrilly. Once more the teacher needs a lot of patience until all the children are sitting quietly on their seats. One or another keeps running to the front to point out or hold the monkey.

In big, clear letters, Master Wennekamp writes the word *Affe* (monkey) beside the drawing on the board. He points to the toy and the drawing and then to his mouth and forms the word *Aff*. He places his chair in front of his desk, sits down and, taking each child in turn, he grips them between his knees, holds their hands firmly, directs each face toward his own, looks compellingly into their eyes, and says, "aff-aff-aff." Master Wennekamp holds one of the child's hands against his larynx to feel the vibrations. He holds the child's other hand close to his mouth so that the child can feel the puff of sharp breath the *ff* makes. Then, for comparison, he quickly puts the child's hands on his or her own larynx and mouth. To and fro it goes.

Maria learns quickly. Some other children can't work out what to do with their lips or teeth to say "ff." Others make a sound, but it is not right. Many children have difficulty switching the shape of their mouths from *a* to *ff*. "Aff," says the teacher, loudly stamping his foot on the floor for the child to feel the force the *ff* should make—not soft and not slow, but rather forcible and fast.

The children have a long way to go before they learn to pronounce the letter *e* of *Affe*. As Master Wennekamp practices with each child and rechecks to see if they can say the new word, some of them forget it. Then they have to start all over again.

Master Wennekamp needs to have an infinite amount of patience. While he is concentrating on the child between his knees, other children come up with their slates and disturb him. He has to look at how they have written *Affe*, correct it quickly or praise them with a smile. Master Wennekamp says everything right out loud when he speaks to the children, as if they can hear.

He takes a cigarette out of a pack and lights it. When he puffs clouds of smoke into the air, the children jump up and try to catch the smoke, scramble onto the teacher's knees, and shout and laugh. Then he walks over to the blackboard and draws a burning cigarette in front of the monkey's mouth. The children go wild with delight. The teacher writes on the board *Aff pafft* (monkey puffs).

With the stare of his eyes, the knocking of his stick on the ground, and vehement banging on the desks, Master Wennekamp has restored the peace again. "Aff," he says and points to the monkey; "pafft," and he mimes smoking with his hand. "Aff pafft." Again he takes each child one at a time between his knees, after he has written both words on each of their slates.

Maria watches the teacher's lips carefully when she is so close to him. She makes her lips pop strongly when she says the plosive *p*. From earlier exercises, she knows that it must not vibrate in her throat. Only when she says *a* must she press in her throat. For *ft* she must blow out air between her upper front teeth and lower lip and then quickly add the *t*, which they have been practicing for days. To say *t* Maria presses her tongue to the roof of her palate behind her upper front teeth, then makes it bounce off again with a quick, short breath.

There are so many things to think of at the same time! She must be careful! Back and forth her small hands go, guided by the teacher's hands: to the teacher's lips, to her own lips, then quickly to the teacher's larynx and to her own. Touch, see, feel, think, remember. Fiercely, the teacher stamps his foot on the floor. "Aff pafft. Aff pafft."

And Maria says, "Aff pafft, aff pafft," over and over again, just like the teacher says to them. She repeats the two words that she herself cannot hear. Her whole body moves to the rhythm. The teacher is satisfied with her; he strokes her head and nods in praise, and she laughs back at him loudly, also nodding her head, her eyes shining. The teacher has to nudge her away to take her seat again so the next child can come forward.

For one boy, Master Wennekamp has to fetch a small mirror and hold it under the boy's nose while he is practicing. *And look!* The mirror mists up with his breath. The teacher shakes his head, unsatisfied. When he himself speaks and is holding the mirror under his own nose, it stays clear. Again, the boy has to speak with the small mirror under his nose and it mists up again. The teacher is distressed. The boy is very surprised. It takes a long time for him to understand and realize that when he speaks no air is allowed to come through his nose, only through the mouth. Now he has to watch out for that too. He struggles. When the mirror finally stays clear he gives a shrill shout of joy, spreads his arms wide open and beams at the teacher. Right away he wants to try again. But with the first *Aff* he says, the mirror mists up again. In sad astonishment he shakes his head.

The Institute for the Deaf in Aachen.

Consolingly, the teacher strokes the child's head. For some of the children, Master Wennekamp makes use of a beautiful peacock feather. He holds it in front of his lips and says "ff" and "Aff pafft," and the feather trembles and flutters. When, for comparison, the children hold the feather in front of their own mouths, they realize that they need to give more strength to their breath to get the feather to move as much as possible.

Maria sits at her slate and slowly writes letter after letter. The teacher goes from desk to desk, bending over each child, observing and helping. One child begins to daydream, a girl nudges her neighbor and gestures with her hands. Two boys are crawling around under the seats, and another boy wants to lay his head on his arms and doze off. All the time, the teacher has to keep their interest and attention going.

During recess in the schoolyard the girls and boys are kept apart. The little ones play tag between the old trees, the older ones talk in groups using quick, clumsy gestures. The teachers would like the children to speak and lipread when at play, too, but the gestures come easy and are convenient to them.

After the break, Master Wennekamp gets out the big mirror at the front of the room. The children have to come up to him individually. He sits in front of the mirror and places the children so that they can see his mouth and their own mouth at the same time. "Aff pafft," the teacher says, stamping his foot twice; the child repeats it and compares the movements of the two mouths in the mirror. But, oh dear, some have forgotten already—between just a moment ago and now, they have forgotten. How did they come together, the breath, teeth, and tongue? the lips and vibrations in the larynx? and the force with which one has to blow out the air? The *a* is no longer full, it is more like an *ah* or an *uh*, a strange, indistinguishable sound. The child has no control and cannot tell the difference between the sounds. Only the teacher can help to find out and say when it is right. Then the child must memorize what the vibration feels like and what happens inside—and must practice and practice, again and again, what was so painstakingly learned so that it doesn't get lost.

In the same way that air makes organ pipes vibrate and resound, the deaf children learn to use their breath consciously. Like virtuosi, like artists, they must one day be able to master the position of tongue, lips, and teeth in an endless number of variations. Master Wennekamp knows it all too well. The speech of his deaf pupils is a work of art, a sensitive instrument for their expression, always in danger of being lost again.

After the strenuous morning lessons, Maria is glad to push her schoolbag under the seat and rush outside. Her foster sisters, fourteen-year-old Juliane and cheerful twelve-year-old Adelheid, are already waiting for her. Together they walk home to Papa and Mama Bunden. For many years, the couple has been taking care of deaf children. Papa Bunden is a carpenter, and this helps Mama Bunden earn a little extra money. The children do well with them.

Lunch is already waiting on the table. After the meal, Papa lies down on the sofa for a nap. The girls help Mama do the dishes and tidy up. They try not to bump into anything, to walk quietly, and to speak without noise, in order not to wake Papa. Except for Saturday and Wednesday, they have to go back to school in the afternoon, from two until four o'clock. Before they set off, Mama points to her sleeping husband, winks with a twinkle in her eye, and rubs her forefinger and thumb together, the gesture for money.

Papa Bunden's moustache is still quivering with his snores, when suddenly he shoots up. His three foster daughters—Maria, Adelheid, and Juliane—pounce on him, pinching and tickling him and ruffling his hair. "Papa! Papa!" the girls cry gleefully, making the gesture Mama has just made. Papa Bunden sits up and with a grand gesture takes his coin purse out of his trouser pocket. Three hands stretch out toward him, and in each he lays a copper penny. From Mama they receive the sign of the cross. Outside they run to Ros Chapel, against which a little stone house with crooked windows is nestled. They step across a well-worn doorstep into the tiny shop. For their pennies they get a handful of sweets to suck on the way back to school.

After the afternoon session, the children change quickly out of their school clothes and into their simple play clothes and do their homework under Mama's watchful eye.

Then, finally, it is time to play.

10

Time flies. Now and then a faint smell of ripe grain wafts over the town. The summer holidays are here!

One afternoon Father is standing in the Bunden's flat. *What a surprise!* For a moment Maria stares at him in astonishment, then she rushes to greet him. She is proud that her foster parents and the girls can see what a strong and confident man Father is. When he talks, Mama and Papa laugh so much that tears roll down Mama's cheeks.

Maria stays close to Father. Snuggling up to him, she would not and cannot imagine that anyone could pinch or tickle him like they do in the afternoons with Papa Bunden. *Why ever is he here? Is she to go with him? What about school?* She taps Father on the arm to make him look at her. She points to herself, then to Father, then to the door, and out into the distance. Now, Mama Bunden turns her around in order to give her the answer. "You will go away with Father, but then come back." Happily, Maria looks back at Father. The smell of another world clings to his clothes. It is the smell of stable and grain, of cows and horses—all of a sudden she feels terribly homesick.

The next morning, very early, Father and Maria set off on the long journey to Freilingen. Maria recognizes much of what flies past the train window. Throughout the long journey, Father does not speak a single word to her. She would be very glad if he would try.

When they arrive home, Mother clasps her in her arms and Grandmother fondles the girl's head. Maria would love to tell them everything she has seen and experienced, but she has not yet learned the words for it all. Still, the grownups are amazed enough at what she has learned in the meantime.

On her first evening back in the village, everything feels rather unfamiliar and strange. She has been away from the little village for too long—and in Aachen life is so different. Maria stands in the summer's evening light at the front door, leaning on the stone frame and looking out at the yard. She is still wearing her pretty school frock, a bright pinafore, and shiny laced boots. A group of children gather and stand silently around her. When Maria walks across the yard, they all follow her.

The next day, she puts on her old clothes, and now it is as if she has never been away. Everyone knows her and has a friendly smile for her.

The vacation passes much too quickly, though, and at the end of the summer, Maria has to go back to school.

Soon after returning to Aachen, the days become shorter. In the mornings, dense fog awaits outside the main door. The three girls have to put on coats and caps for their walk to school. In the classrooms, the great black iron stoves are lit.

Maria learns how to pronounce the consonants *b*, *d*, and *g*. She forms words with them, and the more sounds she learns the more she has to remember. For the *p*, which explodes forcefully from the lips, she has to keep her throat free from any vibrations, and for the *b*, she must remember that it is formed just like the *p*, but more softly and with a pressure in her throat. Master Wennekamp sometimes puts his ear with a hand cupped behind it next to Maria's mouth. She is to speak into it. Why she has to do this, she does not know, nor does she know what ears are for, but she learns that speaking and ears are connected for the teacher. She realizes that the teacher's satisfaction or dissatisfaction with her speaking also has something to do with his ears. The opening in his ear must be a mysterious passage. There it should go in, the teacher points, but Maria cannot see how or what goes in. She imagines that the teacher's ears must have feeling. But her ears only feel when she sticks her finger in.

Maria also learns the art of lipreading. She should, after all, not only be able to make herself understood but also learn to understand other people. One day she should be able to talk with them about anything and everything.

She can understand the teacher well because he forms every word clearly and slowly, but strangers out on the street, or Mama talking to Papa, they all barely move their lips when speaking. They talk so fast she wonders how she will ever be able to understand them.

One evening, Maria, Adelheid, and Juliane are sitting in Mama's room doing their homework by the light of the paraffin lamp. Any moment now,

Papa will come home from work and then it will be time for supper. Mama has just gone out. In the streets below, the gas lamps are burning, but up here the night is dark outside the windows. Cozy warmth comes from the coal oven. There is a smell of paraffin and also of soot.

The flame in the glass cylinder burns calmly, only now and then it suddenly twitches up. Then a light smoke curls up the cylinder and blackens the glass along the upper rim. Juliane, the eldest girl, fetches the wick scissors from the kitchen, pulls the wick out and takes the glass cylinder out of the brass holder. She snips off a piece so that the lamp will not smoke and stink. The shine of the lamp does not spread very far. The corners of the room stay dark.

The door flies open. All three girls feel the sudden draft. They feel something fall on the floor, roll, and bounce. Startled, the children jump up. Maria does not know what is happening. Now she sees Adelheid and Juliane laughing and crawling around on the floor, joyfully picking up and collecting things. Maria stands quite still. *Did somebody open the door? Throw something in? Who did it? What are the children looking for?* They signal to Maria to get down on the floor and also pick things up. Juliane closes the living room door, takes the lamp from the table and places it on the floor. Maria bends down and discovers red apples, *Printen*—the sweet, spice cookies that are a specialty of the town of Aachen—and lots of nuts. She picks up whatever she can find and puts it on the table. On her face is a look of total wonderment.

Juliane, noticing Maria's lack of understanding, describes with her hands a pointed hat over her head, a long beard, and a stick, curved at the top. "Nikolaus," she says.*

Maria tries to read Juliane's lips and forms the word after her, soundlessly. But she cannot understand Juliane. When Mama comes back, the girls encircle her. Everything St. Nikolaus has thrown into the room must be shown to her. The children share the goodies.

Despite the joy and surprise about all the gifts, Maria is lost in thoughts and feels a bit sad because there is so much she doesn't understand. Pensively holding the nuts, apples, and Printen in her arms, she stands and watches fat Adelheid happily gobble up one Printe after another.

---

* Translator's Note. On December 6th, St. Nicholas, or Santa Claus, distributes gifts to the children in Germany.

Snow has fallen overnight, but already by midday only dirty slush remains. Father is there again to take Maria home for the Christmas holidays.

In Freilingen the snow is piled deep. On Christmas morning Maria's brothers Willi and Klöss wake her up. It is still dark outside. Willi is holding Grandmother's night candle in his hand, and Klöss drags Maria out of bed. Barefoot, all three run down the wooden stairs and across the cold stone floor of the hallway into the living room, where a light is shining. Here it is cozy and warm, and Grandmother beckons to Maria and points at four plates filled with yeast pretzels, sweet ropes, and hazelnuts. *A plate full of tasty things for each child? For her, Willi, Klöss, and little Christina?* Grandmother takes her by the hand and walks to the dark window. She points at the sky and flaps her arms like wings, then she points at the bountiful plates. Maria watches Grandmother carefully, then looks out into the darkness and thinks of a bird. Her forehead is all wrinkled because she is thinking so hard. *A bird? At night? And the goodies on the plate?* While she is looking at Grandmother, puzzled, questioning, pleading, the old woman gets an idea. She goes over to the cupboard, gets out her prayer book, leafs through it until she finds a picture, and shows it to Maria. Maria knows the picture—it shows a bright figure in a long white gown with golden hair and huge wings on its back, bigger than those of any bird and as silvery as the stars on a clear night sky. Again Grandmother points at the plates and out of the window. One has to believe Grandmother, one has to believe all grownups. This lovely being that Maria knows from the pictures and statues in the church and chapel, she has actually never seen. But Grandmother says that is where the tasty things come from. Maria smiles a little, looks up at the dark sky and thinks in images. *Angels who are flying over the snow, over the farm, and then . . . ? Who saw them? Where did they get the sweet things? Why did they come in the cold night?*

Mother comes in from the stable with her skirt tucked up. She marvels at the delicious things, and off she goes to work again. In the morning light they can see the snow. It now almost reaches the attic windows. Father has shoveled a path from the front door to the stable, out to the road, and then along the road until it bends past the farm.

Aunt Barbara's two children and Maria's friend Traudchen come to collect Maria and her brothers. Traudchen, who is the same age as Maria and lives in a very small house nearby, is kind and friendly to Maria and also has the patience to explain things to her. From her black apron pocket beneath a large woolen shawl, Traudchen pulls out a handful of raisins for her deaf friend. Maria nudges Traudchen's arm excitedly. She has something to say: Maria makes the gesture for flying and points to the raisins. Traudchen understands. *Yes! Yes!* she nods. And Maria points to herself and flaps her arms again. Yes, Traudchen too has been brought something by the angel.

The children walk along the road to the church in Lommersdorf, as they do every morning, in every kind of weather. Today, for Christmas Mass, they have to walk one behind the other because of all the snow. The square around the fountain in front of the chapel has been cleared of snow. The water in the basin is frozen solid around the edges and a rivulet trickles down thick icicles into the cattle trough. A few children are waiting there and join the others. All of them are wrapped in shawls, only Maria is wearing a coat. The path to Lommersdorf has been trodden hard by those who went to Midnight Mass. Where the road still goes through the village, past the houses, narrow paths lead to the front doors. The snow is piled high, sometimes so high that the children cannot see over the top. Then only the top windows of the bedrooms peep over. The windowpanes are covered with frost flowers. Long icicles hang from the roofs. On the rise to Lommersdorf, next to Stichelchen Cross, the wind has blown the snow into high drifts. They walk through a little ravine of snow there, until they come to the sheltered hedge path where tall sloe bushes line the way to the church.

Inside the church, Maria senses the pounding of the organ. When she feels the abrupt vibrations through the wooden bench, the people around her all move their mouths at the same time, more slowly and distinctly than they usually do. Maria knows nothing of the festive hymns of Christmas. She gazes at the wooden angels on the Baroque altar, thinking that they fly with their wings like birds. *Perhaps,* she thinks, *they were not in this room last night but were flying to the children in the villages.*

Back home, Maria kneels on a chair and lines up her hazelnuts on the broad windowsill. Sometimes her nuts are schoolchildren sitting in a semicircle, sometimes horses with wagons, and in the end she uses them to form rectangles and squares that are meant to be rooms and furniture. If someone passes on the street, all she can see is a head above the piled-up snow. It's funny to see just a head bobbing up and down along its way. Maria feels a draft from the door and right afterwards a thudding. Her brothers come storming in. Mother slaps her hand on the table to get Maria's attention, and Maria immediately turns around to face her. Mother tells Maria to pick up her little sister, but first Maria puts her nuts into her apron pocket. Willi and Klöss follow Mother into the kitchen. Maria holds Christina carefully in her arms. Sometimes she rocks the child back and forth as she has seen Mother and Grandmother do.

Outside it gets dark early. After supper, Mother puts little Christina to bed. Klöss and Willi put on their jackets and caps, and Mother hands Maria her coat, too. *So late?* Maria is very surprised.

"Aunt Barbara," says Mother, and points to the door. Even though Maria cannot yet say "Aunt Barbara," she recognizes the lip movement for the name of her aunt. She goes out with her younger brothers. Icy cold air hits the children. The night is clear. Maria sees that other children, too, are on their way to Aunt Barbara's. Frost bites into their faces. Quick through Aunt Barbara's door! There they stand in the big room and stare.

A Christmas tree! Aunt Barbara lights the candles on it. She has to stand on a chair to reach those right at the top. Light after light shines with a warm glow. Now the tree can be seen in all its splendor, covered with little colored pictures, silver streamers, and cookies. A crib is set up. An angel made of wax hovers above it. It is such a beautiful and overwhelming sight for the children, so unusually festive, that they all stand silent. This is the only Christmas tree in the village.

More and even more children arrive. Under their shoes little puddles of melted snow form. Maria looks at the lighted tree and at the children whose eyes reflect the candlelight. Uncle Ernst, Aunt Barbara, and all the children move their mouths slowly, just as they did in church. The children are singing. Maria feels that, in an unfathomable way, she is left out. The stable there beside the tree, the animals, the woman and man kneeling in front of a crib where an almost naked child is lying, capture her thoughts—*You wouldn't put a child in a crib in a stable!* She waits, watching the golden flames, which flicker and flare from time to time, until Aunt Barbara goes round with a bowl of home-baked cookies and each child is allowed to take two. The candles have burnt down, gone out one after the other, and the children leave, putting on their hats and woolen shawls. The moon shows them their way home.

Maria carries the images of this evening in her memory back to Aachen. Maria, Juliane, and Adelheid return to the Bundens' the same day from their Christmas holidays, and Mama has presents for her darling girls. Maria is given a pinafore, a handkerchief, and a pair of stockings. The prettiest of all, though, is a little, white-lacquered doll's bed with knobs on the bedposts. Papa has made the little bed himself. Everything that goes with a bed is there: a quilt, a pillow, a cushion, a proper mattress, stuffed with feathers, and white lace-trimmed sheets. A rag doll is sleeping in the little bed. Maria has never before owned a real toy, all of her own! She is allowed to play with the little doll until bedtime, putting it to bed, letting it get up again, dressing and undressing it, and is happy.

11

The trains traveling from Aachen to Düsseldorf or Holland have to go past the Institute for the Deaf. The railway embankment reaches halfway up the school building. Only the little schoolyard is in between. Whenever an engine passes the windows, pulling a lot of coaches behind it, the children can feel the school trembling. They look outside and watch the train.

Master Wennekamp has drawn a train on the blackboard. Thick clouds of smoke are puffing out of the funnel, a whole blackboard full. Next to the clouds, the teacher writes *sh sh sh*. He bends his arms as if they were the connecting rods driving the wheels, and moves them so. In the same rhythm, he demonstrates with protruding lips, "sh sh sh." Maria has to learn to emit the "sh" without pressing in her throat. To do this, she holds the back of her hand close to her mouth or to the teacher's, in order to feel the breath. Not until the "sh" comes out correctly does her train run properly, and the teacher can praise her.

But it is much more difficult to learn to pronounce *s*; *ng*, *nk*, *e*, and *i*, too, are particularly troublesome! They all look so similar on the lips. *How is it possible to tell the difference between them?* The sounds *ei* and *eu*, too, are so difficult! Tears are being shed.

Hours, days, weeks go by. Master Wennekamp tells the children to pay attention! Pay close attention! Take note! Practice! Remember! Where is the tongue for the *s*? What is its breath like? Is it warm or cooler? Is it sharp or soft? Do you have to press in your throat, to make it vibrate? And for *ng*? Tongue? Behind the bottom row of teeth. The lips? Slightly open. And the breath? No, it mustn't come out of the mouth. This time it *must* go through the nose!

The children test the *ng* by holding their index fingers under their noses to feel the air. They have to press in their throats, and it vibrates not only there but in the nose and forehead as well. Their eyes squint when they are practicing *ng*. Later the children—and deaf adults too—will, in their conversations with each other, narrow their eyes for an instant and wrinkle their noses with each *ng*. This is the only way this sound can be lipread because the slightly parted lips give no other clue. Often it is enough to quickly crook the index finger for each *ng* in a word.

The letter *r* rolls so nicely in the back of the throat. Maria learns this quickly after feeling her teacher say it. Because the *r* cannot be lipread either, the children place all the fingers of one hand below the chin and do a quick wiggle, as if they are rapidly playing a scale on a piano. When Maria practices with a classmate, she can only indicate the sound with her fingers.

In this way, the deaf children augment their speech with many little movements, gestures, and mime. Some of the movements are so tiny and quick, that an outsider doesn't notice them at all—a turn of the head, a certain facial expression, a twitch of the eyes, of the mouth, or of the eyebrows, all these have meaning: a letter, a word or a frame of mind, things, or qualities. Maria can tell that the teacher is not satisfied with her *i* sound. He holds his hands over his ears. *Why?* Master Wennenkamp says it is high pitched, shrill, and very loud, but she cannot work out how she should change it. So her *i* will stay like that. If she says her own name, "Maria," she carefully pronounces sound after sound: a deep *a*, a rolling *r*, a high-pitched *i*, and again a deep *a*. "Maria Giefer," she points to herself, and whoever takes a little trouble or has gotten used to Maria's voice can understand her.

12

On Sunday mornings, when the weather is fine, Papa Bunden takes his three girls for a walk through the city. The children walk in front and wear starched ribbons in their hair. In the early spring, the sun's rays can barely be felt, but the buds are swelling on the branches of the many trees lining the streets. In the parks, the smell of the earth promises new growth. Blackbirds hop over newly greening lawns.

The town is filled with ringing church bells on Sunday mornings. They peal from the towers, over the rooftops and through the streets. But the three girls know nothing of them. Papa walks with them across squares and along narrow little lanes where the shops are shuttered, stopping now and then at advertising pillars, to read announcements and to look at the colorful posters. Sometimes he raises his hat in greeting.

People are walking or riding in carriages to the many churches and to the cathedral. Others are walking their dogs on a leash. Some small dogs are even wearing little, colorful sweaters on their backs. No one in Freilingen would do such a thing for a dog. Now and then the green tram passes on its shiny rails. Then the ground trembles, and Maria wishes she, too, could sit behind the glass windows and go for a ride.

Father comes to collect Maria for the Easter holidays. On her very first day at home she says everything she can now pronounce, says it and repeats it again. Maria is delighted that everyone is so pleased. Mother has a surprise for her—a new little sister, three months old, whom Maria is allowed to hold in her arms. She has a fresh little face and flaming red-blond hair. Mother points to the new baby and says clearly, "Elisabeth." Then, again, she points to Maria and says, "Maria," then again to the baby, "Elisabeth." Maria repeats it slowly, while her eyes are fastened on Mother's lips, "E-li-sa-beth." Now Mother points to herself and to the child, "Elisabeth."

Maria understands, and now knows Mother's name. She beams and nods her head, "You Elisabeth," and points to Mother, then she strokes the baby's head gently and says, "Elisabeth."

The year is now 1906, and there are five children on the Giefers' farm: two boys who can hear, and two girls who are deaf. *And the newest?* She can hear, Mother is certain. The child responds to noise, which is something her older daughters never did.

It is always hard for Maria to leave Freilingen when vacations are over, but when she is back in Aachen, everything is fine. In her second year at school only eight children sit in the semicircle of desks in her class. Because they found learning to lipread so difficult, five of her previous classmates had to be sent to a special school in Essen; they would only have held back the other more talented children. Maria continues her speaking exercises every day, although she can say the sounds already. Everything has to become second nature to her, so that she will never forget any of it.

The children learn to form sentences out of words. Their eyes move from the teacher's mouth to the blackboard and back again, grasping minute differences and connecting them with each other. Unlike a hearing child, Maria cannot look at the blackboard and at the same time take in what the teacher is saying. Maria has to have swift eyes if she wants to learn. First, she looks at the word on the blackboard and then the teacher's mouth, that only goes one after the other, and yet it belongs together. In this way, she also must learn to do math. But right in the middle of learning new words, ideas, and numbers, it often happens that a child loses a sound that he or she has already felt and formed correctly. Suddenly, the silent knowledge has gone. Then the teacher has to help the student rediscover the feeling of this lost sound, has to show the child the lip movement and tongue position anew, has to teach him or her how to control the air and the proper amount of it. It is a hard struggle, all for a single sound.

Maria learns that there is a God. He is in the many churches, in Heaven above the clouds, and everywhere. Mary and Joseph are up in Heaven and in a stable, like she saw at Aunt Barbara's under the Christmas tree. They have a child, who is Jesus, and the man who hangs on the cross is also Jesus. Maria encounters these holy figures everywhere. She gradually understands the meaning of the pictures she knows from Freilingen and Mama Bunden's house, of the crosses in the fields, and of the angels. She learns how to pray and that this God in Heaven can see into her heart and knows all her thoughts. Even in the darkest night, God can see her. He has a long beard and angels surround Him. His enemy is the Devil in Hell, where there is always fire. She can go either to Heaven or to Hell. God can reward her or punish her. She fears this God more than she loves Him. *Why should she go up there to Heaven or deep down into the earth to Hell?* She would like to be in Freilingen, with Father and Mother and her brothers and sisters, with Grandmother and Aunt Barbara, with the dog, the cows, and the chickens.

But she does like the story of Mary and Joseph and the child. Once, when she is home again on vacation, she says to Mother "My name Maria—Please a brother, Josef." What she means is that they would go together very nicely, Maria and Josef.

Mother smiles and says, "if God wills it. Perhaps." Maria has understood Mother because by now she can lipread quite well, if someone speaks to her slowly.

When Maria is ten years old, she can read and understand the date 1907 on the calendar. During the autumn holidays of this year, she is at home when Mother gives birth to a son, upstairs in the bedroom. Mother is so sweet as to actually name the new little brother, Josef. But, she does not recover from the birth. She cannot even care for the newborn.

Maria is particularly fond of little Josef. She feeds him and washes him and looks after him wherever and however she can. She is like a little mother to him. She also helps Grandmother wherever she can. She does the dishes, sets the table, takes food up to her sick mother, feeds Setta (as little Elisabeth is called), and dresses Christina. She scatters feed for the chickens, peels potatoes, and washes nappies and hangs them on the line in the garden. She collects eggs from the nests and sweeps the front room and hall. She fetches kindling from the shed. In the big iron pan she roasts grain on the stove. She has to keep stirring and turning it so that it will brown evenly. She makes coffee from the roasted and ground grain. With the coffee she also coats the loaves of bread Grandmother has kneaded and shaped before pushing them into the oven. This gives the baked bread a shiny crust. Carefully, Maria ladles the cream from the milk standing in many earthenware pots on the windowsill so that Grandmother can make butter from it with the wooden beater. She takes bread and coffee out to

Father in the fields. Some days, she drives the cows to pasture, leads them to the drinking trough, and takes them back to the stable.

Tirelessly, she is on the go. Only now, since Mother's illness, does she realize how very much those hardworking hands are missed everywhere.

Since Maria has been in Freilingen she has had to comb her long hair herself, although in Aachen, Mama Bunden or Juliane comb it for her. Her hair is so shaggy and matted she can hardly get the comb through it. Maria longs for Mother. Her arms drop with exhaustion. All at once, she feels discouraged and lonely, so she climbs up the stairs to her mother's room. Quietly, she approaches the bed. Mother's face is pale. Maria stands there with her hair loose and the comb in her hand. Mother opens her eyes and smiles at her oldest child. Her lips barely move. "Mother—you please comb!" says Maria. Mother nods and takes the comb into her hand while Maria sits down on the edge of the bed, her back turned to Mother. Through the window in the door, Maria sees Grandmother coming. Grandmother opens the door and her face turns very angry. She walks over to Maria, drags her up from the bed, and snatches the comb from Mother's hand. Mother is so weak that she lets it all happen. Grandmother shakes her fist and scolds her in a way that Maria can understand, "Mother sick—leave alone!" Maria is shocked. Never before has Grandmother scolded her. *Has she done something bad? Done something bad to her dear Mother?* She looks at Mother who is looking back at her, gently, and sadly, and wearily waving her hand.

But Grandmother whisks the child out of the door. So Maria goes downstairs and is angry with Grandmother. She wants to be with Mother and wishes desperately that she will get well soon. Halfheartedly, she returns to her work. There are five children now and she is the oldest—and Mother will surely think *Maria helps a lot.* So she must work hard.

Maria is not allowed to go up to Mother anymore. Grandmother has forbidden it. A few days later, in the middle of the night, Maria is shaken out of her sleep. Scared, she sits up and sees Father standing in the room. The candle in his hand casts a flickering light on the bed and chair, the faded walls and ceiling. Father is fully dressed. He is wearing his Sunday clothes. Maria is wide awake and watches her Father's mouth closely. Father does not like to repeat himself. "Get up! Put on Sunday dress! Stockings, no shoes!" Quickly Maria jumps out of bed and does what Father has ordered. She does not ask why. Never would she ask Father why. Father pushes the child gently into the parents' bedroom. Maria sees two burning candles on the nightstand next to her mother's bed, and a cross between them. Her mother's brother is standing with head bowed at the foot of the bed. Father has taught Maria to say "uncle" to him. Grandmother is kneeling and praying the rosary.

Instinctively, Maria folds her hands. Father is standing behind her, so she cannot see him. She only looks at Mother. More than anything she would like to go over to her. She senses that she mustn't. *Why has Father fetched her? All of the other children are asleep. And what is wrong with Mother? Does something hurt her so much? Why is Grandmother kneeling and crying and praying?*

Maria feels cold. She starts to tremble—and she is frightened. She sees Father going over to Mother, taking her hands into his. Then Father closes her eyes and puts her hands together so that her fingers are intertwined, and gently lays his hand on her face. Then he steps back. Mother is lying quite still. She is not breathing anymore. Something that really hurts tears at Maria's heart. She wants to ask "What is the matter with Mother?" But she remains silent. She does not dare to ask.

Mother was only 34 years old.

Later, Maria will stand at her grave by the Lommersdorf church. There Mother's name is on the cross, and everyone says that Mother is there below the ground. Then they point to the sky and say that she is also up there.

13

In Aachen, Mama presents Maria with a black dress because of the death of her mother. Juliane does not stay much longer with the Bundens on Stromgasse. At Easter 1908, she graduates from school. Maria and Adelheid get a new little foster sister. Mama says, "Anna Dilesio comes from far away, from Italy." Maria likes looking at her because she seems so strangely beautiful. With her dark eyes, her brown skin and black hair, she looks like a gypsy girl. Gypsies can often be seen in the town. The little one has brought dolls with her that can be wound up. They move their legs slowly and stiffly and walk across the table or around in a circle. Maria and Adelheid take their new sister to school.

Maria has to learn so much! Words, that she learns to write, she cannot simply pronounce as they are written, that in itself would be difficult enough. No, there is something more important to learn if she wants hearing people to understand her speech. The teacher writes on the blackboard: *father, ruler, field.* Next to these he writes *apple, sister,* and *run.* Below the word *father* he writes a double *aa,* below *ruler* a double *uu,* and below *field* a double *ii.* The other words remain as they are. Now Maria has to learn and commit to memory that there are words whose vowels are drawn out, twice as long as a simple vowel. In the word *field* she can recognize it by the additional *e,* even though she must not pronounce the *e.* From now on, Maria writes words with drawn out vowels, like *far,* with a double vowel written below them. And there is still something more. If a word has several syllables, one syllable is always emphasized more strongly. *How is Maria to know that?* But, she has to know in order to be understood. So, with each word with more than one syllable she places an accent stroke on the emphasized one. She writes *Chrístmas, páraffin, expénsive.* She cannot feel the stressed syllable herself, she has to take the teacher's word for it and learn everything by heart. She fills page after page with words with emphasized syllables and notes for long vowels.

Of course, there are some words she just cannot manage. She always says "réfusé" when she means "refúse." So, sometimes rather odd sentences come about when she speaks. What hearing people never think about deaf children have to learn with a huge effort. Children who can hear learn words by simply repeating them with the proper sound and emphasis. Slowly, they grow into the language. Every word is spoken correctly if it sounds as it was heard.

In these times of strenuous learning, Maria is surprised when the teacher is sometimes not satisfied with her, although she has made every effort. According to him, she speaks too loudly and too high-pitched, she tries too hard. She yells, instead of speaking normally because she cannot tell the difference between too much and just enough. After the teacher's admonitions, she says sadly, "I don't feel. I am too loud. I don't know what I should do. I am sorry."

"We have patience, the two of us," the teacher says kindly.

With time, it gets better. Anyone who speaks slowly and clearly and uses words that Maria has learned can converse with her. But she must always be able to see the speaker's mouth. In darkness, all conversation stops. That's why deaf children always turn their faces to the last sources of light when it begins to get dark. They want to be able to understand each other.

They have learned from their teacher that they should use their hands as little as possible when talking. The more words they learn, and the better they can use them, the less they need gestures and exaggerated facial expressions. Among themselves, of course, they will never be able to do without these means of expression.

Soon Maria no longer needs to lipread each letter and sound individually, she can recognize entire words. Even when reading, she no longer proceeds from letter to letter but can add word to word to arrive at sentences and at meaning.

She learns to name things she cannot see but only feel or imagine, like invisible attributes such as *sad*, *charitable*, *greedy*, or *patient*. The teacher shows them a big picture, a rider on a horse who is tearing his cloak in two and giving one half to a beggar. This, the teacher tells them, is what it means to be *charitable*. It is what the compassionate do, and that people

Maria with her foster mother, Mama Bunden.

who are like this are called *compassionate* or *charitable*. The idea remains in the children's minds that helping and sharing means being *charitable*.

Maria recognizes that the names of her feelings can express much more easily and quickly what she could only indicate with gestures and mime before, and that other people always understand these names correctly. She realizes that it is good to learn the words for *remorse*, *guilt*, *desire*, and *sorrow*. That hearing people are able to give these words additional expressiveness through the sound of the language, through nuances in intonation, is beyond Maria. Her speech remains monotonous; automatically, though, and impulsively, she will always use facial expressions and body language in order to emphasize what she means.

When Maria plays tag or hopscotch down on Stromgasse with Adelheid and the little Italian girl, there are often other neighbor children present who can hear. Sometimes one of the children stares at her, sometimes they laugh at her or make fun of her by copying her gestures. Then all of a sudden, she loses her courage and all her pleasure at having learned to speak. When she goes to Mama, sad and upset, Mrs. Bunden says, "no matter, Maria! Children are stupid! You speak well, very well!"

Maria cries, "I can't understand children. Only very little. Children talk differently. I don't know why I can't understand."

Mama smiles. "Children speak slang, Aachener Platt. It is Low German from Aachen."

"What is that?" Maria wants to know.

"You speak proper High German, beautifully! The children speak Aachen slang. But, the children can also speak High German. You need not learn Aachen slang. It is not necessary for you! High German is the language you write in." Maria has understood some of this. But, she is still very puzzled. She herself is struggling so hard to learn High German while those children speak that language and another one as well! Maria thinks they must be very clever. She does not know how the hearing children pick up the local dialect so easily, simply by playing on the streets.

14

If Maria wants to go to the center of town from Stromgasse, she first turns right into Rosstrasse. Here, in the middle of the street, like an island, stands the little *Roskapellchen* (Ros Chapel). It is eight-sided, with a domed roof, and if you look through the front grille, you can see the Madonna and child inside. In the attached house there is a tiny shop where, once a week, Maria has a little bottle filled with schnapps for Papa. That costs thirty pennies. In the summer, when it is too hot for Mama to light the fire in the stove, Maria takes a jug, the bottom of which is already covered with ground corn or malt coffee, to the shop and has it filled with boiling water. That is two pennies. Mama does not own a spirit stove for cooking outdoors.

Maria is always surprised when she goes through Rosstrasse at how many children there are. The whole street is full of them. Cats are sitting on the windowsills and in the doorways. Outside the windows of the upper stories, many with green wooden trellises filled with flowerpots, hang birdcages, and the birds in them hop continuously from floor to perch and from perch to floor. From early morning, old men sit on chairs beside their front doors or squat on stone doorsteps. The women often join them, peeling potatoes or darning and sewing.

Some of the houses in Rosstrasse are so old that the doors and windows hang all crooked in their frames. Rosstrasse is unlike any other street in the area. Here, the residents are in the middle of town, in a world of their own, as in a village. Often, families have lived here for generations. On Mühlenberg Street, high above the slanted roofs and the little chapel of this odd little street, stands the splendid church of St. Jakob, Maria's parish church. Its thick walls were built from the stones of the old town wall. In July, when St. Jakob's celebrates its name day, the Ros, as Rosstrasse is affectionately called, celebrates, too. A rope is stretched in front of the decorated chapel from one side of the street to the other, high above the throng of children. An angel with golden hair, a glittering crown, and wings poking out of a white dress glides stiffly along the rope. Maria and her foster sisters gape at the angel, their arms stretched out toward it. Halfway across the street, the angel sways to and fro and sweets spill down from its basket in both directions. The children grab and grasp, scramble and tussle, until there is not a single sweet left on the street, and the fun begins again.

Mama goes through the Ros with the children when she wants to go shopping in town. Maria and Adelheid carry the shopping basket while Mama holds little Anna Dilesio's hand. They walk past the city theatre and come to the Elisenbrunnen, which houses two hot springs. Maria was astonished when she saw the building for the first time: a round, tall, open hall supported by thick white columns, with colonnades on both sides that lead to two enclosed pavilions. For centuries people have come to Aachen from far away to soak in and drink the sulfur-smelling waters that bubble up hot from the earth in various places throughout the city.

Mama never goes past this healing spring without taking a drink from the smelly, steamy water. The children shudder. No, they don't want to do the same! They have tasted it once! Maria pinches her nose and says, "Water stinks!"

In the square in front of the Elisenbrunnen, tables and chairs are set up underneath the shady lime trees. Whoever has the money and the time can be waited on here and watch life and people go by. While the children are waiting for Mama to finish her drink, they, too, are watching what is happening on the Graben. Carriages drawn by elegant horses rush by, followed by heavy farm horses with carts. Some of the carts stop in front of the fancy shops nearby, unloading or loading up goods. Kegs of beer are rolled over the pavement and down into the cellars of restaurants. Somebody is pushing a wheelbarrow. The streetcleaner is sweeping up the horse droppings and other litter. Young men wearing student's caps, girls in white pinafores, and nuns from the many hospitals and convents in the city are walking by. Ladies carry parasols and wear feather hats and tight, long skirts. Sometimes even a motorcar drives along the Graben.

Mama then goes with the girls up Hartmannstrasse. Walking in Aachen is always either up or down a hill. The shops have pulled down their blinds to protect the goods from the sun's rays. On Münsterplatz (Münster Square), near the *Vinzenzbrunnen* (St. Vincent Fountain), baskets and stalls have been set up to sell flowers, flowerpots, and vegetable and flower seedlings. Mama never buys a bouquet of flowers. She doesn't throw away money. At home she cares for her own flowering plants—a busy Lizzie, begonias and primulas; they last longer than cut flowers. The dark walls of the Aachen Cathedral loom close to the flower market. Mama crosses the square with the children and enters the cathedral through a small door. Pleading for silence, she raises her finger to her mouth before blessing herself with holy water from the basin. In the sudden dim light and coolness inside, the children walk shyly up to the Octagon at the center of the building. Mama turns to them and points to their feet, indicating they should tread more softly. Being deaf, they cannot know that their footsteps reverberate on the stone floor. But there is a deep silence here, so different from the world outside, and they can sense the solemnity of the mighty room.

Maria has never before seen a church like the Aachen Cathedral. It really is not just one church, but several churches joined together, and they are all different. In the eight-sided central building, Charlemagne's Palatine Chapel, a heavy chain hangs from the high cupola, suspending the Barbarossa chandelier. Maria thinks that it looks like a huge wheel. The walls of the Octagon and the cross vaults of the gallery are inlaid with golden mosaics. In the upper aisle between valuable, ancient columns stands the marble throne of Charlemagne. In later times a magnificent Gothic choir has been added to the Octagon. For half of a millennium after the reign of Charlemagne, thirty-two German kings were crowned on that throne. Maria thinks that its walls are made of nothing but beautiful windows; from the ceiling down to the choirstalls, they glow in all colors. Shafts of light pour into the width of the chancel and illuminate a Madonna in a halo, hovering high above the stalls. The children gaze in awe. Mama puts her hands together, crosses herself and kneels. The children do likewise.

On Sundays at High Mass, on religious feast days, and at special concerts, the famous Aachen Cathedral choir will sing. The singing unites with the beauty of the building into a profound experience for the listeners. Many people come to the cathedral for that alone. But Maria and her foster sisters will never experience music. After the mass, they go out through one of the adjoining chapels.

Across the Hof courtyard it is only a few steps to Körbergässchen. The children already head for it, as Mama has said that she wants to buy a new broom. Here, lovely old houses are nestled together. In the sunshine, the golden and brown baskets glow in front of the basketmakers' shops. Stacked and piled up into each other are laundry baskets, shopping baskets, travel baskets, dog and poultry baskets, and wicker chairs. Bundles of brushes, brooms, carpet-beaters, and feather dusters dangle from the walls of the houses. There are chests, suitcases, and wicker bags. Funniest of all, though, are the wooden shoes arranged in a long, straight line, the largest first, then gradually smaller and smaller. Mama buys a broom and puts it into the shopping basket Maria is holding. Mama carries the broom handle herself, and the children laugh when she shows them how she can use it to spank their bottoms.

From Körbergässchen it is only a short way up to the *Hühnermarkt* (chicken market). The Town Hall, with its onion-domed corner tower and the tall, austere Granus Tower of Charlemagne's Imperial Palace, looks down on the poultry stands. Mama, who never buys poultry, walks past without a second glance. Only Maria turns around to have a look. She sees geese, ducks, hens, roosters, and pigeons cooped up in baskets and crates, and also dead animals with their heads hanging motionless over the edge of a board.

Adjoining the Granus Tower is an ancient house and right next to it there is an inn called the *Postwagen* (mail coach), which is pretty much how it looks. Its wooden structure is decorated with carvings. Fixed to the windows, with bull's-eye panes, are shutters that can be opened above and below. Mama and the children go up past the domed belly of the Postwagen and on to the Market Square. In front of the mighty Gothic Town Hall there is hustle and bustle. Mama heads straight over to the first vegetable stand, set up underneath a gaily striped awning. She does not have a garden like some people. She has to buy all of her vegetables from the market.

Housewives and maids are inspecting the produce. Maria, too, knows how to compare and points out this or that to Mama. They go from stand to stand, around baskets, boxes, and sacks, from barrows to carts, some of them shaded by awnings. Onions for five pennies, greens for two pennies, and a cauliflower make their way into Mama's basket. Mama cannot resist the bright red radishes. She buys six little bunches. Maria will not eat them; no such things grow in any garden in Freilingen. She does not even want to try what the others find so delicious. She does not like the red tomatoes, the oranges, or bananas either, which are only on sale in the finest fruit shops. She has never seen them grow, and something so foreign and strange, she doesn't want to eat. Fortunately, Mama never buys those strange things: asparagus and chicory!

On the market square, there is a riot of color and activity. The market women talk excitedly to Mama. Maria notices that she often laughs at what they say. Some of the market women wear a striped cape over their shoulders, tied in a ruff around the neck. Over their headscarves, they wear golden straw hats that look like small buckets turned upside-down.

Before they all leave for home, Mama nods her permission for the children to run over to the fountain in the center of Market Square. The fountain has a huge round basin. Cart horses are fastened to the railing all around it. The children climb over the bar, up a few steps, and bend over the stone rim of the basin that receives the water from an upper basin made of bronze. The water glistens in the sunlight. They dip their hands into it. Other children are playing with little pieces of wood, floating them like boats. They push them under the surface and let them bounce back up and dance on the little waves. Unruly boys are splashing water out of the basin. The grownups nearby scold them, and a market woman grabs a broom to chase all the children away. At the top of the fountain, undisturbed by the hustle and bustle below, stands the statue of Emperor Charlemagne in full armor, the Imperial Crown on his head, the scepter and Imperial Orb in his hands. The Emperor Charlemagne has turned all green with verdigris.

15

Maria is sitting next to Father in the passenger train, traveling home for the long fall vacation. Twice already they have changed trains, and now the train stops at Nettersheim, 60 miles east of Freilingen. A thin woman gets into their compartment. They all shake hands. Father helps put the woman's basket up on the luggage rack.

"Nice in Aachen?" the woman asks Maria.

"Yes—but much more so in Freilingen!" Then Maria says to Father, "I recognize girl. Lives on road to Lommersdorf, behind chapel. What name?"

"Helene, works for a farmer in Nettersheim in his house and fields."

"Earns money?"

"Yes," replies Father, and turns back to the woman. The grownups talk and laugh with one another and Maria watches silently. She has not seen Father so merry for a long time. She looks at Helene's hands which are rough and raw from hard work. Helene's face is tan and has little wrinkles round her nose and eyes.

Maria then looks out at the late-summer landscape flying by.

They all get off the train at Blankenheim-Wald. From here the three continue on foot. Father carries Helene's basket. Maria walks silently beside the chatting couple and thinks of her dead mother. *Mother*—the thought of her makes Maria sad. At home there is no longer a kind, good Mother waiting for her, and Maria distinctly feels it. The house seems empty. In need of comfort herself, she picks up little Josef in her arms, kissing and caressing him, and says, "You my dear brother Josef. You my dear brother Josef," and even in her hard-to-understand voice, the words sound tender.

The very first Sunday Maria is at home, Helene comes for coffee. She has combed her hair prettily. Her dress is simple and clean. Her light gray eyes look more serious today.

When Maria goes upstairs, she finds Aunt Barbara, her mother's sister, sitting on the edge of the bed, crying. "Why you cry?" Maria asks, alarmed.

Her aunt wipes her eyes. "Because your mother has died. Your father wants to marry Helene." Maria is sad about Mother and that her aunt is crying. But she also thinks of Father and her five younger brothers and sisters. She pictures Helene, healthy, nimble, with industrious hands. "Poor Father must have wife," she says. "Grandmother too much work alone!"

The month of August is hot. Early in the morning the sky is already blue, the air still with only a few white clouds passing overhead. Reluctantly, Willi and Klöss tug their slates under their arms and trudge off to school. Their vacation is not until October. They never like going to school. But if they stay at home they will have to work hard, and Father does not stand any nonsense when it comes to work. Maria has put two slices of bread in her apron pocket and looks around for Grandmother. Father is threshing some sheaves of rye in the open barn. That afternoon, the wheat is going to be harvested. But because the wheat stalks are too short, rye stalks will be used to bind the wheat sheaves.

Setta is playing in the yard with some old shoes she has found somewhere. Her hair hasn't been combed, but Maria has no time to see to it just now because Grandmother is letting the animals out of the stable—a calf, a bull, and two cows, one of them lumbering heavily. Maria quickly fetches her stick from behind the open stable door. The cows stand waiting in the yard. One already has left a cow pat, right in front of the house door. Christina is looking at it, with her finger in her mouth. She is five years old, a chubby little thing with curly hair and soft features. She is a quiet child, and she needs to be handled quietly and gently. She can't bear angry faces. She cries when she sees one. Maria flicks the big cow lightly. Slowly she deigns to move. Christina takes her older sister's hand, and the two deaf girls drive the small herd past the half-timbered houses and out of the village. Maria looks out toward the far, rolling hills. From the road, a meadow slopes steeply down into the valley and flattens out toward the lonely mill down by Mühlen Creek. Maria drives the animals down to the middle of the pasture where she lets them graze.

The children have to watch and make sure that the animals do not stray onto someone else's land or the road. Large stones in the grass outline the boundaries. All of the children from the village have to "drive to pasture," to tend the cattle every day, often far out on the commonly held property, which is full of broom and low shrubs. Out here, there are no hedges or barbed-wire fences.

This great meadow had been Mother Elisabeth's dowry. It is called *Im Reech*. From here, Maria and Christina can see the village people with their animals, and wagons moving along the road on their way to the fields. It is hot—and nowhere is there a tree or a tall bush to offer some shade. Leisurely, calmly, the animals pull the grass with their pale red, rough tongues, in regular movements while swarms of flies hover around their eyes and nostrils. Constantly, their tails flick back and forth to chase away the pests. Maria and Christina have no idea that the flies are making a buzzing sound, that the gnats in the air are humming, the swallows are twittering, and that all the birds are singing different tunes. They can't hear the farmers in the distance calling out orders to their draft animals in the fields. The children can't hear the screeching when a farmer has to put on the brakes on the steep road above them.

Maria and Christina lie on their bellies. Christina has stuck her face into the grass and breathes its smell and feels its coolness. She cannot speak at all. Maria has tried to teach her, but without success. She has to rely on gestures to communicate with her. Slowly, and extremely clearly, she pronounces the words at the same time. On the first days out here in the pasture, she pronounces for Christina "cow," "flower," and "sky,"—everything one can see, touch, or point out. But, Christina does not understand what Maria meant. Maria puts her finger on her sister's mouth, then on her own, and then points to the cow and says "cow." But the little one only looks at her blankly. *So,* Maria thinks, *maybe it is too hard to say "cow." What does a cow say?* The teacher has said it in school—and if you look at a hungry cow or one that wants to be milked, you can well imagine that she makes the sound "moo."

"You say moo!" Maria addresses her little sister again, "Moo, moo, moo!" Again she points to the cow. Christina looks anxiously at Maria and starts to cry. She sobs, rubs her eyes, and tears run down her cheeks. Maria puts her arm round her sister's shoulder and wipes away the tears with her apron. She wonders why her little sister is so scared; she did not mean anything bad. All she wanted was to make her talk.

One cow has wandered and is grazing in the neighboring pasture. Maria runs over with the rod in her hand and chases it back. The other two cows are grazing peacefully on the slope. The cumbersome cow has lain down wearily in the pasture. She turns her head and looks at the girls. *Why cow tired?* Maria wonders. *Cow must eat. I let lie.*

Maria waves at Christina and gestures *come.* Christina gets up and follows her big sister almost up to the road, where two massive rocks protrude from the neighbor's pasture. The angular limestone rocks are light gray and covered with black specks of moss. The rain has washed out hollows in them. Little blackthorn bushes grow in the cracks and crevices. The children move their hands over the firm moss. Maria and Christina climb on one of the rocks. They sit side by side, dangling their legs and leaning back on their arms. From here, they can keep a close eye on the animals grazing peacefully in the Giefers' pasture. The heavy cow is still lying in the grass. She is not eating. Maria is very surprised because normally the two cows and the calf always eat their fill before lying down to chew their cud.

All is quiet on the road. The siblings eat the slices of bread that Maria has brought along in her apron. They can see the farmers on the surrounding hills, busy with their work. Now and then a breeze blows across the slope. It feels good. They are sweating in their long dresses and woolen stockings, but they are used to that. Christina slides down from the rock and picks a harebell, common along country lanes, she has discovered at the edge of the rocks. She hands it to Maria. Maria looks at the flower and thinks of the bell that hangs visibly in the chapel tower. The bell swings back and forth when someone pulls the rope. She knows that when the farmers hear it they will make their way home. She holds the dainty stem with its tiny leaves in front of her face. Gently, she moves it, and the flower swings like a little bell.

Do people hear everything that moves? If the flower moves, can they hear that too? And to hear—what is that? Can those who hear know when something is moving, even without seeing or feeling it with their body? Without sensing it? Maria is lost in thought.

Suddenly, she jumps off the rock, grabs her stick, and runs down the path to the meadow. Christina follows as fast as she can. The calf is busy munching in the neighbor's meadow. Maria scolds it, "Away! Away! You must not! Away!" The startled calf makes some high leaps and only gallops deeper into the neighbor's pasture. Maria moves around the animal in a wide circle and drives it back into her mother's meadow. Christina has followed her, brandishing a branch. Now soaked with sweat, the girls lie down in the grass, red-faced.

Maria lies on her side with her head on her arm, keeping an eye on the cows. The heavy one is still lying down and Maria thinks she seems restless. *Isn't she mooing, when she raises her head and opens her mouth, over and over again, mooing? Perhaps she is sick! She has lain down after hardly eating anything at all.* Maria gets up and goes over to her. The cow turns her head and looks at her. "You get up! You eat!" she says to the animal and wants to urge her on a little with her stick. But the cow will not get up and Maria is at a loss. Then she sees something peculiar. She looks once and then again, to make sure she is really seeing it. Below the cow's tail the little hooves of a calf are poking out, two tiny little hooves are poking out, just a bit.

All at once, she is very excited. *The cow is dropping a calf!* Now Maria suddenly knows where baby animals come from—the kittens, the foals, the piglets, and the little calves. Until now, she had not realized that they have to be born from the animal mothers. Maria's heart is pounding. If the calf comes now, what should she do? What if the cow is in pain? But she doesn't dare leave. The farmers that she can see in the fields are much too far away to call or wave to for them to come and help. Maria knows from experience, and feels it as well, that her voice does not carry that far. She runs over to Christina. Hastily, using both hands, she makes the same motion as Father does when he twirls his moustache, and gestures that Christina shall go and fetch the moustache, and points to the cow. Christina sees how excited and worried Maria's face is, so she runs up the meadow, toward the village. Maria hopes that Christina can make herself understood and that help will really come. How fortunate that Father is working in the barn this morning!

She goes back to the cow, kneels down beside her, strokes her hide, and speaks to her sweetly and calmly, "You get baby calf. You brave!" She is thrilled with the miracle. Now she is quite alert and quite conscious of her responsibility to tend to the cow. She keeps an eye on the other cows, tearing away at the grass without haste or greed. She caresses the animal lying on the ground, shooing away the pesky flies and all the time looking up toward the village.

Finally, Maria sees her Father coming. She lets out a sigh of relief. *Christina good,* she tells herself, glad that Christina understood and was able to get Father to come. She also is proud that Father can see how attentive she has been. Father knows right away what is going on. He kneels behind the animal and takes hold of the calf's legs by its hooves and begins to pull. Every time the cow moves and presses, Father pulls firmly. Then he slackens and waits. Fascinated, Maria sees the calf's head appearing, pressed on its front hooves. Now Father gestures to Maria to run home and fetch Grandmother. Maria would like to stay and watch. She is excited. She is also worried about the cow and the little calf. But, she knows she must follow Father's bidding. Never before has she run so fast. Grandmother meets her on the way and she seems to know what is happening already. She indicates to the excited Maria to go home to look after Setta, while she herself hurries to the meadow where the calf is being born.

In the evening, Maria finds the newborn calf in the stable. It is lying in a corner on fresh straw behind a high board and is gazing with big, wondering eyes. As Maria comes closer, it tries to stand up, but it has no control over its legs yet and staggers back and forth. Maria leans over the board and stares as if she had never seen a calf before.

Vacations at home in Freilingen are wonderful! Every time, Maria wishes she could stay here for good. It is such fun to drive the team of Father's new horse and the cow and lead it slowly across the stubbled field when the sheaves are being loaded. And when the heavy cart is rumbling home, Maria is sometimes allowed to sit on the horse! Its hide is warm, smooth, and soft. She laughs and waves, and her eyes are happy and bright.

Toward the end of the vacation, Father gets a threshing machine. It is a real monster, very long and high. Behind the barn, Father has a capstan built, a long, iron shaft with a couple of cogwheels. Two cows or one horse have to keep walking in a circle to turn the wheels, then the machine runs and the tiresome work of threshing is done much faster and easier.

It is time for Maria to depart again. Very early one morning, Grandmother wakes Maria. She has prepared a basin filled with warm water. Father stands bare-chested in the front room, washing himself with cold water, dripping and splashing it everywhere. He smiles at his daughter and makes fun of her. "You are an old grandmother," he says. You are a spoiled *Aachener Printe*. Washing yourself with warm water! Bah!"

Maria is not in the mood for teasing. She would like to stay here, like her siblings. She alone has to go away to that strange town, which, like the school and her foster parents, she forgets during vacation. To be sure, once she is in Aachen she is happy there—but she would rather stay at home in Freilingen. Once Maria is dressed and her hair is combed, she slinks out into the gray dawn across the yard and into the barn. There she hides in the threshing machine . Her heart is pounding, but she tells herself, *I stay here! I not go away—Father scolding—I not care!* She does not feel quite right, though, in the dark box. Never before has she done such a thing. Never before has she made a decision on her own—let alone gone against Father's will. She starts crying with sorrow. When, after a while, the lid is raised and Father peers in anxiously, she climbs out of her hiding place, a heap of misery, sobbing and begging. "Please Father, I here stay!"

But Father just shakes his head gruffly and says, "Christmas you come again!"

16

The fresh snow has thawed. Only on the sheltered slopes does it still glisten in the late December moonlight and falling frost. When Maria got out of the train at the lonely station of Blankenheim-Wald, she was freezing. But after the brisk walk, her body has warmed again and the north wind blowing frosty dust along the Ahr road does not bother her. Only a few people got off the train with her and Father; the others went to Blankenheimerdorf and the larger town of Blankenheim. Now, she and Father are walking past the dense fir forests that reach down from the hills to the road at the valley floor. Bare chestnut trees line their way. The waters of the Ahr River glitter like silver.

Maria's few belongings are in a cardboard box, which Father is carrying tied to a strong stick over his shoulder. Father has given her his hand to hold. He has never done that before. It is wonderful to walk holding so tightly to Father's hand.

The moon travels with them. In the vast sky, the stars are also traveling. *How many there are!* One cannot count them, and beyond the many bright and faintly flickering lights, there are even more twinkling. The longer Maria looks, the more she can sense the infinity of the heavens. How tiny man is in comparison—it is good that Father's hand is holding her. Maria looks up at him, sees his quiet face and his eyes fixed on the road ahead. *Does Father know everything? Does he know why the moon is there and the stars, why the heavens are so vast?*

Where the road splits at the bare hazel bushes, they leave the Ahr valley behind. Maria is thinking only of home now. The road rises, and ice glistens between frost-hardened ruts.

Maria sees two figures approaching, and a dog comes bounding up to Father. Maria does not know the dog, a German shepherd, but Father gives him a pat and talks to him. Klöss and Willi have come to meet them. Maria hugs them and notices how they smile with embarrassment because they are not used to such a show of affection. "Whose dog? I don't know dog!" Maria asks her brother. Klöss points to Father. So they have a new dog. "Where is old dog?" she asks. Klöss turns his mouth toward the moonlight so that Maria can see it. "Dead," he says. Silently they walk on. Soon Maria sees the whitewashed walls of the mill. When they are crossing the bridge over Grindel Creek, the dog dashes off like an arrow. He runs up the high Stein, a steep hill opposite the pasture where Maria and Christina had tended the cows in the summer. At the top are a number of other fields, and behind them lies their village. Suddenly, Father throws the cardboard box at Maria's feet and runs off with the stick in his hand. The brothers follow him. She watches in bewilderment as they clamber up the steep slope, until they disappear behind the top of the hill. *What does it mean? Where have the three of them gone? Is she meant to walk on alone, through the night, up the road to the village?* She decides to wait at the bottom of the rocky hill. The rocks hold many secrets. Once some archaeologists came and searched and poked around, digging on the Stein and they found Roman urns and coins, ancient coffins, bones, and weapons. One of the coins dated from the time of the Roman Emperor Caligula. They also found a Franconian grave with a complete human skeleton. Higher up on the Stein there is a cave. Sometimes, villagers find round light-red bricks that once belonged to the heating system of a Roman villa and Roman floor tiles that the villagers in Freilingen use for their kitchen and hall floors.

In later years, when Germans became Christian, innocent women and girls were burned as witches on the Stein. Since then, ghostly, mysterious things have been seen on the Stein and stories have been told about them in the village—stories of dogs with eyes of fire, a headless man, thousands of cats with glowing eyes, and the Midnight Ghost who shoulders a boundary stone, but does not know where to put it down.

Maria is relieved when, at last, she sees her father and brothers returning to her. Klöss laughs and shows Maria what he is carrying on his back: a fox, a fully grown fox. Klöss is carrying the fox fast by its hind legs. He has wrapped the fox's beautiful, bushy tail around his neck and its head hangs down between its dangling forefeet.

Father pats the panting German shepherd. Through gestures, Willi tells Maria what has happened. Willi almost never talks to her, but, he is so excited that, still gasping for breath, he simply has to tell her. Maria repeats out loud what she understands from his story. "Dog has smelled fox, has run after it, has caught fox. Father, Klöss, and I have heard animals fight. Father has killed fox with stick."

Father turns toward the moon so that Maria can clearly see his mouth, putting his forefinger on his lips and says, "You not say anything about killed fox!"

When they finally arrive in the village, all the lights have long since been extinguished. It is the middle of the night, no one is awake.

Maria is tired from the journey and the three-and-a-half hour walk from the train station. The next morning, she watches Father in the stable skinning the red fox. It has a fine pelt. But, she will never see it again. Father must sell it.

17

In October 1908, while Maria was at school, Father married Helene. Now she works everywhere in the house. Father tells Maria to call Helene "Mother," and although it is hard for her at first, she does what Father wants. Mother Helene barely says a word to Maria; she has no time for that, anyway.

The first afternoon that Maria is home, Grandmother tells her about the terrible thing that happened to Christina and little Setta. An early frost came suddenly in November. Christina and Setta ran indoors to warm their hands at the stove, but the stove wasn't throwing out enough heat for them. They hurried across the yard and into the barn, where they found enough straw lying around to gather up and take into the house. Christina opened the little door of the stove, and inside a log was still smoldering. Setta watched as Christina stuffed all the straw into the stove. They knelt in front of the stove door and watched little red flames lick at the straw. They were so pleased with their warming fire. Christina felt a cold shiver run down her back, so she turned around. Setta, too, turned her freezing back to the stove. Neither of the children noticed how the little flames increased in number, grew larger, and devoured more and more of the dry straw, until they reached the ends poking out from the stove door. Soon they were no longer little flames but had become a single, raging one. Christina did not feel the tongues of fire licking at her little apron and dress, she did not feel it until she was all ablaze. Setta, to whom nothing had happened, screamed at the top of her voice. Alarmed, Grandmother came running, saw the child burning, grabbed sacks and jackets and threw them over the child. She pulled Christina to the floor, rolling her back and forth, and slapping the flames dead with her bare hands. Meanwhile, Setta ran screaming out of the house. Grandmother then carried the unconscious Christina upstairs into the bedroom.

Completely horrified, Maria looks at Grandmother's face and immediately goes up the stairs to Christina, with a sinking heart. As she opens the door to the cold room, she can smell a nasty, sweetish odor. She feels like turning around and leaving again, but she pushes herself forward. Christina is lying in the bed, so gaunt that Maria hardly recognizes her. Grandmother has said that Father has no money for the hospital, but a nurse who lives in Lommersdorf comes to Freilingen every day to apply fresh salve and dress Christina's horrible wounds.

Maria feels sick. She cannot stand the awful stench or the sight of her helpless little sister. She goes back into the hall, opens the attic door, closes it behind her, and quietly climbs up the curved stairs. The sky shines through cracks and skylights in the attic ceiling. Up here there is the pleasant smell of wheat, rye, and barley grains, which lie on the floor in small heaps. The cat is curled up in the wheat and lifts its head to blink at Maria. Spider webs are draped like curtains. Bunches of chamomile and peppermint and bundles of dry onions hang down from the beams. Maria detects a spicy scent in the air and also the smell of dust. She sits down in the grain, a little distance away from the dozing cat. The grain is cold, smooth, and heavy. Here she can cry at last, cry and cry. She longs bitterly for her dead mother, pities her sick sister, and is sorry for herself because she cannot hear.

Now, because of her wounds, Christina will not be able to go to school with Maria in Aachen. *Life is so hard.* They are poor, and that means work and more work. No one has the time to show love.

The cat looks warily at the sobbing child and twitches its ears. *Can the cat hear her crying?* That animals turn their heads toward her when she approaches, even when they cannot see or feel her, surprises Maria again and again. *Even animals can hear!—and she can't.* Maria has been careful to cry without using her voice. She must not press in her throat. She does not know if anyone downstairs can hear her, and does not want them to. She is cold. Slowly, the cat gets up, stretches itself, and comes over to nudge Maria's leg. Maria does not like cats and finds no comfort in the animal's affection. She pushes it away.

Lost in thought, she lets the grains trickle through her fingers. She waits until her tears dry up, cautiously blows her nose, not knowing how far that sound carries, and goes back downstairs, freezing.

Christina will stay in bed for a long time. It will be five years before she can get up again.

18

After Christmas, in the middle of the school year, the little Italian girl departs with her parents for a faraway country. A new foster sister comes, a small, quiet child. She is called Gertrud. After Easter the jolly Adelheid is no longer with the Bundens either, because she has graduated from school. Maria is sad. *To whom is she going to pass the fried sausage she doesn't like, under the table? Who will make her laugh now, until tears run down her cheeks?*

There was one place the girls were particularly fond of—a landing with a window on the stairs leading up to the attic. From here, they could look down on many roofs and courtyards. Here, they could play undisturbed all the fun games Adelheid invented. Here, it was cozy.

Maria will never forget how she played Mass with Adelheid. Adelheid would drag up a little bench, cover it with a white cloth from their dolls' things, and place the figure of a saint on it. They would smooth silver paper with their thumbnails and make a chalice from it. From white paper they would cut out wafers, and for a missal, they would place a thick prayer book on the "altar." Adelheid played the priest and Maria was the altar boy. Then they acted out everything their eyes had observed in St. Jakob's church. Adelheid would even give a sermon. She'd stand at the banister as if it were a pulpit. Maria would make wide sleeves for her out of cloths, lace mats, and safety pins, just like the lace sleeves on the priest's surplice. Then, Adelheid would give a soundless sermon. She'd roll her eyes, brandish her arms in the air, and move her mouth exaggeratedly as if she were speaking loudly into the high church. She'd wipe the wide sleeves across the banister pulpit and stretch her arm and forefinger toward the heavens, letting her sleeve fall back. She would then bring her arm back down, as if the wrath of God were descending upon the listening congregation, her sleeves falling nicely back into place. Adelheid rocking back and forth on her feet, bent over the pulpit, almost falling over it, spread her arms wide, as if to embrace heaven itself. She'd pretend to wipe the sweat off her forehead, hit her palm against her chest, and shake her fists toward Heaven. At the end, she would make the sign of a huge cross over an invisible congregation and, deeply moved by her own sermon, step down. Maria would be doubled up with laughter on the stairs.

But now, Adelheid has gone. Now that is all over. The new girl, Gertrud, is not interested in such things, and Maria just doesn't have the knack for making other people laugh.

Mama Bunden takes in two more deaf girls: Eva and Therese. Now there are four of them sleeping in the little room upstairs. Mama had to put in another bed, and Maria now has to climb across three beds to reach her own.

Mama is quite taken with dainty little Eva and dresses her up in bows and ribbons and starched frilly pinafores, like a little doll. Maria, too, likes Eva and does not mind when Mama buys the little one an extra piece of cake in the middle of the week. Therese, though, feels offended and is cross with Mama. Maria cannot understand why. Therese loves Maria. She brings whatever Maria needs, presents her with toys or special morsels, even shines shoes for her and is always trying to please her. Maria is wondering a lot about it. Never before has she known anyone who wanted to serve her.

On Sundays when the weather is bad and raindrops are running down the windowpanes, the four children play dominos or with building blocks. Mama has bought these new toys for the girls, and even Papa joins in. On Sunday afternoons when the weather is good, all six of them go out for a walk. Papa walks on ahead. Now and then, his hand slips into his trouser pocket and then a wrapped piece of candy appears on the ground behind him. The children pounce on it noisily.

In the wide grassy valleys outside of Aachen, the roads are bordered by hedgerows. With some of these, the banks on both sides are so high that the hazel, hawthorn, and blackthorn bushes and the hornbeam trees join their branches overhead. It is shady and cool on these sunken roads. When the group reaches the edge of the forest, they have a wide view of the countryside, all the way to the Eifel Mountains. They can see the houses of the town nestled in the valley below. Sheltered by the high woodlands and surrounded by gentle, bare hills, the town leans up against Lousberg and the smaller Salvatorberg. Two locomotives, puffing thick clouds of smoke, pull a long chain of coaches through the rising valley toward the wooded border to Liège in Belgium and further on to Paris.

The Linzenzhäuschen coffeehouse in the old watchtower is situated on the Aachener Landgraben, which can be followed easily in the forest as it is the remains of a land defense system that surrounded and protected the entire realm of Aachen during the Middle Ages. It is a double bank of earth walls, planked with double rows of oaks and beeches whose branches have been cut back to a man's height and so intertwined as to form an almost impassable thicket. The children like to walk along the banks past the strangely knotted tree trunks.

In summer, the carriages of the narrow-gauge railway have no side walls. That way one can travel out of the town and into the forest in the open air. Mama, Papa, and the children take a tramcar when they do not want to walk; they hike on many a Sunday through the Aachen forest with a rucksack and picnic bag. They sit wherever it suits them, on a grassy slope or in a clearing, to eat and play. On other Sundays, they climb the many stairs and narrow paths up the Lousberg hill, which is much overgrown. The birds there are so tame, they hardly flee from the human intruders. From the top of the hill, the town lies directly at their feet. Tallest of all, the slim spire of St. Jakob's points up to the sky. On November third, the celebration day of Saint Hubert (the patron saint of hunters), colorful lights will be lit around the spire. The lights will burn from evening until morning to show the hunters their way back home.

One road leads straight out of Aachen and right into the Eifel. Traveling along that road, which Napoleon allowed to be built and which leads all the way to Trier, one would come to Freilingen. When Maria turns around, away from the town, meadows and fields spread out before her, and white-washed farmhouses dot the landscape. The black cones of slagheaps where miners dig coal out of the earth loom in the distance.

Maria stretches out her arm and points toward Holland and the little church steeple that belongs to the Dutch village of Vaals. She was there in May with her class, and she tells Mama how they walked through the forest up to the lookout tower on Vaalserberg. They climbed the wooden stairs and looked out over Holland, Germany, Neutral Moresnet, and Belgium. The teacher explained to them that the lookout tower stands on the highest mountain in Holland. Maria had been astonished because the

Lousberg in Aachen appeared to be higher than the Vaalserberg. Later, not far from the tower, they had also seen the four boundary stones, marking the point where the four countries meet. In Vaals, the children also visited the large tannery. Maria tells Mama about the animal skins and great vats, and of the men in their leather aprons, rubber gloves, and rubber boots. It smelled very bad. Maria also remembers the church in Vaals that was built of red bricks—she had never seen a red brick church before.

19

In school, Maria learns how to construct clear, short sentences. By using the past, present, and future tenses correctly, one sentence can be made into three different ones. But she does not learn the simple past tense: "He fetched the pot"; instead, she learns the perfect tense: "He has fetched the pot." This is because "has fetched" is much easier to lipread than "fetched." Nor does she learn "I travel tomorrow," but instead, "I will travel tomorrow," since that is also easier to lipread.

Maria gets used to thinking in sentences. There are articles and their inflections, singular and plural affixes, ordinal numbers, infinitives and participles, and verbs, both passive and active, and—oh dear!—the four cases. The teacher has the almost superhuman task of helping the children understand the difference between them all and how to use them properly.

A small glass inkwell is set into each desk. Maria dunks the sharp steel nib of her pen into it and begins to write letters neatly in her blue exercise book, the *Aachen Notebook*. She is learning to write *Sütterlin*, the German handwriting script, and Latin characters. The teacher is very pleased with her work, and she beams when he nods his head and says, "That is fine." Then, he dictates to the children a short paragraph titled "YOU."

> Your body is mortal, your soul immortal. Your heart and soul are one. God will one day separate your soul from your body, then your body will be buried. Where will your soul go? Your soul will go to God. Your body has eyes and ears. You can open and shut your eyes. You can see with your eyes. Can you also hear with your ears? You cannot hear with your ears.

Maria has to think a lot about what the teachers says—that all deaf children will hear in Heaven after death. *But then, she will not have any ears! And without ears, she will not be able to hear?! And why does God not let her hear while she is still on earth? She has got healthy ears! Why and what is invisibly broken inside?*

After Easter vacation in 1911, Maria gets a new teacher, Master Wirtz, a short man with a white moustache and a little beard. In May, it rains buckets for days. Thunderstorms rage and hailstones fall, too, turning the earth white in no time. When the lightning flashes across the gloomy sky, the children are frightened. "Already, two people in Aachen have been struck by lightning," Master Wirtz says, and he prays with the children for God to protect them.

And, oh, how much Master Wirtz has to say about farming and cattle breeding, animals, and plants! *Does Father know all these things?* Maria wonders.

One day, a classmate brings a little box to school, with two maybugs inside. What excitement! Master Wirtz tells them that the maybugs can fly, but they are not birds, they are insects. They eat the leaves off the trees. At the end of May, they will crawl into the earth and lay their eggs. Out of the eggs will come grubs, which will eat the roots of the plants. The plants will then die. Good thing, the birds like to eat maybugs! "It is all right to kill maybugs, but not to torment them," Master Wirtz says.

Maria learns that fish have scales and fins and that roses were brought to Europe from Asia. There are many varieties of roses in Aachen, in parks and in gardens. But in Freilingen, there are only wild dog-roses.

Wednesday afternoons, in their needlework class, the deaf girls learn from Miss Jonas. Mama has presented Maria with a white cloth bag. Into it go a long, rectangular piece of nettle cloth, embroidery and sewing thread, scissors, a thimble, needles, a small wooden embroidery hoop, and a few pieces of cloth for practicing. The girls learn to do simple seams and hems, hemstitches, cross-stitches, backstitches, and herringbone stitches. When they have mastered a stitch, they are allowed to sew it neatly in a crosswise row into their long samplers. Maria sews small and large buttonholes into her sampler. Tight and firm, the individual stitches with their tiny heads sit around the edge of the buttonhole. Two patches are underneath—one laid on and one set in, and both so neatly done as if they had been sewn for decoration. She stitches designs, sayings, and pictures into the cloth, and crotchets delicate laces. She even knows how to handle the many confus-

Maria at age 13 in Aachen. She sent this photograph home to her family.

ing bobbins, and all is put on the sampler. She learns how to mend her pinafores, underwear, dresses, and stockings.

Now and then, Maria writes a letter to Father and Mother and Grandmother. But she never gets a letter in return. She also sends a photograph home and is very proud of it. Mama goes with her to the photographer on Jesuitenstrasse (Jesuiten Street). Before they go, Mama puts new earrings into Maria's earlobes. She wears her best Sunday dress. It has smocking, double-puffed sleeves, and a wide collar trimmed with beads and braids. Mama combs her hair straight back and binds it at the back of her head with a large bow. At the photographer's, she poses with a book in her hand, and she is photographed! How impressed they will be at home!

Every weekend, Maria goes with her whole class to the public baths called Klosterbongard. In the changing cubicle, they change into their long bathing suits that reach from their necks down to their calves, and then they take showers. The teacher has told them that they should always look straight ahead when washing themselves. One should not even look at one's own body—that is indecent, and to see another person naked is unthinkable. So, it is more convenient to wash under the shower in one's bathing suit.

Once a week, they do gymnastics in the schoolyard. The children will do exercises in their school clothes, without moving their legs from the spot. Only their arms and heads move.

A photographer is coming! All the pupils of the Institute are to come to the school at two o'clock in the afternoon in their Sunday best. The teaching staff, too, is dressed up, more than Maria has ever seen them. In the courtyard in front of the school building, they all form a group. The teaching staff sits in the front row on chairs, with the headmaster and the chaplain in the middle of the row. Behind them, in three rows, the children are lined up. The ones in the back row have to stand on benches.

The camera stands on three legs. The photographer puts his head under a black cloth hanging over the box. Then he walks over to the group, adjusts a child here and there or shows one where to turn his or her head. He goes back again to disappear under the cloth. In the front of the box is a large, round glass and in the middle pleated bellows. The photographer pushes the bellows together, or pulls it out again to get the right focus. Finally, he is satisfied with everything. Now the children have to stand completely still and must not move.

But again, the photographer runs back and forth, puts an arm into place here, plucks at a skirt there, runs back to his box and looks under the black cloth. He tells the headmaster that the children are not to make the slightest move. The teaching staff immediately admonish the pupils. In order to do that, they have to stand up, of course, and turn around, so that the children can read their lips. The photographer is desperate, for now he has to rearrange clothing and move a head a tad here or there. Then, finally, finally, the photographer raises one hand and takes a small, pear-shaped, red rubber ball in the other. All the grownups and children hold their breath as the photographer squeezes the rubber ball. Spellbound, the children keep their eyes on the camera, but they don't notice anything. Then, the photographer lowers his arm. Everyone exhales—it is done. They begin to chatter and move around, relieved, and they gesticulate with their faces, and hands.

In twenty days, the pictures will be ready. The children are full of anticipation and curiosity. But, Maria is worried about the cost and whether she has saved enough money to get her own copy.

In the sweltering summer of 1911, the schoolchildren take a trip to Cologne—how exciting! More than once in the weeks before, lessons were canceled because the temperature rose over 90° F. It is on such a summer's day that they travel to the big city. With her heart in her mouth, but greatly impressed by the Rhine, Maria boards a small boat that takes the children downstream to the zoo. They walk for a long time between cages and enclosures, looking at the animals. After, the zoo, the small boat brings them to the Institute for the Deaf, which is much larger than theirs in Aachen. They are glad to be in the city again. *What a lot of traffic there is!* There are many coaches drawn by four horses, countless horse-drawn carts, and in between, on high wheels, automobiles, many more than in Aachen. In Heumarkt Platz (Square), on their way to the cathedral, the teacher points out the monument to Friedrich-Wilhelm III and his generals.

The children marvel at the west entrance of Cologne Cathedral and look up at the tops of the spires. Inside, they stare in amazement into the huge vault of the middle nave. It is so high and wide that they stay close together because they feel so tiny and lost in there. They walk slowly through the cathedral with their haversacks hanging on a cord or a basket or cloth bag in their hands. Around one of the columns bordering the nave, the children hold hands and form a chain. It takes nineteen children to encircle such a column!

Leaving the cathedral, they return to the Rhine and walk upstream to the harbor. Standing against the railing, they watch steamers glide slowly along the river. The shipping bridge is raised to let the vessels pass underneath. At last, they can cross the bridge. Maria is scared walking across on the broad wooden planks. She does not dare to look at the rushing green water below.

In the Deutz section of Cologne, they get something to eat and drink. Across the new, high-arched Hohenzollern Bridge, high enough to allow ships to pass underneath, and with railway tracks on it, they leisurely walk back. The teacher has to pay a toll of two pennies per child.

The children can see the mighty river flow far into the distance. They admire the silhouette of the cathedral, the many churches and towers of the city—and then they become rather scared, as next to them, separated only by a wire fence, a train rumbles across the bridge. The locomotive spits steam. The children can feel the swaying and shaking of the bridge under their feet. They stand still, until the monster with its long tail of coaches has passed.

The teacher points his walking cane upstream and downstream to show where Bonn and Düsseldorf are situated, where Switzerland lies with the source of the Rhine, and where the Rhine empties into the North Sea. Maria is glad when they get off the bridge.

At the end of the day, the children return to the huge railway station to take the train back to Aachen.

20

There are poems in Maria's reader. When she reads the lines, she can sense a rhythm to the verses. One of them is,

The Emperor is a kindly man,
in Berlin does he stay,
and were it not so far from here,
I'd travel there today.

Next to the poem is a picture of German Emperor and King of Prussia, Wilhelm II, with his wife, Empress Auguste Viktoria. The emperor looks handsome; his uniform is decorated with many gleaming medals. The empress is wearing a lace dress with bows, a gem-studded diadem, and a heavy pearl necklace. Many stories of the noble deeds done by these two for their subjects accompanying the picture. Maria has read them all, and she loves the emperor and empress because they seem to be so good and beautiful to her; in her mind they come right after God and Emperor Charlemagne up in Heaven. Each year on January 27th, the emperor's birthday, all the people wear their Sunday best, and the school and many of the houses are decorated with black, white, and red flags. The whole class goes to church to pray for the emperor. In school, they don't have to study on that day. Instead, they sit in the art room in front of a bust of the emperor, and a teacher delivers a speech in honor of their ruler. Some children recite poems, and, at the end of the celebration, each child is given a sweet bread roll.

In January 1911, Maria stands in Friedrich-Wilhelm-Platz at noon to watch the magnificent parade. Feather plumes are fluttering, helmets and sabers are gleaming. Officers ride by on fine horses. The soldiers' legs move like jumping jacks, pulled by a string, always up and down, up, down—higher than anyone would normally kick their legs. Flags are carried, cannons are paraded. The onlookers stand packed tightly together. The emperor must be a wonderful man! Maria has learned very early that everyone has to obey him; but who would do otherwise? If called upon, one even has to lay down one's life for the emperor. The many soldiers in their uniforms belong to the emperor, as do the towns and the lands and the schools and the train stations and much more. The market woman pays him money so that she is allowed to sell flowers and fruit, and the laborers and farmers and all other people, they all give money to the emperor. *The emperor is so powerful!*

The summer is hot and long and there seems to be no end to it. The people complain that it is dry and dreadful. Maria feels sorry for the farmers back home. The fields and pastures will be withering. On October 18, 1911, when it is still so summery hot that it does not seem the least bit like fall, Maria stands with all the other children of her school at the *Fischmarkt* (Fish Market). Emperor Wilhelm II is coming today to Heinrichsallee (Heinrichs Avenue) to unveil a monument to his father, Emperor Friedrich III, who ruled for only 99 days. Also today, a new fountain will be unveiled at the Fischmarkt. The people look at it with amusement because it is a naked boy, a sturdy little lad holding a fat fish under each arm. Water gushes out of the fishes' mouths and splashes into the stone basin underneath. Normally, the Fischmarkt smells of the fish that women sell from large baskets. But today, it is gaily decorated with garlands, flowers, and flags.

Maria is wearing a white bow in her hair. Like a long ponytail, it falls down her back. She wears her best dress. From ten in the morning until half-past noon children watch as more and more people gather in the square. All the children are holding flowers in their hands, but the flowers gradually begin to droop. Policemen with spiked helmets and long, curved sabers at their side keep the street clear. There is a succession of triumphal arches. Many of the policemen have moustaches like the emperor's. The sunlight glitters on the shiny buttons of their blue uniforms. Hussars, mounted high on horses, form an honor guard in a semicircle. The horses prance nervously while agitated sergeants and officers dash to and fro, coming and going, and seeking their places. All the windows in the surrounding houses are packed full, young lads even sit perched on the rooftops. The streets are lined with a dense crowd of people.

Maria has never seen so many people in town before, not even for the pilgrimage in the summer of 1909. At that time, pious pilgrims came from far away to see the holy relics in the cathedral. The streets and all the squares were full of parked carriages, and the air smelled of horses. The sparrows had the time of their lives finding plenty to eat in the streets. Procession after procession of pilgrims made their way to the cathedral. Maria and the other deaf children also made their way to the holy relics, full of hope.

Earlier in the day, they had prayed for a miracle with their chaplain and the teachers, asking for something in their ears to open so they would be able to hear and talk like everyone else. Maria had no idea whether the rough ancient cloth with which the bishop touched her mouth and ears was the Virgin Mary's dress or Jesus's loin or swaddling cloth. Her heart was pounding. Now it would come to her, the thing she does not know—hearing! Her mind was fully concentrated on her ears, but a miracle did not happen. Nothing changed. Everything stayed the same.

She still secretly hopes that this miracle will happen. Perhaps one day, she will be able to hear after all. Once, Grandmother had made a pilgrimage on foot from Freilingen to Kevelar on the lower Rhine to the Virgin Mary, consoler of the afflicted. She prayed ceaselessly all the way there and all the way back. Maria had asked herself, *Is it really so bad not to be able to hear? So sad, that one should walk so many days on foot, and pray because of it.*

Suddenly, everything starts happening at the Fischmarkt. Top hats, black hats, and handkerchiefs are waved in the air, and flowers are scattered. What a good thing Maria is standing right in front! At the head of the *cuirassiers*, the special regiments wearing armor breastplates, the emperor rides by on a black stallion, saluting graciously in every direction with his shiny field marshal's baton. The heavy bronze main door of the cathedral stands wide open; the emperor dismounts and strides inside.

And Maria has seen the great man from Berlin up close! That she will tell them, back in Freilingen!

Despite her adventures in Aachen, Maria longs for Freilingen. The Easter, autumn, and Christmas vacations always mean a return home. When she is back at school afterwards, she usually has to write a composition. After Christmas 1911, she writes,

The holidays began on December 22, 1911. My father came to collect me. I worked hard at home. I washed dishes, swept, made the beds, scrubbed the floors and polished everyone's shoes. I washed laundry and mended it. I played with the building bricks, too. I came back to Aachen, all by myself. I would rather be in Freilingen than in Aachen. Today, I am sad.

One morning, Maria stays in bed with a headache. She has told Mama that her head hurts, and Mama wants her to stay in bed. Never before has Maria missed a single day at school. The headmaster sends one of the older girls to the Bundens' house to ask why Maria hasn't come to school. Later, the girl returns and tells Mama, "The headmaster says a headache is not so bad! Maria is to come to school." So, Maria gets up and goes to school, with her aching head.

21

Winter comes late to Aachen. Not until February does it bring snow and frost. March 17, 1912, the day when Maria will take her first Holy Communion, is coming closer. She is now fourteen years old. With the preparations for Holy Communion, which are additional to schoolwork, the weeks fly by. She takes pains to make herself worthy. The teacher and the chaplain help her to understand the miracle. Two days before the celebration, she writes in her composition book, "We were a bit anxious," and she puts a stress mark over every syllable that should be emphasized.

Eight deaf children are to receive their First Communion. Maria is looking forward to it. But, to be quite honest, she is looking forward to the visitors from Freilingen most of all.

The day before the event, the children make their confessions in St. Jakob's church. Maria has written down on a slip of paper all the sins she can think of having committed, and has added that she repents them and has resolved to amend her ways. She sticks the note through the lattice of the confessional, and the priest writes her prayers of penance on it and hands it back to her. With the sign of the cross, he absolves her of her sins.

As she leaves the church, there is no holding her back. Like one truly redeemed and knowing only happiness, she exults with joy inside and rushes off, her prayer book in her hand. She races and jumps until she has to slow down because she gets stitches in her side and is out of breath.

She does not run down to Stromgasse, but instead hurries along the ruins of the town wall to the main station. This afternoon, her guests will arrive! At Marschiertor, she can already see Father and her beloved Grandmother. Maria runs toward Grandmother and throws her arms around her neck.

Grandmother is wearing her best black dress and her beautiful scarf. She has brought a basket full of good things to eat and Father has his heavy backpack on his shoulder. Maria is overjoyed and says, "I am so glad Grandmother has come! For the first time, you in Aachen! I hoped perhaps Grandmother also will come with Father. I am so glad!" Grandmother laughs as Maria takes the basket from her, and Father gives her a friendly nod.

Maria has something else she wants to say right away. She has something on her mind, something that she wants to get out before they arrive at her foster mother's house. "Father, Grandmother, I do not want to stay with the Bundens anymore."

Grandmother asks in surprise, "Does Mrs. Bunden not treat you right anymore?"

"Oh, yes, Mama is very good to me. But, I have already been there for seven years, I'm getting bored. Other children are always getting new foster homes. They always have something new to tell. Please, Father or Grandmother, you can talk with the headmaster, please? I wish to have a new foster mother. Mama Bunden is too old for me. Twice already, I have found hairs in the soup. Please, I do not want to stay with the Bundens during my last year of school."

Early next morning, at six o'clock, Mama wakes Maria. The new dress Maria puts on is made of heavy black woolen cloth. The skirt is stiff and reaches all the way down to her ankles. Grandmother had the dress made in Lommersdorf and brought it with her. At home, in the Eifel region, anything that wears well and lasts a lifetime is a good value. Maria looks down at herself and thinks, *oh, I look like a farm girl. Other girls wear fine town dresses. They are much prettier*. But, she does not let her feelings show. Mama places a green wreath on Maria's head and is excited and deeply moved; her "oldest" is having her celebration today! Her younger foster sisters sit around Maria in their nightgowns and watch her being adorned.

Papa Bunden, in his best clothes, goes on ahead with Grandmother to the church. Maria carries her prayer book in a little white lace cloth, and Father goes with her to An der Schanz where all the communicants from the Institute for the Deaf meet. Four boys and four girls, all dressed in black, are collected by the pastor, chaplains, and altar boys, and then led together with their teachers to St. Jakob's church. While they are being led up to the chancel, Maria's eyes dart back and forth over the crowd until they spot Grandmother.

The deaf children's chaplain gives a sermon to the children. He speaks in such a way that they can read his lips while the hearing congregants can listen to his voice. The children light their candles to renew their baptismal vows. It has become very quiet in the church. The priest puts his question to the children: "Do you believe in God?" They answer in unison in their discordant voices, "Yes, we believe!"

Grandmother cries. Father listens out for Maria's high voice. Before receiving the sacrament, the children pray, singly and aloud, "Lord, I am not worthy that Thou shouldst enter under my roof, but only say a word and my soul shall be healed."

Today is a great day of celebration. There are sausages, bread, and ham from Freilingen, and fresh, slightly sour tasting Eifel butter. There is a letter from Aunt Barbara. Maria's teacher comes to visit, and he presents Maria with a picture of a saint. Mama Bunden attends to everything and showers Maria's guests with love and happiness.

After the two festival days, Father returns to the Eifel. Urged by Maria, Grandmother goes to the headmaster of the Institute and speaks to him about a new foster home for Maria. Grandmother does not feel at ease about it. She thinks of kind Mrs. Bunden and fears that Maria might not do so well in another place. Maria, however, is looking forward to a change, to a new way of life. But, first she travels back home with Grandmother for Easter vacation.

22

Each time Maria is home on holidays, people marvel at her. She is that smart girl who owns a coat for winter, who wears slim laced-up shoes, and who so often goes by train to the big town to attend school. Many of the adults in Freilingen have never even seen such a town. When the villagers talk to Maria, they have to speak High German; with anyone else they would speak the Eifel dialect. After the first day back, of course, Maria belongs fully to Freilingen again, but she is still seen as being different. The warmhearted kindness she is shown by everyone also contains respect and admiration.

Maria knows that she experiences and sees much more than the hearing children in her village, and perhaps also learns more in school. But even so, anyone who can hear appears to her to be infinitely superior. She is somewhat afraid of the Aachen children in Stromgasse, Rosstrasse, and on Mühlenberg. Maria is often surprised how assertive they are and how privileged they act. If someone is drunk or strangely dressed, has peculiar habits or features, is very old or ugly, deformed or mentally challenged, some of the children will make fun of him or her. The children in Freilingen are more reserved, friendlier, and more considerate. They know that hard work can only be done with everyone's cooperation, and that it does not matter how someone looks or what peculiarities there might be, as long as the person can lend a hand and is industrious.

Maria enjoys working in the garden. She pushes the spade into the ground, turning the heavy clods, cut after cut. The earth smells fresh and rich. The raw wind tousles her hair. The chickens are looking for worms and grubs in the newly opened soil. Maria is sowing lettuce and a variety of vegetables. A man with a small cart pulled by a dog passes through the village, offering winter plants for sale. Of these, Maria is planting in the garden what will be ready to eat by June. For a few days, she regularly weeds and waters the small plants.

She joins Mother in the fields, where, with their backs bent, they set potatoes in the furrows. Father laughs when Maria comes home aching in the evening, barely able to straighten up. He has spent the day spraying fertilizer from manure in wooden barrels on the meadows and turnip fields.

On Saturdays, Maria sweeps the road in front of the yard with the big birch broom Father himself bound during the winter. Straw lies scattered around, horses and cows have left their dung. She sweeps a parquet pattern in the ground. All of the people in the village do. Spring is in the air—the skies are becoming brighter, and the buds are swelling. But, in between the spells of sunshine, there are often sudden heavy rainstorms and even snow. Sometimes, the nights are still frosty. It is a typical April, impetuous and unreliable, moody and full of surprises.

For Easter, Mother boils the onion skins that she has collected all winter long in a basket by the cellar door. In the brown broth, a whole apron full of eggs are dyed golden yellow. Maria gets four of them for Easter. That is quite a lot.

After Easter Mass, Maria watches the young men in front of the Lommersdorf church tapping their Easter eggs together. They make bets as to whose egg will crack first, who will win or lose.

During the Easter vacation, Father tells Maria that for Whitsun she is to travel to Kohlscheid, to distant relatives, the Schmitzes. Father has written already to "Aunt" Schmitz. Seven weeks later, Aunt Schmitz picks up Maria from Mama Bunden's. She is a capable housewife, and her husband "Uncle" Schmitz dresses every day as if for Sunday mass. They have two pretty daughters who catch on quickly to Maria's voice and diction, and they are attentive and polite to her.

Uncle Schmitz is a school principal, and he reads a lot at home. Maria has never before seen so many books. In his room, there are shelves from floor to ceiling, full of books, one next to the other. Carpets lie on the floor of every room.

Maria helps Aunt Schmitz with the housework, weeds the garden behind the house, embroiders, and crotchets lace. They walk together through the village and to Kermis, the outdoor festival where Maria is allowed to ride the Zeppelin carousel.

Kohlscheid is a mining town near Aachen. Maria sees long lines of dumping trucks full of coal sludge being pulled by horses along one of the town's streets. On rainy days, the air can be bad, despite the wind blowing from the Dutch plain in the west.

All in all, the Whitsun vacation is wonderful and, at the end, Aunt Schmitz brings her back to the Bundens' in Aachen on the narrow-gauge railway.

Maria is in her final year at the Institute for the Deaf. *Will she ever be able to return to Aachen when she has finished her schooling?* she wonders. How nice it is, therefore, that her teacher, Master Wirtz, takes the entire class on a walk through the town every Thursday. They choose a specific destination, talk about it, and then go and see it.

In the thirteenth century, Aachen was a fortress with eleven strong town gates. The children visit the remnants of the town wall, the two remaining gates—Ponttor and Marschiertor—and the tall tower in Turmstrasse, where gunpowder was stored in earlier days. Maria already looks at the sights with a feeling of farewell. On one occasion the class also visits the Kaiserbad thermal baths on Büchel Street. Underneath the three-cornered cobbled square of Büchel, the hot springs are diverted into the sewers. The sulfurous steam rising from the drains, and looking so sinister sometimes at night, smells of rotten eggs. In front of the fountain monument, the children huddle together: a fearsome animal looms over the fountain rock where a boy is filling his jug with water. Scared, the boy turns to flee. Master Wirtz tells the children the legend of the *Bakauv*, an evil monster with glowing eyes, sharp claws, a shaggy coat, and long teeth that lives in the sewer canals of the hot springs by day. But at night, it lurks about to frighten people who are staggering home late from the inns and taverns. Maria does not like the fountain and thinks that she will never cross Büchel on her own at night, even though it lies in the very center of town.

Back at school, the children write compositions about the outings. Writing compositions is not easy. Rough drafts are made first, then corrected by the teacher, and then finally entered into the composition book with pen and ink in neat handwriting. Maria enjoys writing compositions, even when she is not describing her own life. The teacher hangs a big picture on the wall that shows something typical from a particular country, and

Maria writes about it. All her compositions on foreign countries begin with the same phrase.

> ***In the picture I can see*** *a vintage wine crop. The region there is France. The people are gathering the grapes into baskets. The grapes are squashed in a press, so that their juice will flow out. From the juice, wine is made. This wine is called 'champagner.' My teacher, Master Wirtz, has already tasted it.*

> ***In the picture I can see*** *an area in Southern Russia. We have talked about Russia. In the north of Russia it is very cold, but in the south, very hot. Russia is a large Empire. The Emperor of Russia is also called a Tsar. I have not yet been to Russia. From Germany you must travel north to Russia. In the picture, Southern Russia is very sandy and barren. I can see three riders and a cart. Two farmers and a woman are sitting in it. The cart and the riders are swirling up a lot of dust. A boy is running away, because the cart is coming. He is afraid of being run over. The geese are fleeing, too. A woman is selling fruit. So she is a fruit merchant. She is holding a melon in her hand. Many people in Southern Russia eat melons in the summer. A melon is similar to a pumpkin. I have not yet eaten a melon. But Master Wirtz has eaten melons quite often.*

> ***In the picture I can see*** *a high and broad wall. It is the Great Wall of China. China is a vast land in Asia. Asia is the largest continent. The Great Wall of China has been built to keep out its enemies. The people in China drink mostly tea and eat rice. China has too many people, so many of them are poor. In China, much tea and rice is grown. China has 400 million inhabitants and often suffers famine. Chinese men all wear pigtails.*

23

Mama Bunden is crying. Maria stands there feeling ashamed of herself because she feels no sorrow for Mama's tears. Mama keeps wiping her eyes.

The silent, speechless work of packing up is like a reproach. The clothing, underwear, and toys of the child Mama has cared for like her own for seven years are being packed into a cardboard box.

Maria is glad that the headmaster has arranged a new foster home for her and that she will get to know something new. She is tired of always having to go to the same room, always having to look at and do the same things. Other children have much to tell and get to know different things because they change their foster parents so often. Admittedly, there are very few children who are being treated as well as Maria is by the Bundens. Some are starved or beaten, but do not dare tell their parents or their teachers.

Maria picks up her cardboard box and says goodbye with hugs and thank-yous. Mama bears it in silent grief. With Papa Bunden, Maria leaves the home where she has been so well looked after for so long. They go across to Hubertusstrasse. It is not far. At house number 11, they climb up one floor and Papa pulls the doorbell. The woman who opens is still very young, and pretty and friendly, as well. When Maria sees her, the last trace of remorse and bad conscience about Mama Bunden disappears.

Mrs. Salzburg, her new foster mother, has everything clean and cozy in her three-room flat. She shows Maria where she and another deaf girl named Hedwig will sleep. A fat dog comes crawling out from his box under the coal stove. Mrs. Salzburg tells Maria his name, Ali. He sniffs at the newcomer inquisitively. Above the kitchen sink hangs a birdcage with a canary. Old photographs decorate the walls. The water tap is right in the kitchen, not in the hallway like at Mama's.

Later, that evening, Maria meets Mr. Salzburg. All day long, he works in a large needle factory.

Mrs. Salzburg treats Maria with such kindness that, after a few days, she barely spares a thought of Mama Bunden anymore. Mrs. Salzburg enjoys talking to Maria and helps with her homework. After lunch, Mrs. Salzburg lies down on the sofa. Maria sits at the kitchen table with Hedwig. The sun is shining, and Maria writes about the newspaper:

> *My foster parents, the Salzburgs, subscribe to a newspaper. It is called the* Volksfreund. *This newspaper comes out in Aachen. It is also printed in Aachen. Master Wirtz also shows us another newspaper, called* Westfälisches Volksblatt. *In the newspaper, there are news and advertisements. The newspaper has reports from Germany, from Russia, from all states and countries. It also has reports on aviation. I do not like to read the newspaper, as I do not understand it. In the newspaper, there are also death notices, sales advertisements and housing advertisements. Many people like to read the newspaper. The* Volksfreund *costs ¾ of a Mark, every three months.*

Father meets Maria's new foster parents for the first time when he comes to take Maria home for her last summer vacation. Mother Helene has kept Maria in constant suspense over the last few years. Each time Maria has come home she has watched Mother carefully. *Was she working more slowly? Was she bending with difficulty? Was she getting rounder?* Upon arriving in Freilingen, if it appeared that the nimble and tiny woman had changed at all, the first thing Maria did was to look into the cradle. Sisters Lena and Anna have both been born while Maria was at school, and now, this time, a little brother, Mathias, lies inside. The ninth Giefer child!

It rains for weeks on end, from the beginning of August until deep into September 1912, throughout the entire summer vacation. In the fields, the oats have already been ruined. They never had a chance to ripen and are now lying waterlogged on the ground. The potatoes, too, are rotting in the soaked earth. Maria says to Grandmother, "When potatoes are scarce, Mrs. Salzburg in Aachen will have to pay more for them." There is plenty of fruit, though. Tiny, shriveled pears and apples grow in the orchard behind the house.

On cool summer evenings, one or the other of the villagers will drop in at the Giefers' for a chat, gathering around the warm stove. Maria thinks they must be talking about the bad weather and how they cannot work. It smells of damp clothes. The young ones have the sniffles.

When Maria wakes up in the mornings, the first thing she does is to look out the open window. Hopelessly, ceaselessly, the rain falls from the sky; a desolate world of gray and more gray. The yard and the street are drowned in water and mud. The few passing carts grind through it, and anyone who comes into the house brings in the sticky mud. Only the two ducks that Father has recently bought enjoy it; they waddle across to the chicken patch where a small pond has formed.

Maria goes with the others to church in Lommersdorf every morning, returning soaked to the skin. The people pray for better weather. Maria knows how hard they struggle to wrest their daily bread from the stony ground and how the weather can ruin everything. Grandmother often carries her rosary in her hand in between her chores, praying.

Setta is now six years old, and although the sun seems to have forgotten that it is summer, her face and arms are full of freckles. Christina's pretty face is also slightly freckled, and her thick hair has a dark chestnut-brown shimmer. She walks around the house cautiously, afraid that she might bump into something or that the children will run into her during their play, because her wounds are still festering and painful. She holds herself at a slant because some of the wounds have healed so badly as to form contorting scars. Christina is now nine and still cannot speak. Shyly she looks at Maria who is always trying to teach her. *Poor sister!* Maria thinks.

Now and then, Grandmother secretly boils a fresh egg, one time for Christina, another time for Maria or five-year-old Josef. Then Grandmother will put her finger to her mouth to tell them it is their secret. No one is to know because eggs mean money. Maria loves the taste of fresh eggs. In Aachen, she never eats an egg if it has a stamp on it because she doesn't know who put the stamp on the egg. *A stamped egg?* It makes her cringe.

It is uncomfortable in the house in this eternally wet weather. The children don't know what to do with themselves. Willi and Klöss are in school in the mornings, and in the afternoons they struggle with their homework. Maria is pleased when her brothers come to her for help and advice on their homework. Otherwise, they don't bother themselves much with their older sister. Maria does the washing and hangs it up in the shed. But, in this weather it just won't dry. The chickens perch with ruffled feathers on the wheel axles and equipment or have scratched out a hole in the ground in the shed and sit there, blinking their sleepy eyes. In the front room, the dog shakes his coat when he comes in, dripping wet, and Maria scolds him.

It is still raining when she walks with Father all the way to the railway station in Blankenheim-Wald. The Ahr valley looks desolate. For two years on her trips, Maria has been watching the progress of the work on the new railway line that will go from Blankenheim-Wald to Ahrdorf. The rain streams down incessantly on wooden shacks, heaps of earth, rubble tips, piles of gravel, and stacks of wooden planks, on carts, tippers, barrows, tools, and machine saws, junk, and iron rods. Not far from the steep country lane that leads from the Ahr road up to Freilingen, a high bridge will span the Ahr valley. Near the bridge, the new station is already under construction.

Father and Maria have to walk through mud and mire. The construction workers labor with grim expressions on their faces. Others sit in the shacks and stare out at the two lonely wanderers. On dry days, a cloud of dust would rise up here, and hundreds of weather-beaten workers would be carrying, lifting, chopping, shoveling, banging, and drilling. Never has Maria seen so many people in her homeland. Father explains that the workers come from different countries; there are Poles, Italians, and Frenchmen. On Sundays, they come to Freilingen and sit in the inn; they stroll in small groups through the village, chatting and gesticulating with the villagers in the courtyards.

Soon Freilingen, too, is going to get its own railway station. From there it will be less than an hour to the village. Maria wonders if it will be finished while she is still in school. But today she and Father must march bravely through the Ahr valley for three and a half hours through incessant rain, over soggy roads.

24

Sometimes Maria wishes young Mrs. Salzburg could be her mother. Maria is really fond of her, so she always behaves obediently and is never unfriendly. At least she tries not to be.

They are sitting at the table for the midday meal. Maria is really hungry. Mrs. Salzburg sets down dishes of steaming lentil soup. Maria looks horrified at the dark brown liquid. There are flat round things glistening under blobs of fat. No! She is not going to eat that! She has never seen anything like that before and certainly never eaten it, neither in Freilingen nor at Mama Bunden's. And she was so looking forward to something to eat after school. She gets cross. With a defiant face she says: "No, I won't eat this soup! I have never eaten this soup!"

Mrs. Salzburg is upset and sad. "It is lentil soup, it tastes very good. You only have to try it. It is made with bacon. Please, Maria, just try it!"

But Maria sits there stubbornly: "No, I won't eat the soup!" Hedwig follows her example. She shakes her head and say she won't eat the soup either.

Sad and sighing, Mrs. Salzburg takes the soup back to the pot.

The headmaster of the Deaf and Dumb Institution happens to visit the Salzburg family later that very day to inquire about Maria. He also wants to get to know her new foster home. Mrs. Salzburg praises Maria and mentions in passing the incident with the soup. The headmaster calls Maria over with his forefinger! "You wouldn't eat the lentil soup? Well, well, well!" Then he leaves her standing there and takes his leave of Mrs. Salzburg. Maria breathes a sigh of relief and thinks she has heard the last of it.

The next morning it is raining, as it has been for weeks. The rain splashes onto the shiny wet cobblestones. Rivulets trickle toward the gutter. Maria lifts up her skirt, pulls her scarf down over her forehead, and tries to avoid the puddles. Hedwig runs behind her and Maria turns round to her now and then to check that she is still following.

When the girls finally get to the school, they are wet almost through and through. All the children have taken cover in the hall. Lessons have not begun yet. Puddles of water form on the stone floor. Wild boys are throwing wet caps around; it is an unpleasant, damp crush of bodies. The children see the headmaster coming and let each other know. Gradually it becomes quieter. They all look at the man who they fear, more or less. More than once he has sent the most defiant and obstinate of them to the cellar, where they got only water and a slice of black bread the whole day.

Now he looks angry. "Maria Giefer is to come to me!" All the children turn to Maria. The headmaster looks at Maria sternly. He has never been angry with her before, but as he stands there in front of her with wide-open eyes, she thinks *He has eyes like an owl!*

"You did not eat your lentil soup! You are very obstinate!" the headmaster says, and he brings out a cane from behind his back. Maria has to hold out both hands and is given two hard strokes on each palm. She presses her lips together and does not make a sound. She looks at the man's face and thinks, *You are an owl! You are an owl!* Her hands burn like fire, but, she waits until the headmaster has gone before she begins to cry bitterly. She has been beaten for the first time in her life.

Maria looks at the school barometer every day. Gradually the weather gets better, perhaps because she prays to God to send the sun "for Freilingen's sake!" She notices that Mrs. Salzburg seems to be getting paler and weaker. Maria does not know what is wrong with her. She sees that the young woman has to lie on the sofa or in bed more and more often and that the work remains undone. Sometimes the doctor comes to see Mrs. Salzburg. When Maria comes home from school, she often sees his bicycle parked by the front door.

"You have to go away from here soon. I am too ill to keep any children," Mrs. Salzburg says to Maria, who is very alarmed.

"If I have to go away I will cry a lot. I will be sad."

"So will I," Mrs. Salzburg says.

Then the time comes. Maria has only been with the young Salzburg couple for six months. One afternoon, an elderly lady dressed in black comes to fetch Maria. She is tall, almost skinny, and looks serious. Maria is terrified and flies into Mrs. Salzburg's arms. She cries and clings to her and does not want to go with the strange lady. But it is no use. Her things are packed. Maria says goodbye to the Salzburgs, to fat Ali, and the little bird, too.

25

Maria walks beside the strange elderly lady up Hubertusstrasse to a square bathed in the warm October sunlight. Here stand the ruins of a tower that was built from massive, rough stone. The remains of the town wall can be seen. A wide street runs alongside the square exactly where the ditch outside the town wall used to be. The street is called Boxgraben. It comes from the Schanz, one of the highest spots in the town, where the Westgate used to stand. The square with the remnants of the tower and the chestnut trees is called Am Lavenstein. Out of the old walls that are overgrown with ivy, sprout tufts of grass, little bushes, and flowers. In the square, children are romping around, throwing chestnuts.

Maria enters a tall corner house with the lady. They climb up three flights of wide wooden stairs that smell of floor polish. They stop in front of a door with a nameplate that reads *Rögert*. When she enters the strange living room, she is choked with homesickness.

A friendly little woman comes toward her with open arms. She gestures for Maria to sit down and offers her coffee with milk and black cake, a round cake topped with a puree of dried pears and plums. Maria is not hungry, but she does not like to refuse. She looks around the large kitchen that also serves as a living room in the colder months. She reads the labels on the square stoneware pots lined up on a shelf: *Flour, Salt, Sugar, Rice, Cinnamon, Pepper, Nutmeg*. A strong rod is fixed from one wall to the other about a meter in front of the windows. Maria cannot imagine what it is for. There are no curtains to be seen.

The older woman who brought her to the house leaves. Now, the other lady shows Maria where she can wash her hands and then leads her through a bedroom into a smaller one. She opens a high wardrobe door and says to Maria, "You can hang your clothes in here and put your underwear in the drawer below. That is your bed. Do you like it here?"

"I like it very much here," says Maria, "everything is clean and tidy." She opens her cardboard box and starts to stow her few belongings and her doll's bed and little doll's chair from Papa Bunden.

"Have you done your homework already?"

Maria answers yes and is glad that the little lady is so easy to understand.

"My name is Fine, and my sister's name is Käthe Rögert. You can call us Miss Fine and Miss Käthe."

"Yes, I understand," says Maria. They go back to the kitchen, and Miss Fine puts a chair near the window for Maria, puts the flowerpots to one side, and tucks up the curtains.

Dusk falls bringing a slight fog. Behind the square, carts and carriages jolt past on the cobblestones. Women stand chatting in a doorway. Two old men are sitting on a bench under the chestnut trees. The smoke from their pipes curls in the twilight. Soon, they stand up and go.

It has become too cool, Maria thinks to herself. The golden-red glow of the leaves has disappeared. The evening eats up the colors and gradually shrouds everything in gray.

Miss Käthe returns home and lights the gas lamp. On the embers in the stove, Miss Fine puts shiny black coal sludge she has brought up from the cellar in a bucket. After the evening meal, an elderly lady comes in. Miss Fine says this woman lives above them on the fourth floor and comes to visit every evening because she lives alone. Maria shakes hands with the neighbor. She is easy to understand, too, when she says, "The Misses Rögert are good people."

"Yes," says Maria.

Maria cleans her shoes over the coal box, washes herself, and says good-night. She wonders why Miss Käthe always looks so serious. She has not yet seen her smile. Miss Fine accompanies Maria to her room and removes the ornamental cushion from the bed. Maria puts on her long nightshirt and slips under the sheets. The bed is wide and soft. While Miss Fine tucks her in affectionately, Maria says, "Thank you. It is a fine bed. I will sleep well." Miss Fine dips two fingers into the bowl of Holy Water and blesses the child.

Maria is alone, in a strange house, with unknown people. There are no curtains on the windows, and the October night peeps through the sheers.

She can make out the contours of the room. She does not know that the nights are quiet or that the people in the next room are instinctively speaking more softly. But she can sense the stillness of the night that comes with darkness. Colors are alive, and light and shadow create movement. At night, the eyes rest. *It is very still,* Maria thinks.

Maria also thinks of Mrs. Salzburg and of Hedwig, who used to share her room. Never has she slept in a room on her own before. She thinks of Freilingen and what Father will say about her living in a new place. Homesickness raises its head again—but sleep finally overtakes her.

The rhythmic thud of weaving looms can be heard in many streets of Aachen. Miss Käthe has worked as a darner at the Croon Textile Factory on the corner of Annastrasse for many years. By the time Maria gets up in the morning, Miss Käthe has already left for work. Miss Fine makes coffee and sandwiches for her sister every day, as she usually doesn't get home until evening. Maria is amazed at how hard the two unmarried sisters work, and at how they can earn their living all by themselves. They have no relatives, nobody who belongs to them, Miss Fine has told her.

Soon after moving in with the sisters, Maria discovers the purpose of the rod in front of the window. She often goes with Miss Fine to Annastrasse; they pull a handcart in order to fetch two long, heavy bolts of cloth or *Ballen.* Together, they carry the bolts up to the flat and lay them on the floor in front of the windows. The floor is smooth and clean. Miss Fine and Maria lift the end of the cloth, throw it over the rod, pull it down on the other side and fasten it with clothes pegs.

Miss Fine examines the cloth for flaws and irregularities and marks these with chalk. She pulls the cloth she has examined through until it lies in layers on the floor. Then, she lays the end of the cloth over a long, tilted wooden board and weighs it down so that the cloth is stretched flat over the board. Her hand skims deftly over the cloth feeling every patch for flaws. With the nap-nippers, she plucks out wrongly woven threads or bits of wool and smooths the spot out with her thumbnail. Miss Fine pulls down the parts she has examined so that the cloth lies in folds at her feet. Every so often, she shakes out her right arm or stretches her tired back. After this procedure, she sits down and takes the cloth across her knees to darn the places that are still marked. She uses a special needle to replace missing threads in the warp and weft with the spare threads she has already pulled out. Sharp little scissors are at hand to cut off any loose ends. Then she examines the cloth once more over the rod.

There is not enough light to do homework in the room behind the hanging cloth. So, Maria takes a seat next to Miss Fine at the wide window ledge and does her own work. When Miss Fine has finished, Maria or Miss Käthe help to roll up the cloth. Then, they carry it back to the textile factory on the handcart, in exchange for money and new work.

Now, Maria knows at last why she has so often seen bolts of cloth being carried through town.

Though it is still fall, on some mornings there is already frost on the roofs. The trees at Lavenstein are losing their leaves. The square is strewn with them. Often a gust of wind swirls them into the air and sometimes a withered leaf flutters past the windows where the three ladies live. To get ready for winter, the Rögert sisters have a few hundredweight of potatoes delivered to their cellar. One hundredweight costs three marks. They also get briquettes of coal, which are brought by horse and cart, but the shiny, wobbly coal sludge is tipped onto the pavement in front of the house. Then there is a lot of work to be done. They carry the heavy black stuff in buckets into the cellar, and afterwards the bottom of the house wall, the pavement, the long hallway and the cellar steps all have to be scrubbed down.

At school, Maria learns about what happened long before she, and all the people she knows, existed. That is *history*, and she likes to learn it. Only, it is teeming with war and victory, armies, enemies and brave heroes, generals, battlefields, and slaughter. At the word *slaughter*, Maria cannot help thinking of the pigs and cattle slaughtered on Father's farm. Throughout history, emperors, kings, and popes waged wars. *Why was it like this?* she wonders. *Why do the hearing people kill each other? Why? When they can talk to each other about everything and listen to and understand each other?* And now, there is yet another war somewhere in the world. That is what she has to write about today in her composition book.

> *18.11.1912. At the moment there is a war in the Balkans. The Balkan states are: Montenegro, Serbia, Bulgaria, Rumania, Greece, and Turkey. Montenegro, Serbia, Bulgaria, and Greece are fighting against Turkey. So far, Turkey has always lost. Rumania did not want to fight against Turkey.*

The four Balkan states will take a lot of land and various towns and villages away from Turkey. War is terrible. A lot of soldiers are killed and wounded in war. Afterwards, the wounded are mostly cripples.

Maria really enjoys the arithmetic lessons with Master Wirtz. The teacher leans back in his chair, twirls his white moustache with the thumb and forefinger of one hand and holds a small cane in the other. After each question he asks, the little cane shoots forward and points to a pupil who has to work out the answer in his or her head. Quickly he asks, 17 and 94 is? 24 and 116 is? 103 and 36 is? 99 minus 37 is? 53 minus 17 is? The children must pay attention! Maria enjoys doing sums in her head and fractions, percentages, and calculation of interest; she learns easily.

When she goes shopping for Miss Fine, arithmetic comes in handy. Maria writes a shopping list, and she later writes down the prices and goes through the bill with Miss Fine.

1 pound beef costs	*0.80 Marks*
1 pound coffee costs	*1.60 Marks*
1 pound white beans costs	*0.30 Marks*
2 pounds flour costs	*0.18 Marks*

What a lot of money that is! There are many poor people in the city who do not have enough to eat. Some of them get free meals at one of the many convents in Aachen. *What a good thing that no snow has fallen yet,* Maria thinks, and she hopes the winter will be mild. *Then the poor people don't need so much fuel.*

Master Wirtz and the two Misses Rögert have told her that snow has already fallen in the Black Forest, in Westfalia, and in the Eifel. Maria doesn't like snow, but it is good for the winter seed. It protects it from the bad frost.

In winter, it is agreeably warm in Misses Käthe and Fine's kitchen. When the coal sludge is aglow in the black kitchen stove, the silvery blue hotplate glows. Mama Bunden and Mrs. Salzburg, too, heat their kitchens with the cheap mixture of coal and water. The coal sludge burns longer then the best oak wood, but it does not smell as good as a wood fire. If you are careless, and the fire under the sludge has no air, then there is a little puff and a bluish little cloud of smoke rises from the stove rings and stinks. Such a way of heating also creates a lot of dust from the smoke. If

Miss Fine does not clean the kitchen every day, little balls of fluff gather, especially below the stove.

During the long evenings, the three sit together with the neighbor and do needlework under the lamp. Miss Käthe sits up straight at her sewing machine and turns a little wheel. Busily, the needle bobs up and down in the cloth.

It is December, and for St. Nicholas' Day at school, Maria receives a linen towel, red embroidery thread, and some blouse material. The presents are placed in front of her name card, between fir branches and burning candles, with a *Printenmann* (gingerbread man), nuts, and apples as well. St. Nicholas, with his bishop's miter and long white beard, comes to visit with his companion, the hunched, black-clad Hans Muff, who threatens to punish the naughty children with his broom of twigs.

At home, Miss Käthe uses the new material to make a blouse for Maria. Maria sits nearby embroidering her towel. There is a picture already printed on the cloth—it is a young woman just coming home from shopping, carrying a handled basket and a net bag. The basket contains small packets and bags, and the net bag is full of cans. The saying *Buy well, Cook well* is framed by carrots and their leaves. Embroidering the piece of linen with red thread will keep Maria busy all winter.

This year, she is not going home to Freilingen for Christmas. Miss Fine has invited her to stay with her and her sister because Miss Käthe does not have to go to the factory over Christmas. Instead, she wants to sew clothes for Maria.

Maria helps to undo the seams of old clothes, which Miss Fine washes and irons. From these, Miss Käthe sews two new dresses for Maria, and she adds deep hems and concealed tucks at the sleeves and waist, so that the dresses can be let out later. Maria is certain to grow in the next few years. Miss Käthe also makes a skirt, blouses, two white and two colored pinafores, chemises, drawers, and nightshirts. Everything is made as good as new out of old things. Maria has never had so much to wear before. This Christmas, she does not feel homesick. The church and the Rögerts' kitchen smell of fir trees; there is a little Christmas tree decorated with silver and colored balls, angel hair, and lots of tinsel in the Rögerts' living room. The three of them visit the churches and look at the various nativity scenes on display in the city.

One day during the Christmas vacation, the headmaster of the Institute arrives unexpectedly to inquire about Maria. She sees that the Rögert sisters praise her and that the headmaster is satisfied. Maria tells him with a radiant face, "Sir, I like being here. Both ladies are good to me."

January 1913 is cold. In Aachen, children toboggan from Lavenstein down Hubertusstrasse. Maria watches them from the window, not at all envious. Funny snowmen stand in front of the ruins of Lavenstein. Some boys throw snowballs at the tobogganers. The coach drivers are wrapped in long, thick coats. If they have to wait, they stamp their feet and slap their upper arms, some of them keep blowing their noses and coughing. Maria thinks to herself that she has never had a cold or a cough. She likes standing at the window, looking out. There is always something going on in the street and on the square. When twilight falls on winter evenings, the lamplighter comes. He goes from gas lamp to gas lamp, some set on ornate green posts and some hanging on the house walls from curved iron brackets. Their light falls softly on the snow. People hurry home from work through the cold. Oil lamps sway to and fro on the carriages driving up and down Boxgraben. But the lamps next to the drivers' seats are fixed, so only their light flickers lively.

Maria knows it is not very long now before she will have to leave Aachen for good. Father has said she is to stay at home in Freilingen because the family needs her help. Christina is coming to Aachen in her place after Easter, and she will stay with the Rögert sisters. But, what about herself? What about Maria? Everyone in Freilingen can hear, no one is like her, no one is deaf. *Why am I deaf?* Maria wonders. She tries to remember if it was ever different. There are children who were able to hear once. But, she can find no memory of ever being able to hear. As long as she can recall, it was always like it is now. She takes out her composition book and writes, *My teachers say I have been deaf from birth. Yes, I have been deaf for a long time.*

In the last weeks before she leaves school, Master Wirtz talks a lot about the "Fatherland." Once more, her class walks through the city to the Bismarck Tower at the edge of the Aachen Forest. The students watch the teacher's mouth while he talks about the Imperial Chancellor, Count Bismarck. Master Wirtz tells them they should honor Bismarck. Then, they go to the War Memorial at the railway station, which honors the Prussian soldiers who were killed in the wars against Austria in 1866 and France in 1870. The teacher impresses on them that the dead are the heroes of the Fatherland.

Finally, in March 1913, Maria writes her last composition. It is a summary of all she has learned since Christmas.

> *On March 10, 1813, the Iron Cross was founded. The Iron Cross is a medal or a decoration. It is put on someone's chest. It was donated in honor of the Queen Luise. She was born on March 10, 1776. She was the spouse of Friedrich-Wilhelm III. Whoever is a very brave soldier on the battlefield, receives the Iron Cross. On Monday, a celebration is to take place. The people are meant to remember the founding of the Cross. It is now 100 years since the Prussians drove the French out of the land. We remember that and are glad.*

Soon enough, Palm Sunday comes. It is Maria's last Sunday in Aachen. She carries some boxwood sprays in her hand that will be blessed by the priest. She is going to take one twig with her to Freilingen, and she will tack it up over her bed. Spring is truly here. Snowdrops and primroses are flowering in the front gardens. The willows have put up their catkins. The sun works to dry up the puddles and damp, soggy paths. A mild breeze is blowing. Maria is overcome with a longing for freedom!

The children who are going to be released this Wednesday are feeling ecstatic: Free! No more school! To be young and healthy! No one knows what good will be coming their way, and each is full of anticipation. Something has come to an end, something new is about to begin.

Eight children sit at their desks, which have become too small for them. Master Wirtz twiddles his moustache nervously; the whole teaching staff, plus some visitors from the outside are watching the students take their exams. While Maria was out in the schoolyard, she looked quickly through her schoolbook of facts. Now, everyone watches the teacher's mouth when he asks the exam questions. Maria has to answer questions on geography. The teacher and the headmaster nod their heads with satisfaction. Later, they hand out the certificates showing the students' grades and achievements. Maria is very proud—she has earned the highest grades! Afterward, the headmaster makes a farewell address to the children, advising them not to forget what they have learned in school. "You have learned what is good and what is useful," he tells them. "For that, you must be grateful."

It is all over quickly—the handshakes, best wishes for the future, the goodbyes from former schoolmates. No one is sad. For eight years, Maria has attended the Institute for the Deaf. For eight years, she has been at home with strangers in Aachen. She can speak and make herself understood, and she can lipread and understand.

The world is wonderful! Even for a deaf child!

She runs all the way back to Lavenstein. She is looking forward to seeing Father and going back home to Freilingen.

26

The month of April is really only there to prepare the house for the first Sunday in May, which is the outdoor festival of Kermis (May fair)! Father has ordered a general cleaning of the house. He hires their neighbor Johann Neu to come paint the house. All of the rooms upstairs are emptied one after the other so Johann Neu can whitewash the ceilings with chalk-white paint. Then, he paints the walls different colors—blue, green, or pink. But that is far from being all! He has also brought stencils with him. Maria helps him to put them up on the wall. He holds several of them up, one after the other, and paints over them with different colors. Then he adds flowers, scrolls, circles, and loops on the walls. If Maria stares at them for a long time, the shapes and contours blend and she seems to make out new figures: faces, animals, and things, as if looking at drifting clouds. When the work is finished, the rooms look fresh and clean. But, the color will not last long. Over the beds and by the doors they fade fast, wherever people brush against it.

Maria scrubs the floors clean with lots of water, so that they don't look gray. Up and down the stairs, she hauls the water. When the house is clean and the painting finished, the furniture is moved back into the house, put back into place, and wiped clean. Finally, fresh straw is stuffed into everyone's bedding.

Downstairs, the front room is painted as well. Over time, flies have dirtied the edges of the ceiling beams, and the smudge marks made by the children above the long bench are also a sorry sight. Maria scrubs and washes them with old rags, and wipes the doors and the window panes clean, not forgetting the window frames. While she cleans the house, Father and her brothers tidy up the stable and barn. The stable is whitewashed as well. Father has also checked his tools and repaired them.

What a pity, it is still so cold outside! All of a sudden, fat snowflakes will begin to fall, or there is a hailstorm or thunderstorm. When the low, dark clouds disperse, the sun breaks through. Sometimes it brings out a beautiful rainbow over Lommersdorf, and the children stand in the Giefers' doorway and marvel at the display of colors on the pearly bridge.

On reasonably dry days, Father harnesses the horse, ploughs the fields, and sows seeds. Turnips are already in the ground, and potatoes, too. On the flat fields, sometimes the water forms shallow lakes. Flocks of crows fly across them.

After a cloudburst, water collects in front of the Giefers' farm, and more and more flood water gushes down the street. Father, Klöss, and Willi wait until the worst of the storm is over, then they each take a sack, turn one corner inside out, pull the sack over their heads like a pointed hat and run out with spades and shovels to dig a channel for the water to drain away.

At the end of April, Willi takes the last of the wheat grain down to the grist mill. Maria quickly climbs on the cart to go with him. She hasn't been to the mill for a long time. On top of the sack of grain, she has a soft seat. Inside the mill, there is a good smell of bran and flour. The huge millstones turn continually. Everything is powdered white. The miller greets Maria with a nod. He is busy because at fair time everybody needs their saved wheat to be ground so they can bake cakes. Since no one pays any attention to Maria, she goes to a little door she knows well and opens it cautiously. Immediately, coldness and wetness hit her; water foams and crashes from above, falls on the paddles of a wheel, and keeps it turning. The waterwheel is enormous. Father once told her that it was the biggest waterwheel in Germany. It measures 29 feet in diameter. For a while, Maria watches the regular rhythm of the wheel turning and the play of the water, and she senses the tremors coming from their movement.

Meanwhile, Willi has unloaded the cart and loaded it again. Maria can tell by his face that he has to make an effort to talk to the miller. She has sometimes seen that hearing people have to speak with more emphasis and has noticed that it has to do with the tremors she can feel, as right now, here in the mill.

Now it is time for the big baking. Maria is glad to be present for the first time. Mother has rolled up her sleeves and stands bent over the wooden kneading trough. With both hands, she kneads the dough made of wheat flour, yeast, and one full bucket of milk. Then she adds half a pound of sugar. Maria has learned in Aachen that you can use sugar every day—sugar in coffee, sugar in milk pudding, sugar in a lot of foods. But in Freilingen, a household uses only one pound of sugar in a whole year. Every year in April, Mother buys a one-pound sugarloaf from Aunt Barbara, and it has to last the family the whole year. One-half is used for the May fair cakes, and the other half is saved for the St. Barbara Fair on December 4th. Otherwise, sugar is never used. If any delicacies are baked in between, then they are large oblong dried fruit tarts and semolina cakes made without sugar. Sugar is precious and expensive.

While Mother is kneading the dough, Grandmother gets the oven ready. Into the dark hole she shoves a lot of kindling and straw Maria has dragged from the woodshed. From the stove, where the fire is never allowed to go out and which is carefully banked up with ashes at night, Grandmother takes a glowing piece of wood and uses it to light the twigs in the oven. At last, thick oak logs are placed on top of the fire. The oak logs burn long and hot. When the embers have died down, the stone walls of the oven are white with the heat. Grandmother dips the birch broom into a bucket of water and sweeps any smoldering ashes and still glowing or charred bits of wood aside. In the meantime, Mother Helene has covered the large baking trays with dough and spreads it with peeled apples, dried pears, and crumble. One tray after another disappears into the huge belly of the oven, which seems insatiable.

And, of course, a cinnamon ring must be made. Mother sprinkles raisins, sugar, and cinnamon on the rolled-out yeast dough, rolls it up and forms it into a half-circle. She mixes the rest of the dough with bread flour and stuffs a cooked ham inside. This lump is pushed into the oven with the wooden spade last of all, and then the iron bar is bolted across the oven door.

Soon, a delicious, wonderful smell wafts throughout the house. The little ones come in sniffing and can't tear themselves away from the smell. Neighboring housewives look in to see how far the Giefers have already got. The chickens flee from the house of their own accord, there is too much activity. Later, the freshly baked white loaves are set to cool on the stairs, and the delicious cakes cover the bedroom floors.

Inside the chimney hood, newly made fat sausages are hanging. The meat of a freshly slaughtered pig lies in salt in a wooden vat. Father has slaughtered a pig for the second time this year. Most people in the village slaughter a pig in January or February when the frost is crisp and the meat can't be spoiled by heat or flies. The one pig usually has to last a family for a whole year. The farmers' wives save a smoked shoulder for the May fair, which is then boiled in the soup and is the best part of their holiday midday meal. The poorest people in the village can't even afford to eat their own pigs. They drive them to the butcher in Münstereifel or to the cattle market in Hillesheim to sell them. But, Hubert Giefer has enough pigs, and, now and then, he can afford to buy a piece of beef from the Dollendorf butcher who comes to the village on some Saturdays. The butcher harnesses his two dogs to the little cart loaded with meat.

On the day before the fair, Maria cleans all the floors in the house again. In the early evening, the brass band marches through the village. Colored ribbons flutter from the musicians' jackets and hats. The children follow them excitedly. All the people watch and listen, stopping their work for a few minutes. Later, Maria's friend Traudchen comes to get Maria. In a long line with other girls, they go up to the Meiers-Hof dance hall. Maria stands in the doorway with Traudchen and watches the dancing couples turning and shoving each other back and forth. Why people dance to enjoy themselves is something Maria cannot understand. Leaning against the door frame, she can feel the rhythmic vibrations of the big kettledrum, and she sees Traudchen moving in time to the rhythm. The hall is decorated with garlands, and in the glow of the many paraffin lamps, the girls and young women look pretty in their finery. Everyone is in good spirits, including the many strangers in town who have been working on the new railway. Tomorrow is May 1st, 1913; the railway line will be officially opened and a train will travel for the first time from Blankenheim to Ahrdorf.

What a procession there is the next day after the midday meal! Almost the whole village is afoot or in carts drawn by cow or ox. They are on their way to the new railway station. Father has hitched his horse to the cart, and Maria, Mother, and all the siblings pile on, as do the relatives who have come to visit for the festivities. They take pieces of cake with them wrapped in colorfully checkered cloths, in case they get hungry on the way.

There has never been such a crowd in the Ahr Valley! Richly decorated, the new bridge spans the Ahr River, the road, and the meadows, in four wide arches. The new railway station is also decorated with garlands and flags. Maria sees brass bands, marchers in uniforms, the workers in their Sunday suits, strangers from Cologne in top hats and derbies, and all the farmers and their children from the surrounding villages. The Giefers stay seated in their cart on the road, where they have a good view of the bridge and the station on the opposite hill. Everyone waits in excited anticipation. After a little while, the little ones knock on Maria's arm and point to where a train decorated with paper flowers, fir branches, and bunting is approaching. The people wave their hats and kerchiefs. Some just stand and stare; they have never in their lives seen such a hissing monster.

The train stops at Freilingen Station. Someone stands and makes a long speech, then somebody else gets up to make a speech. Music plays, hats are thrown in the air, the stationmaster in his new uniform and red cap gives the signal, and the train starts moving again. Slowly it passes over the new, high bridge. The engineer waves to the cheering crowd below and blows the whistle.

The new stretch of railway is nearly fifteen and one-half miles long and has cost 8,000,000 Reichsmark (almost $2 million) to construct. At home, Maria never tires of asking Aunt Barbara about it, as she knows so much and has the patience to tell Maria.

Shortly after the May fair, Christina goes to Aachen with Father for the first time. They board the new train at Freilingen Station, just as if it had been built especially for Christina's school days.

27

At last, spring arrives. The swallows appear overnight. Speedily they flit across the yard, into the barn and stables where they build their nests in the beams. They breed, and soon, gaping little beaks poke out over the edge of the nest. The swallow parents are kept busy catching enough food for their little ones.

In the barnyard, the mother hen struts with her fluffy chicks over the steaming manure heap. The cat lies on the warm wall and pretends to be bored.

Father has been out mowing grass since three o'clock that morning. Grass is easier to cut when it is still wet with dew. Maria is to take his breakfast out to him and spread out the grass that has been cut. She has taken the three-pronged hayfork from the barn with her and carries it on her shoulder. She waits at the front door for Grandmother to tell her where to go. But, Grandmother stands there not knowing what to do. *How is she to tell Maria that she should go to the Ruede Borre field, where Father is working?* But Ruede Borre is not High German, it is Freilingen dialect, and Maria cannot lipread the dialect of Freilingen. Everyone in the village speaks in dialect to each other, and they know the names of the fields only in dialect. And what names they are—Mixdell, Löfjesdell, Stöckebähne, Ühlers-Nöck, Schohn, Nehrbröck, Schaafer!

All the melodious names of the fields and meadows are ancient. Many of them are derived from Old and Middle High German, some of them even originate from the Romans. They indicate springs and streams, woods and fields, and old roads that no longer exist. They tell of encounters with animals, or of a hollow tree, or of a hedgerow of blackberries all long since vanished. They refer to things that happened in a certain spot or describe the differences in the land compared to the surroundings, emphasizing distinguishing features. In the huge land register book in the Land Registry

Office in Blankenheim, the field names are written in both the Freilingen dialect and in High German.

A villager passes the Giefers' yard on his way to work in the fields. Grandmother asks him to show Maria the way to Ruede Borre. He does so. Maria knows the field where Father is working well, but she does not know what the field is called. She asks Father about its name, as she knows that was somehow the cause of Grandmother's helplessness. Father, who has sat down on the edge of the field to eat his breakfast, considers this for a moment, then he says, "Rother Born," and explains to Maria that there used to be a spring here for the big Roman villa called *Am steinigen Morgen*, (Stony Acre), which he points out to her. Maria will remember the names Rother Born and Am Steinigen Morgen. Over time, she gradually learns the names of many of the fields, and her family gets accustomed to using the High German names with her.

The tall grass with its colorful flowers and herbs falls under the blade of Father's sharp scythe. The freshly mown grass smells wonderful. Maria loosens the cut grass and spreads it out so that it can dry better. Bright and blue, the sky arches over the fragrant land.

On the way home, they do not say a single word to each other. Only when Father meets others returning home does he smile and talk to them. Everyone is friendly to Maria, smiling or nodding at her, but nobody speaks to her. What a good thing Grandmother and Aunt Barbara are there, as they at least sometimes talk to her. Maria cannot understand Mother very well because she speaks too fast and has thin lips. Mother does not have time anyway; talking to Maria means stopping her work and gesturing to make Maria understand. Mother often goes for many days without saying a word to her, even though they are always together in the house or out in the fields. It often happens that when Maria asks a question, people do not answer but only nod *yes* or just smile. Then she is sad because they haven't taken her seriously, or haven't listened to her properly. Even Traudchen, her girlfriend, does that sometimes. But, Traudchen is nice. She comes to get Maria for their Sunday walks. Every Sunday, Traudchen puts on her fine black pinafore, which she wears for church in the mornings, but as soon as she gets home, she takes it off, folds it, and puts it away. On the street, Traudchen and Maria meet other young girls. They walk along together, and the other girls chatter among themselves, laughing and giggling all the time. Maria walks silently beside them. It is not easy for her.

"Why you always laugh?" she asks her friend. But Traudchen has no time to explain at the moment.

At home Maria asks Grandmother, "Why girls always laugh? Why girls always merry? I don't know why."

"Young girls always laugh," Grandmother replies. "They don't know why."

Strange, Maria thinks, *I would like to know why.* There is a lot she would like to know—where a calf has been born in the neighborhood, where a cow has had to be put down, if anyone is ill, or what other news there is in the village. Sometimes, she goes round to the neighbors in the evenings to see if anyone will talk to her.

She calls everyone she knows by their first name and surname because this is what she learned in Aachen. She is the only person in the village to do this. All the villagers call each other by their first names and their house names, for in Freilingen even the houses have names. Everyone, regardless of their real surname, is known by the name of their house. There are seven farmhouses near the chapel that have girls' names. The legend is that a Freilingen nobleman had seven farms built near his castle, one for each of his seven daughters: Eva, Maria, Ursula, Klara, Anna, Cäcilia and Gertrud. In the Freilingen dialect, these names are *Eve, Mähr, Uschele, Kläre, Ännches, Zeye,* and *Jiedrögge.* The houses are still known by the daughters' names. All the other house names are very old, too, and have been handed down through history. They usually go back to the original builder of the farm.

Aunt Barbara's surname is Riethmeister. The name goes back to an ancestor who was a *Reidtmeister* (ironworker) in Eifel. But no one would really call Aunt Barbara "Mrs. Riethmeister." She comes from the Giefer house, and so she is called "Jivesch Bärb" (Giefer's Barbara).

Anyone who has business at an office or with the authorities must remember their real names. Now that Maria is in the village, the villagers use their proper High German names, so she will never know the names of the houses.

The days fly by while the family harvests the grain. When the barns are full and haymaking time is over, Father says to Maria one day, "Go upstairs to your room. Put on your Sunday dress, we are going to Hüngersdorf. You are to learn to sew."

Maria is quite shocked. "Must I go away? Can't I stay here? There is a lot of work here!"

"You are deaf and dumb. You must learn a trade," Father replies. Maria is sad. But, Father means well for her, she knows that.

Grandmother tells her, "You will come home every Saturday night. Learn to sew. It is better for you than only work in the fields."

Maria carries her folded pinafore in her hand and some slices of bread in a knotted headscarf. With her silent father she walks down to the Ahr road. Behind the new bridge, they immediately turn left and go up a country lane. They climb over a hill and come to Hüngersdorf. It is a small village, like Freilingen with little farms all around. They go into a cottage where two sisters live. Below the window in the front room stands a sewing machine like the one Miss Käthe Rögert had. Sewing things lie on the bench and tables, dresses hang from hangers on the walls. One of the two ladies has a club foot. She limps over to the visitors to welcome them. Maria realizes they have been expected. They have coffee with milk. Maria eats the bread she has brought with her. The two women talk with Father about Maria. When the woman with the club foot says something to her, Maria does not understand a word.

She turns to Father, "Please, Father, you must tell the woman to speak slowly and clearly." Father repeats her request, and the woman tries again. "I am a seamstress. You can learn to sew with me."

As Maria lipreads, she repeats the words aloud, as she often does. Then she nods her head and says, "Yes, I want to learn to sew well. I have already learned a lot at school in Aachen. I have already learned a lot at school in Aachen." Maria has a habit of repeating her last sentence. She doesn't do it consciously, she is simply uncertain as to whether she has been understood. Then she speaks even more loudly than she normally does, as she is making a particular effort. The seamstress looks a bit puzzled, but Maria knows it will take a while for the seamstress to get used to her voice.

"We will understand each other well, later on," Maria says confidently.

Maria is always away from home during the week. But, the days pass quickly because it is never boring in Hüngersdorf. While the seamstress's sister looks after the house, the cattle, and a bit of land, the seamstress and Maria walk from village to village—to Ripsdorf, to Waldorf, to the Dollendorf Mill, to Vellerhof, to villages near and far. Sometimes they stay for days, sometimes even weeks, in one place. If it is too far to walk home at the end of the day, they stay overnight in strangers' beds. Whatever village they happen to be in on Saturdays, Maria walks the whole way to Freilingen on her own, on field and forest paths, through valleys and over hills. Then, on Sunday evenings, she makes her way back to Hüngersdorf.

Only the richer farmers can afford a seamstress. Bed linens and clothes have to be sewn or patched up. Maria sews hems, mends seams and tears, sews on buttons, and does all the simpler needlework. She gets to see inside many different peoples' houses and eats at many tables. Children often sit with her and look at her curiously or shyly when she speaks. The housewives are friendly to her. They have already heard about the two deaf sisters from Freilingen. Maria is polite and attentive. Father will never have cause to be ashamed of her.

Everything has to be sewn by hand as nobody owns a sewing machine. The seamstress only uses her machine when they stay in Hüngersdorf. She has an iron like a real tailor. There is a little shutter in the base with a small hollow space inside. The seamstress uses fire tongs to take a glowing iron bar from the fire and put it into the iron.

Maria does not earn any money for her useful help. After all, she gets her board and lodging, and she is learning a trade. So far, Maria has never had any money of her own. Maria sees what the seamstress earns. For a skirt sewn from scratch she gets 80 pennies. For a good Sunday dress with braiding, bead embroidery, flounced sleeves, and tucks, she receives two to three Marks (200 to 300 pennies). The seamstress is satisfied with this amount, especially as a woodcutter doing piece-work earns up to 98 pennies a day.

The smoke trails of potato fires drift across the empty fields. Cranes fly overhead, heading south, and the harsh wind blows over the hills. The colors of nature are fading. Just before the hard winter sets in, Father decides that Maria should stay at home. That is fine with her. There is enough mending and sewing to be done at home. With scissors, needle, and thread she bravely sets about repairing linens and clothing for her family of eleven.

In December, strange men from outside Freilingen come to the village and stay until March. They sleep in barns or in the hall of the Meiers-Hof Inn on piles of straw. These day laborers work as woodcutters felling oaks and, toward spring, as bark strippers. Maria goes to the woods with Father early every morning to help the laborers. Maria ties the sawed-off branches into bundles. Her fingers grow numb with the cold. The forests belong to the parish and the church. They are mixed woods, mainly oak trees, with grass and bush underneath, and so thin that the farmers can graze their cows and pigs there in summer. The real Eifel forests have always been mixed woods, mostly of oak and beech. But, the former ironworks used up whole groves for making charcoal, and during Napoleon's military campaigns, entire forests were destroyed. When the Eifel became part of Prussia, the Prussians forced the Eifel people to plant fir, pine, and spruce trees. For a long time, the Eifel villagers were opposed to that Prussian wood, but gradually the fast-growing conifer trees replaced the mixed forests and supplied more wood more quickly.

In spring, when the sap rises in the trees, the young oaks, thick as an arm, are stripped. Maria watches Father tap the trunks with a wooden mallet and then peel off the bark with a curved knife. Soon, Maria can do it almost as well as he can. She learns to recognize the barks of the different trees. The young trees have green bark up to the age of eight years. Then, it becomes silver-gray; this bark, before it hardens, is preferred by the tanners. Maria knows from school and the Zinzius Tannery in Hillesheim that oak bark is used to make a special liquid to soak animal skins in to make leather. Whole cartloads of bark are transported from Freilingen and the other villages to the Blankenheim-Wald railway station. The stripped young forests stand there, pale, naked, and ghostly. Later, the laborers cut these trees down. The stripped wood is used as firewood in Freilingen. These logs burn long and hot.

The work in the forest is hard. Maria's hands become rough and calloused. In the evenings, she is exhausted.

28

There are people in the village who have so many bedlinens that they only need to do the washing twice a year. On the Giefer farm, too, they let the dirty linen pile up for six months until the women do a big wash.

It is spring. In the open shed, a big wooden tub is set up. The dirty linen is put into it. Mother stretches a worn sheet across it and scatters white wood ash on top. The ash has been collected from the stove. In the kitchen, the Grandmother and Mother boil water in large pots on the stove. Mother finds it hard to work because she is expecting another child.

Maria carries buckets of boiling water to the shed. She is strong, even though she is only sixteen. She slowly pours the hot water over the ashes and it seeps through the fabric into the tub. Maria keeps on fetching boiling water until the sheets are covered. Then, Mother pulls out the plug and lets the water run out. Again, Maria has to fetch water. Grandmother stands sweating at the stove, keeping the fire going. The process continues—fill up the tub with hot water, empty it again, several times over until the tub is as hot as the water itself. Only then does Mother allow the linens to soak in the hot water. After a few hours, she lays a board into the tub, takes a piece of wood, and she pounds the wet wash. Then Maria helps her to load the linens into a tub and to carry it past the chicken patch to Dörfer Creek. The water in the stream is clear, the gravel bed clean. Sky blue forget-me-nots, mauve lady's smock, and golden marsh marigolds grow along the banks. Mother and Maria spread out the sheets lengthways in the brook. The clear water flows over them and rinses away all the dirt. The linen is clean.

They hang it behind the house on wires stretched between the old fruit trees. It takes a whole day to do the great washing. Maria thinks of the soap she had never seen before her time in Aachen. Who on the Giefer farm or anywhere in the village has ever seen soap?

The small wash is boiled in a large vat every Saturday. A bag of wood ash is hung in it. The clean dry linen is pulled smooth over the edge of the table on Sunday morning. *That's as good as anything,* Maria thinks, for no one in Freilingen owns an iron.

The people in Freilingen say, "Hubert Giefer can hear the fleas sneeze in his sleep," and by that, they mean he knows very well how to make a buck. Maria is used to Father driving off early in the morning with his horse and cart, but she does not know where he goes. When she asks Grandmother, she gets the reply, "Cattle, buy and sell." *How does he do that?* Maria wonders. Often, there are strangers in the front room who stay for dinner. They are usually given something special, like Father, too. They are cattle dealers or hunters who come from the cities of Aachen and Cologne, and they meet in Blankenheim to go hunting in the forests. Father can talk to them for hours on end. A bottle stands on the table with small glasses, and Father's face becomes red, and he often laughs with the strangers.

In June, a new brother is born. He is to be called Hubert, like his father. Maria likes that.

When the weather becomes warm, Maria goes to work with the seamstress in Hüngersdorf again. She returns home on the weekends. She knows that Father is managing without her help on the farm so that she can learn a trade.

After only a few weeks, her brother Klöss turns up in Hüngersdorf to take Maria home for good. Without receiving any explanation why, she packs her things in a bundle, takes her leave and walks home deep in thought beside her silent brother. Father now wants to have her at home, but *why?*

During the next few days, in the middle of harvest time when everybody has to work especially hard and there is no time to waste, Maria notices a change in Freilingen. Men and women stand in groups on the street and in their yards when there is so much work to be done. When they finally leave, they stand around in the fields talking. In the evening, when the cattle has been fed, the people from the village gather in front of Giefers' farm. They all have worried faces, no one laughs. Maria is troubled. She joins the people and waits for the right opportunity to ask Grandmother.

"What is the matter?" she asks. "What has happened?"

Everyone seems to know. Only she, Maria, does not know.

"War! Grandmother says. There is war!"

Maria is scared. "War? Where is war?"

"Germany is at war with Russia and France. Bad! Bad! That is why you must stay at home," Grandmother says and turns back to the others.

Maria asks her friend Traudchen, "Why is war?" But, Traudchen cannot tell her.

Maria feels lonely for the next few days. Shut out. Then, she remembers that it is her birthday. Today, August 4, 1914. She had almost forgotten. No one else thinks of it. She is now seventeen years old.

She secretly steals away from work. It is oppressively hot. In her parents' room, she climbs onto a chair and drags out the big cardboard box lying on top of the wardrobe right at the back. It is covered in dust. She takes down the box, hoping she won't be disturbed. She tries to move as slowly as possible and not to bump against anything because the younger children are having their afternoon nap. She carefully opens the box. There is the doll's bed Papa Bunden made and the little white doll's chair. They both look like new, as if they had been freshly painted. Her exercise books and readers are neatly tied up with string. She finds pencils, penholders, needlework, and hair ribbons wrapped up in tissue paper, plus her school photographs and the photograph of her First Communion in St. Jakob's church. She slowly unties the string around her books. *How long is it, since she has done any reading?* Much longer than one year. Father does not get a newspaper, and there are no books in the house. She starts to read, one page and then another. Then, she unties her exercise books and reads what she herself has written. She has to read slowly, and suddenly she realizes she has forgotten how to write, she has already forgotten how. Did she write that herself? Those long, beautiful sentences? She can hardly believe it. She was able to do that all on her own? She couldn't do it anymore now; she has simply forgotten how to form sentences properly, how to write everything correctly.

The people who speak to her, they use only short sentences or only single words strung together. And she does the same. This realization is a blow to her. She does not know much anymore. She does not know what is happening outside in the world, either. There is war! If only someone would explain everything to her. Sadly, she packs all the things together again and puts the box back, out of reach of the children and hidden from her bigger brothers who make use of everything.

The sun is beating down outside. The cattle all seek shade. It is hard binding sheaves in the field in the afternoon heat. The air is shimmering. Maria has tied a white scarf round her head. Her woolen stockings are too warm, but, together with her heavy hobnailed boots, they protect her from the scratchy awns, thistles, and stubble. The flies are a terrible nuisance. In the west, huge clouds are gathering, getting bigger and bigger and coming closer. The sun is still blazing, but a cool gust of wind brings relief. Nine sheaves of grain are stacked quickly into shocks in long rows, then everyone hurries to get home. The sun has disappeared. Flashes of lightning make them hasten even more. Fierce gusts of wind tear at the women's skirts and blow off the men's hats; nervously the animals hurry home. Man and beast, the whole of nature, waits for the coming rain. It grows dark, the black sky gets nearer. When the Giefers reach the farm, lightning tears open the sky, thunder crashes, and a violent downpour starts. Hens scuttle cackling into the barn and stables, glossy swallows swoop close to the ground to seek shelter. Some villagers get caught in the rain on their way home, and men, women, and children rush soaking wet into their houses.

Maria has her hand on the iron door handle of the front room and is just about to press it down when the dark passage is suddenly lit up by a bright flash of lightning. At the same time, she is startled to the bone by an overwhelming, dreadful sensation. *Did the house tremble? Did she hear or did she just feel something?* She is so shaken that she goes weak at the knees and has to lean against the wall, breathing heavily. It was in her head, all around her, inside her. *Did she only feel it?*

"Thunder," Grandmother says, seeing Maria's face turn pale. "Thunder is very loud!"

Maria's knees tremble. She has learned about thunder and read about it at school. But, she thought people could only hear thunder. Maria has never experienced it before. She did not know thunder. But now—*did she hear it? She couldn't just have felt it, could she?*

Later, when she has calmed down, when the thunderstorm has passed and the long rain gushes, she tells anyone who will listen to her. "I heard thunder! Very loud in my ear." She does not want to experience it again. It was awful to hear something like that.

A few days later, the first men set off to war. Evening after evening, they have sat in the inn, drinking, talking, and singing. The whole village stands in the doorways or in the streets. Everyone waves. Many women cry. But the men, who are now soldiers going off to war, laugh. They have posies on their hats and jackets and wave back cheerfully. For them, war is still a great adventure.

The post office is the only link to the soldiers away from home, and the telephone in the post office is now particularly important for everyone. Aunt Barbara has explained to Maria that from the telephone in Freilingen you can speak and hear from far away. Maria has registered this fact without believing it. She cannot imagine how you can understand people who are a long way away. Aunt Barbara gets news every day through the telephone. She writes down all the news of the war and from the front on a big sheet of paper and hangs it in the window. No one passes without stopping to read it. In the evenings, they come down from the upper village and stand in groups in front of the window. One of them reads aloud. Maria goes to look every day, too, and tries to understand what is written there.

Otherwise nothing else really happens to call the war to Maria's mind. Yet, they all pray every evening in their rooms, on their knees in front of the crucifix. One day, someone tells Maria, "Heinrich Josef Klären has fallen and so has Karl Mungen." The village is stunned. Never will those two return.

As time goes by, the children forget war and all the other troubles for the winter's delights. When the valley of Dörfer Creek between Freilingen and Lommersdorf turns into a single sheet of ice, there is no stopping them. At the Giefers', so many jackets, scarves, headscarves, caps, and hats have to be put on that half of them fall to the floor in the scramble. Maria fashions handkerchiefs from old cloths, and gives one to each child. She tells the smaller ones to wipe their runny noses with it. And then off they go!

When Maria has time, she likes to join the other girls on the ice, too. Aunt Barbara has given the children some old barrels. They have made skis out of the curved staves. With them, one can glide wonderfully across the ice. Homemade sleds are there, too, with real little seats on them. But, it is best to go to the upper end of the village with the sleds. There it slopes quite steeply down to the valley. There are several bumps, which make the sleds take to the air in their downward rush. Then, the sleds make a little leap over the thick ice on Weiler Creek and gradually come to a stop on the flat ground. That's great fun for the brave and adventurous. Maria would never join them, she is much too scared. Rather, she watches with amusement and admiration until she gets too cold, and runs the long way back home, down through the village.

For supper, there is warmed-up sauerkraut or green beans or turnip greens from the stoneware pot. And with that, delicious golden potatoes with cream or vinegar and, very occasionally, melted bacon fat. The whole day, Father drives manure out to the fields, over frost-hardened tracks. There the manure for the potato fields will lie in heaps until spring. In the village, the wood smoke, curling white out of the chimneys, smells good.

29

"Have you got an exercise book for me?" Klöss asks his big sister. "I have to write a composition." With a heavy heart Maria gives him one of her exercise books from the cardboard box; it still has some empty pages in it. Father will not buy a new exercise book, the slate does well enough for the eight years of school in his opinion.

"When you finished, please give me exercise book back. I want to keep it to remember my school" she begs Klöss. He promises. But, she still has to be careful that it does not get lost. Sometimes she looks in the boys' room. It smells of straw, hay, leather, the stable, and rotting wood. The floor is soft and gives way when you walk on it. There are places where it is already rotted through. Bits of straw and hay that have dropped from the boys' clothes fill mouse holes, gaps, and cracks. Klöss's schoolbag is sewn from a sack. When Maria finds her exercise book in it, filled up, she takes it to put it back in its old place. What a difference there is between her compositions and her brother's, who can hear and is now thirteen. As his last sentence for a composition on the emperor's birthday celebration, he has written, *When the lessuns have finisht, we will give thre cheres.*

Maria does not know whether to laugh or cry. But, she knows how hard her brothers have to work all day. Father does not stand for any nonsense. Willi, who has already finished school, has to work like a grown man. Father gives him no money for it though; no one in the family is paid for work on the farm.

The year 1915 passes, and more and more men have to go and fight at the front. Everyone in Freilingen fears for them. Maria always hears about it when one of the men from the village is killed. The women and girls work even harder while the men are away at war.

Maria longs for Christina to return from Aachen for the autumn holidays. She is glad that each time they see each other, her younger sister has made more progress with her speaking, and Maria tries to ask questions about Aachen. She can hardly contain her curiosity. However, the result is usually too meager for Maria's liking.

"When you go to Aachen for Christina?" Maria asks Father. He shakes his head and tells her, "Christina is coming with visitors. The two Rögert ladies are coming with her." Maria's mouth drops open with astonishment.

Then, she shouts for joy and asks, "When?"

"Soon," he answers.

Maria has to clean and tidy the house plus her work in the fields! She tidies, wipes, and sweats, and is full of excitement.

Finally, the day of the visitors' arrival has come. In the heat of the August afternoon, Maria runs to the station, so as not to get there too late. When she reaches the Ahr road, she sees the train crossing the bridge to Ahrdorf. The visitors must already have gotten off! She runs down the last stretch of road and when she gets to the bridge, she sees the two Rögert ladies and Christina coming down the stony path from the station. First Maria flings her arms round tiny Miss Fine, who hugs her for a long time, and then Miss Käthe, who puts up with this jubilation somewhat stiffly. Christina stands there awkwardly, as if Maria were an incomprehensible creature to her. "I'm so glad! I'm so glad! I am very glad you have come!" Maria exclaims. She beams and hugs Miss Fine again.

"You have become a big girl. A lovely girl!"

"Yes, I am big now. All the dresses from Aachen too small and tight for me. I have made longer and wider."

"You are so brown and healthy!" Miss Fine marvels.

Maria says eagerly, "Yes, I always work very, very much in fields. I always in fresh air." Christina is dressed from top to toe in new clothes, a smart little city miss. Maria tells the ladies so, and they look as proud as if Christina were their own child. Maria takes their bags and small suitcase. She does not want them to have to carry anything. "I young. I strong and healthy. I want to carry!" she says. Miss Käthe asks if it is far. "Oh no!" Maria replies. "Not far." Then she tells them how far she had to walk before and about the opening of the new railway line, and talks and talks. She asks about the town of Aachen and whether there is any sign of war there. From the Ahr road, they go up the steep path lined with hazel bushes. The ladies' faces grow red. They wipe their faces and necks with white lace handkerchiefs. They lift their skirts to avoid the light dust that has settled on the blue chicory bordering the stony path.

At the top of Zollstock, they stop to rest and look around. Maria points to the rooftops of her village behind the shelter of the Stein and to the unprotected Lommersdorf on the hill. She points out the harsh, spreading Eifel country, points to Father's fields, meadows, and new wood, and to Father, who is hard at work. When they continue, they meet the villagers in the fields and on the road and Maria calls out, "My foster mothers have come from Aachen!"

A cow-drawn cart turns onto the road from the field and the luggage is loaded on it. Everyone greets the ladies warmly and waves to Christina. Maria is proud of her visitors and proud of the people of Freilingen. The Rögert sisters have had a long journey, and they are tired and perspiring. Finally they arrive at the Giefer farm. Maria makes sure that the chairs the sisters sit down on are clean. When her parents and brothers come home in the evening, there is a cheerful welcome. After supper, they have a look around the house, stables, barn, garden, and village chapel. The younger Giefer and neighbors' children tag along, too.

The following day is a wonderful Sunday for Maria. They all go to church together in Lommersdorf, and when they come home Miss Fine and Miss Käthe sit with Father on the bench in front of the house. While they are preparing the meal, Grandmother says to Maria, "The ladies from Aachen speak funny."

"Why funny?" Maria asks, almost accusingly.

"Aachen dialect is like singing," Grandmother says. But this answer does not mean a thing to Maria. For her, singing means opening your mouth wide and swaying a little with your head and body. But, Miss Käthe and Miss Fine don't do that.

After the midday meal, the visitors wish to rest. Maria tidies up the kitchen corridor and takes the bucket full of kitchen refuse to the stable. The youngest of the children are asleep upstairs, and Maria's other siblings have gone to the church service in Lommersdorf. Mother prepares coffee. Grandmother is sitting outside with the neighbors, talking softly and sleepily. Just before it is time for coffee, Father comes and asks Maria where their visitors are. "In front room, resting," she says and follows Father to the front room. He stops in the doorway. In their smart dresses, the two ladies are sitting stiff and bolt upright on the bench side by side. But their faces cannot be seen. They have spread large white handkerchiefs over their faces, and the swarming flies are walking about without bothering them. They have also stuck their hands in their sleeves so the flies cannot get at them. Father suddenly bursts out laughing. Startled, the hands fly out of the sleeves and whip away the handkerchiefs to reveal two reddened, sleepy, peering faces. Father curls up with laughter. Only when the ladies start laughing, too, is Maria relieved, as she was worried that the ladies might be angry with Father. Embarrassed, they dab at their faces with the handkerchiefs. Then, Father picks one after the other up from the bench, carries them struggling out to the yard, and swings them round in a circle before setting them down. Maria claps her hands with glee. The ladies smooth down their skirts.

The next day, Father takes them all to the station on his horse and cart. Maria waves goodbye to them until they disappear from sight.

30

Klöss has obviously been up to something. Maria comes into the front room and sees him getting a beating from Father, who is enraged. Father has unbuckled his belt, taken hold of the boy by the scruff of his neck, and is lashing him with the belt on the seat of Klöss's pants. The younger children are sitting nervously on the bench and in the corners, watching. Maria shrinks back. She can see that Klöss is yelling. His face is contorted. He is kicking his legs about. But, Father, who is infuriated, holds him firmly. He shakes him back and forth a few more times and then lets him go. Klöss stoops quickly to retrieve his hat that has fallen on the floor and runs out of the door. Maria goes after him and sees him crying and rubbing his bottom and then disappears into the barn.

Poor Nikolaus! Maria thinks. She stays out of Father's way for the rest of the day.

That evening the petroleum lamp on the wall is lit, and the family are all seated at the supper table. Potatoes are steaming in the bowl. Then, the door opens, letting in a cold draught, and Klöss stands in the doorway. Mother and the children look at him in surprise. Finally, Father raises his head, too, and he looks grimly at the culprit in the doorway. Klöss's face is still smeared with tears, but they all notice his shining, triumphant eyes. Straddle-legged, defiantly, he stands there. Using both hands, he holds out his shabby hat handed down to him from Father. The brim is wide, soiled, and floppy, and it is far too big for him. But, heaped up perilously in its depth there are brown and white eggs. Everybody looks at Klöss in silence. Maria goes to him, brings him in gently, and closes the door behind him. Doing so, she glances quickly at Father from the corners of her eye. Christmas is not far away. The hens tend to lay badly at this time of year, and eggs are money!

Father stands up very slowly. Klöss without moving, looks at him proudly. Father asks him something and Klöss replies. Mother carefully takes the hat with all the eggs from him. Father raises his hand and drops it on his son's shoulder, making him buckle a little. Then, Father slaps himself on the knee and starts to laugh; he bangs his fist on the table with such gusto that the plates bounce, and he laughs and laughs. The tension in the family is released. They all become cheerful.

Klöss sits down at his place at the table, grinning. Maria fetches a stoneware bowl and places the eggs into it, one by one. There are over forty eggs! "Where have you found?" she asks Klöss in amazement. But he is busy with his boiled potatoes with cream and just tilts his chin toward the barn.

Grandmother has to tell her the story. In his shame and pain, Klöss had hidden in a dark corner of the barn behind a stack of beanpoles. He didn't want anyone to find him. After he had sniffled and moaned quietly for a while, his eyes grew used to the dimness. He suddenly became alert. He could see a hole in the wall. Hay was hanging out of it and something white was gleaming inside. He sniffed hard, wiped his eyes with his hand, and stood on tiptoe. Slowly and carefully his hand slid into the hole and groped for the white thing. Then he felt the many, many eggs. They lay in the dark, right up to the back of the hole. He took his hat, filled it, put it down on the floor of the barn, and waited, delighted and sure of victory, for the evening, when they would all be gathered around the table. With relish he anticipated his great entrance, his enjoyment, twice as great after the humiliation of Father's beating.

Maria looks at Klöss affectionately. There he sits, stuffing himself with potatoes.

31

For Maria, the year 1916 does not start well at all.

She has a toothache. She feels a gnawing and piercing and hammering in her lower jaw. With a disgruntled face she does her work. She has put a scarf over her head as she thinks the warmth might drive out the pain and cure the sick tooth. At night, too, she wraps her head up well, but she still can't sleep. It gets worse and worse each day. Sometimes she cries quietly. She feels absolutely miserable with the pain and the lack of sleep. Her left cheek swells up, bulges more and more, and is taut and shiny.

Maria is in so much pain that she doesn't feel like working any more. She goes upstairs to Grandmother's cold bedroom where the old woman is lying sick in bed. Frost flowers have formed on the windows. Maria pulls off her heavy boots and crawls under the blanket at the foot of the bed. There it is warm, and she curls up and whimpers with misery. Grandmother stays quite still and Maria knows that she feels sorry for her. After a while, she is shaken roughly. Tortured, Maria raises her wrapped-up head.

Father is standing there, the corners of his mouth turned down contemptuously. He makes a mocking face. "Get up! Work! Not so weak, so soft! Not to bed with toothache! Get up! Get up!" Maria obeys and gets up. For two weeks, she drags herself around the house, the picture of misery. She sits at the stove sometimes, cradling and rocking her head in both hands. She cries. "Tomorrow we go to Blankenheim to the dentist," Father says when he has had enough.

"Thank God!" is all she can answer.

The next morning, Maria puts on Grandmother's bonnet. It has a shoulder cape knitted to it, and it is pointed at the top. Grandmother urges her to take an umbrella. There is driving snow outside, and she should protect her face. "Umbrella too good for that!" Maria exclaims. How many people have an umbrella, and one with a mother-of-pearl handle at that?!

"Take it," Grandmother insists.

The snow is so deep that the trains cannot run through the Ahr valley. Maria and Father have to trudge all the way to Blankenheim. The telephone wires mark the way. On the top of the hill, it is difficult to hold the umbrella against the bitter, icy wind.

When they finally reach the dentist's office, they find other people sitting in the waiting room. They have come from the town, the surrounding villages, and isolated farms. The dentist is not there yet. Father signals to Maria to sit down. "I wait in the fresh air. I pick you up here," he says and disappears.

Maria waits until the dentist arrives and it is her turn. The dentist works very quickly, but she does not care what happens to her if he can help her. And then, out comes the bad tooth! Dazed, her mouth full of blood, she sits on a chair again to wait for Father. She waits for a long time, and when she is tired of just sitting there, she goes out to the street, where she can spit out the blood into the snow.

She walks up and down the street, looking into the narrow side streets. There is no sign of Father. Maria is exhausted and shivering with cold. It must be well past midday. Then, at last, she sees Father approaching. He comes swaying down the street arm in arm with another man. She knows straightaway how he has been passing the time. His face is bright red, his twinkling eyes are tiny, and he keeps bowing in front of Maria. She takes a step back. She cannot stand the smell of an inn right now.

"Tooth is out!" says Maria, pointing to her cheek and spitting more blood into the snow.

"Come," Father beckons and goes on ahead with his pal.

The people stop and grin and turn around to stare at the three of them. Maria can see Father opening his mouth wide and waving his free arm about, which means he is singing loudly all the way down the street. *My God!* she thinks. *How will I ever get home?* When they arrive at the square below Blankenheim Castle, the two men make for a closed carriage. The driver has fitted wide runners under the wheels, turning the carriage into a sleigh. Father begins a long discussion with the driver, and finally they come to an agreement. Father takes out his leather pouch and gives the driver some money. The men climb clumsily and unsteadily into the carriage followed by Maria. She squeezes into a corner and looks out of the window, shivering. She holds her handkerchief over her mouth.

Actually, she is glad that Father is drunk; otherwise, he would certainly not have hired a carriage. The two men chatter and laugh. Maria has never seen the other man before. Her cheek is still numb. She is glad to be rid of the pain; now she can feel human again. She puts the umbrella next to her, holding onto it tightly. The carriage glides along the white road. It is still snowing, and an icy wind blows snowflakes thick as curtains past the window and across the meadows. Maria gazes into the whirling and swirling. She gradually begins to feel the pain of her wound. If only she were already home! She wants to lie down immediately. She longs for her bed. She shivers and dozes.

There is a bend in the Ahr road where the wind has blown up a snow drift. Suddenly the carriage tips over. Everything happens very quickly. Horse and carriage are lying in the ditch. The three passengers try to steady themselves with their arms and legs. They tumble over one another. The carriage is lying on its side. One door is buried in the snow, the other pointing up to the sky. They scramble out awkwardly. It is not at all easy.

At a loss, they all stand beside the carriage in the snow. The driver, who had been sitting up on the box, comes crawling out of the snow-filled ditch on all fours. The horse struggles desperately to get up. But the reins and shafts hinder it. The driver unhitches the horse and the men try to help it up. They have to wade deep into the snow. Maria holds the reins so that the horse cannot run away when it gets out of the ditch. At last, the horse gets up on its front legs, and then its hind legs, and is standing on the road again. It snorts white clouds of steam from its nostrils, tosses its head, shakes itself, and paws the ground restlessly. Then the three men push and pull the carriage out of the ditch and set it upright. The driver hitches the horse again. The men brush the snow from their jackets. They check the carriage to see if the crash has caused any damage. Luckily, everything has remained safe and sound.

The door of the carriage is wide open. Maria sees Grandmother's umbrella lying inside. She leaps into the carriage and comes straight back out. "Umbrella is broken! Umbrella is broken!" She shouts in horror. Part of the cloth has been ripped from the spokes and hangs in tatters. She holds the umbrella under father's nose accusingly, and in her rage she starts to cry. "Umbrella is broken!" she shrieks angrily. Father takes it from her and steps back. He holds it in both hands—crack!—the umbrella snaps in the middle—rip!—the cloth is torn in two. He holds the two halves high in the air and, with a cheer, he flings the pieces far across the ditch into a field of snow. Snowflakes swiftly begin to cover the black cloth. And Father starts to laugh. He laughs and laughs. The other two men who have been watching the little drama start laughing, too, and the shock of the carriage turning over is dispelled by their laughter. Maria stands there and thinks disconcertedly: *That is my Father!* When they drive off she turns around for a last look at Grandmother's abandoned umbrella.

When Maria tells Grandmother what has happened, she doesn't dwell on it for long. She has other things to worry about. Grandmother is lying in bed, more angry than ill. She has withdrawn because she cannot get along with Mother Helene anymore. Maria has often seen the two women arguing with each other. Why and what about, she does not know. When Father interferes, doors are slammed so hard that the house shakes. Maria thinks that perhaps there is also trouble because Mother overlooks a lot in her work, as she cannot see very well. *Why Mother no glasses?* Maria wonders. But, getting glasses costs time and money.

Maria loves them all: energetic, warmhearted Grandmother; Father, who she knows loves her; and little delicate Mother, who she respects because she works so hard for all the others. Mother is never impatient nor does she contradict Father. She is the first to get up, and by the time she brings Father his coffee early in the morning and sits down to talk to him, she has already done a lot of work in the stable and house. She fights with Grandmother in a dogged, quiet way. *Why can't they get along with each other?* Maria senses and notices the tension between the two women. For Grandmother, the farm is still her property. Here she worked with her husband, bore and brought up her children. *It is hard for everyone*, Maria thinks sadly.

In February, Mother gives birth to her fifth child, a boy called Toni. At the time of the birth, Father was out hunting wild boar in the Lommersdorf woods. He has a hunting permit and a shotgun. The snow lay freshly fallen over the Eifel, and this helped to see the boars' tracks. With hunters and beaters from the surrounding villages, they began to encircle the wild pigs early in the morning, after the first blast of the horn. Father shot a wild sow and had to buy rounds of schnapps and wine at the inn after the hunt. Proudly, he brought his bag home, where he met the latest addition to the family.

All the children Mother Helene has borne can hear, and, together with Elisabeth's six children, she is the mother of eleven children. With this large family and the farm to take care of, Maria, as the oldest, must work very hard. She takes this for granted, as she does the fact that she never gets any praise for it. Only later, when she is older, does she decide that she does not want to look as work-worn as many of the women in Freilingen do. These women work hard in the fields in addition to their work in their homes and stables. *The Eifel has beautiful girls, but no beautiful women,* the people say.

Spring comes, bringing fresh courage. Maria is chopping wood in the shed of "Eve," a house named for its former owner. It adjoins the stables of the Giefer's farm and is so old that the half-timbered wall leans forward about three feet. Father has bought it and turned it into a shed for storing timber. It smells good in there, like the woods. Maria chops the sawed up oak logs on the block, which is crisscrossed with notches. She throws the smaller pieces of wood into a basket, which she is going to carry to the stove in the kitchen. Suddenly, she sees a shadow and looks up. The moment she recognizes Father, she chops the hatchet into her hand. Blood drips onto the soft, sawdust-covered floor. Alarmed, she runs into the house to wrap up the gaping wound with some cloths. She makes a thick bandage around her hand. But she cannot stop working. That's impossible. She has to fetch water from the well. Her injured left hand cannot do anything now. *How stupid and annoying!*

On the way to the well, she meets the parish priest from Lommersdorf who asks why her hand is bandaged up. "I have cut with hatchet. I have a big wound," she replies. The priest goes into the house with her and tells her to remove the blood-soaked bandage and show him the wound. He goes across the yard and looks for Father in the stables and barn and shed, and then speaks to him. Father goes off. The priest says goodbye to Maria with a reassuring nod. When Father comes back he is holding a bundle of ribwort. He puts it in a small bowl of warm water. After a while, he takes the leaves out and shakes off the water. Then he tells Maria to hold out her injured hand. He squeezes the ribwort and dribbles the juice into her cut.

"You do this every day. Priest said!" Father orders her. Maria does so, and she is surprised at how quickly her wound heals.

In early summer it rains long and hard. The hay making will be late. On the first dry, sunny day Father says to Maria, "Come, turn hay." Klöss goes with them. Silent, but pleased, she carries the light rake across her shoulder. Father has cut two new prongs from soft plumwood and repaired the rake with them. Behind the Stein, they turn right and continue past Grindel Creek toward the woods. Hazelnut bushes arch across the meadow path. Dragonflies hover above the clear water of the brook. Dew still hangs in the grass and the valley is pleasantly cool.

Maria, in her contentedness and well-being, would like to talk to Father. "Father, I think time of rain is over. Hay dry well I think in the next days." She looks at Father while she is talking, as she always does when she speaks to someone. She has moved a little to the side to see Father's mouth better in case he answers her, and suddenly she steps into thin air. She falls and lands in the brook. The water is icy cold. Desperately, she tries to break her fall on the slippery stones with her left hand, her right hand is still holding the rake up in the air. Immediately her left wrist hurts quite terribly. Father first looks baffled, then he laughs, just laughs at her. Klöss grins and drags her out of the water. Maria does not feel at all like laughing. She is wet, and her wrist is beginning to swell up. "I can't turn hay! I can't possibly turn hay!" she groans. Father agrees when he looks at her hand. Maria wants to go back, but Father keeps hold of her.

"Wait!" he says. He gives his rake to Klöss and lies down on his stomach in the grass. He stretches his arm out over the brook and lets it slide into the flowing water. Red speckled trout dart to and fro in the water. Maria sighs. *How long will it take Father to catch a fish?* Father holds his hand very still in the water. Klöss crouches nearby and watches eagerly. Suddenly, Father makes a grab and holds in his hand, a big, fat trout, squirming wildly. Father throws the fish into the grass and waits until it stops thrashing about. Maria is disgusted. Klöss is delighted at Father's clever trick. The fish is hardly moving anymore. Father picks it up and orders Maria to take the animal home with her. Maria shudders with horror. She does not want to and shakes her head.

"No! I can't touch fish!" Father presses it into her good hand and says she must! Then he goes on with Klöss. The fish is cold and slippery, its mouth and eyes are open. It is horrible, revolting for Maria to carry it. A moment ago, it was still alive. If it starts to wriggle or twitch, she will drop it and run away.

Just a minute ago, the world was so wonderful. Now she is walking home with a dripping wet dress, a shooting pain in her wrist, and a dead fish, held way out in front of her. She feels like crying. *Fish is much nicer in water,* she thinks.

She is glad to be home and get rid of the fish. She wraps cool compresses around her throbbing wrist. At midday, she sits at the table with the others and watches Father eating the trout, fried in butter, all by himself and with great relish.

32

The people in the village are shaking their heads. Maria is surprised, too. A man came to the farm and brought twenty sheep with him. Father drives them out to the chicken run where he has built a pen out of slats. Twenty sheep. But just look at them! Nothing but old ewes, naked, without a single curl of wool and with rotting teeth. When Maria asks Father why he bought the sheep, Father only answers, "Cheap, cheap."

It has been many years since anyone in the village has owned sheep. In the past, everyone used to have two or three. In the morning, the community shepherd would walk through the village, and the sheep would run out of all the stables toward him. He would lead them out to the barren, sparsely covered hills and bring them back again in the evening. Sometimes, a great flock of sheep from the district of Daun passes through the Freilingen area. Then the farmers hire the flock to graze on the poorer parts of their land for a while, and they bring food out to the shepherd; in return, the farmers have sheep manure on their fields. Manure is so scarce that many fields must lie fallow for three to five years. No one has money for artificial fertilizer or any understanding of it. *Who will take sheep to pasture?* Maria wonders. She thinks Klöss probably will do it, and then remembers that she hasn't seen him around for several days. She asks Grandmother, "Where is my brother Nikolaus?" She learns that Klöss is working on a farm in Hillesheim owned by a family acquaintance whose sons are in the war and who desperately needs help. Maria is sad because Klöss didn't say goodbye to her.

Father goes out with the dog and the sheep by himself. On his shepherd's crook there is a little shovel with a hook on the top. Buying those sheep was not such a strange thing after all. They won't get fat, but there is still meat on them, and that is important; food is scarce in wartime. By now, everyone is feeling the effects of the war more and more. The state demands high crop and cattle yields from the farmers. In the mill, only a certain quantity of grain per person is allowed to be ground. People come from the neighboring towns and go from house to house begging or offering all kinds of stuff in exchange for food.

The farmers find the situation bad enough as it is, but a year later, in 1917, it becomes unbearable. The people flock to the villages like the plague, begging for food. Father has brought out the big front door key and locks the door with it at night. He has locks fitted to the stable and barn doors. Everyone in Freilingen has to do the same, and when they are out working in the fields during the day, they cannot leave their houses unlocked. Locking up has never been done before in Freilingen!

Maria sees the thin figures, the starving children and mothers at the door, and feels sorry for them. "War! Famine!" That is all she is told. In the mornings, Father counts the slices he cuts from the big, round loaf of bread. Each of them gets one slice. The bread, baked from wholemeal flour, is dark and heavy. In the feed store behind the stable, there is the small mill in which wholemeal is normally ground for the animals. Every week, Maria pours the grain into the top of the mill's funnel and grinds the grain herself. Now, in addition to the quantity of flour they are allowed to have ground at the mill for their animals, they can also bake wholemeal bread. Sometimes, Father sits with Maria in the feed store, thoughtful and silent. Now and again in the course of the year, he slaughters a sheep to provide enough food for all the hungry stomachs of the Giefer family. He buys additional new sheep, so he always has a small flock.

One day, Maria spends hours grinding grain in the fodder mill. Her back aches. Mother will use the wholemeal flour to bake ten loaves of bread, which will be stored in the dark cellar vault. Grandmother has made a fresh lump of butter. Salty drops of water still glisten on it. The butter goes into the cellar, too.

The next morning, there is a great commotion. Mother is standing in the hallway, holding her apron to her eyes, crying. Grandmother looks very angry, and the children are distraught. "What is the matter?" Maria asks, alarmed. Setta, her eleven-year-old sister, takes her by the hand. Setta hardly ever speaks to her big sister. Outside in the yard, she points to the low cellar window. The glass lies shattered on the cobblestones; Maria understands immediately. Dismayed, she claps her hand to her mouth. She has cried out loud.

"Quiet!" Setta says. "Father is asleep upstairs. Don't wake him up!"

Maria does not want to ask her furious Grandmother and instead runs to Aunt Barbara to find out what has happened. Aunt Barbara tells her that Father heard the dog barking in the night and called from the window, "Who is there?" But everything was quiet. Father went back to bed but could not sleep. Finally he got dressed and went downstairs and across the yard with a lamp. Then he saw the broken glass. Fearing the worst, he ran into the cellar—all the bread and butter was gone. So, he took the dog and hurried to the station to catch the thief before he could get away on the first train. But he found no one who had stolen his ten loaves of bread and the butter. Maria is in shock; nothing had ever been stolen from them! Now she has to return to the feed store to grind more grain, but much less than the day before. No one will get enough to eat in the next week. Butter is out of the question. There is no cream at the top of the milk churns yet. For now they eat curds and bread and, once in a while, scrambled eggs.

Weeks pass. Then a man comes to see Father, tormented by a guilty conscience. He confesses to taking the bread and butter. He is a basketmaker from Lommersdorf, "a layabout," Father says, who has eleven children to feed. Father listens to him but says not a single word. He lets the man go unpunished, which surprises Maria.

Father exchanges fat and meat for a sewing machine. *Father is clever,* Maria thinks. *Sewing machine is very useful.* What she has learned at school from Miss Käthe Rögert and the seamstress in Hüngersdorf, she is now able to put to good use. Every day, she sits at the sewing machine. She turns the small wheel by hand and the needle jumps up and down. At first Maria's siblings are fascinated; they stand around the machine watching her work. Setta would like to be in Maria's seat. Later, they become used to it and only come when they have torn something. What luck to have someone at home who can mend everything quickly! No linen or clothing is wasted in the large household. Maria tries to fashion new things from worn-out garments. She is successful, and the work gives her pleasure. Her sister Lena, a child with delicate features, who is unobtrusive and obliging, sits for hours on end at Maria's side, eager to learn how to sew by hand and by machine. Maria feels appreciated. Neighbors come and ask for help. They are impressed with her industriousness and skill and the care she takes when sewing. When she is praised, her eyes shine and she smiles cheerfully. At harvest time, the sewing machine is put upstairs in front of the bedroom window. Then, due to lack of time, Maria only sews and mends on Sundays.

One day, a careworn woman who lives in a humble cottage comes to her. No one in the village wants anything to do with her because she is dirty. She stinks. The poor, overworked woman has many children and a good-for-nothing husband. Maria is sitting at the sewing machine when the woman comes into the front room with Father. The woman tries to smile at her and Maria looks with alarm at the contorted face. "You mend blouse!" Father says and points to the garment the woman is holding out to her. Maria looks beseechingly at Father. Can he really expect her to do that? Father nods sternly and leaves Maria to her task.

Maria takes the blouse from the woman; it is unwashed. She says, "Yes, I will mend blouse. Pick up this evening." The woman gives a pleased nod and leaves. Maria sighs. She wants to get the unpleasant job over with, so she pushes the other sewing to the side. Reluctantly, she picks up the blouse and examines the damage. She forces herself to mend the filthy garment. But suddenly she feels so ill that she has to run outside and vomit on the manure heap. She is pale and and her knees tremble. Then she looks for Father and tells him, "I can't sew the blouse. Blouse stinks!" That only makes Father laugh. Maria gets angry with him. She furiously goes back to work and mends the blouse. *No, you can't talk to Father about that.* He has no pity for her. She hangs the blouse on a nail and washes her hands thoroughly.

In the evening, the woman comes to fetch her blouse. She sits down for a while and chats with Mother. Then she thanks Maria and leaves. Father beckons to Maria and points to the chair the woman sat on. "You take chair into yard. Chair must be aired!" His face is stern. Maria does not dare disobey. She carries the chair out to the yard where it stays all night. She understands that Father wanted to help the poor woman, but he has shown that he disagrees with her uncleanliness.

Willi is wearing his Sunday clothes in the middle of the week. It is the beginning of August and work abounds. "Why Willi not work?" Maria asks Mother.

"Willi is going to be a soldier tomorrow." Maria watches Willi, the oldest of her brothers, running around exuberantly with the small children. *I have never seen Willi so cheerful,* Maria thinks. *Face is happy.*

In the evening, Mother packs his things. Maria has checked that everything is in order. The next morning, she makes a large package of slices of bread with butter for him. After the midday meal, his friends come to collect him. There is a little posy of flowers on Willi's jacket. He says goodbye to his family, shakes hands with the neighbors in the yard, and goes off laughing with his friends to the station. Father follows his son with his eyes for a moment, then he goes into the stable, hitches the horse to the cart, loads the harrow, and gestures to Maria to take the hoe.

"You come with me!" Father says, and drives off. Maria walks behind, carrying the hoe. Father wants to prepare a small field on the Stein for sowing rape later. It won't be ripe until the following June, when they will pick the pods. Rape yields valuable oil.

The sun blazes down. There is always a wind on these heights, but today it has no cooling effect. Father and Maria can see the departing Willi and his merry band on the Zollstock until they disappear into the Hüngersdorf valley.

In the field, Father walks beside the harrow, holding the reins, with a weary step and a grim expression. Maria trudges behind him. The earth is lumpy and dry as dust. The summer sun has baked it hard. Maria breaks up the big clods of dirt with the hoe. Row after row, the harrow is dragged through the earth. Then Maria sees Father stop the horse, throw down the reins, and walk to the edge of the field. Under the blackthorn bushes he lies down, pulls his hat down over his face, folds his arms across his body, and does not stir any more. Maria does not know what to make of it. She has never seen Father like this before. He did not even turn around to look at her, as if she were not there. He just flings himself down and goes to sleep.

As she goes on breaking up lumps of earth, her thoughts turn to Willi. She didn't know anything about him having to go to war. Nobody told her anything. How happy her brother seemed! How glad he was to get away from home! *But, war is terrible,* Maria thinks; *doesn't Willi know that?* He will be afraid—and what if he dies like the others from the village who have fallen? Since the two men who were killed at the beginning of the war, many more have died. Willi went away as if heading for freedom. And

Nikolaus? When Klöss comes home for a visit from the farm where he is working, he is always glad to go back.

Maria can understand why her brothers would want to leave. Father is very strict with them. They have hardly any freedom. They never get money from Father. *Willi is eighteen,* Maria thinks. *And I? I am twenty.* She is overcome with forlornness. Melancholy rises in her. She is totally alone. She starts crying. While she continues to work, endless tears run down her face. She realizes how utterly alone she is: She cannot hear. She is deaf. She will always be shut out, always live on the edge of things and never really belong to anyone who understands her fully, who is like her. The others talk and laugh with one another. She has to be grateful for a single patient reply.

For years she has worked on Father's farm. Years of hard work from morning to night. What kind of a future has she got? It will always be the same. She is quite prepared to work, work is life for her. But, will it always be like this—*nothing but this?* Willi is going away, Nikolaus has gone, and Christina is in Aachen. *Who else will go away?* What will become of her?

Father is lying there, asleep. She longs for his love, for a long talk alone with him. But he just lies down to sleep as if she did not exist. Perhaps nobody would miss her? Only her work? Father can live without her, they can all live without her. She feels superfluous. How senseless and useless her deaf life is. She is not necessary to anyone, and there is no one in the world for her. She cries bitterly, as she has never cried before.

The sun is sinking in the west. When the first farmers begin coming home from the fields, Father stretches and gets up. He walks over to the patient horse and pats it on the neck. He unhitches the harrow, leaves it in the field, and goes home with the horse. Again, he has paid no attention to Maria. Carrying the hoe on her shoulder, she goes home too. There is activity at home. Lena and Anna tease her affectionately. Little Toni is pleased to see her again. Josef hangs on to her pinafore. The security of her familiar surroundings dispels her misery. But a trace of wistfulness remains.

33

The first straw from a newly cleared, cultivated field is as fine as grass. Threshed with the flail and tied into small bundles, it is used to thatch many of the roofs in Freilingen.

Straw is scarce in the high Eifel. The fields are meager and stony. Spring comes late and winter early. The stalks of the sparse grain do not grow very tall. The farmers need straw in winter to mix with the cattle fodder. For the stables, they use gorse and heather. To thatch the roofs, they buy long rye straw from the fertile Jülich region—"the lowlands," as the people of Freilingen say—and transport it back to the village on cow-drawn carts.

With the straw come the rats, which nest in the thatch and create leaks. They also get at the food stored in the cellars and attics. Maria is afraid of rats and loathes them. Father has several cats, two of which hunt rats. Mice are mostly found at harvest time, when Father mows the grain with the scythe. Then, stirred up, they scurry through the fresh stubble. Hundreds of mouse holes become visible. To get rid of the rats and mice, Aunt Barbara has set up some traps at home, and she also sells them to the neighbors.

Maria has been cleaning her aunt's shop every Saturday for years. In exchange for the cleaning, Aunt Barbara gives her a length of dress material. Maria is happy about it. Since she left Aachen she has had nothing new to wear. She has grown out of all the clothes she had, although she has altered and patched them again and again. She takes the material to Mrs. Appels, a seamstress in Lommersdorf. She asks her to cut out the material for a dress. Maria does not dare cut the new material herself, but she will sew the dress herself. At last she has something nice to wear again for Sundays. In her new dress she takes a walk to see her Uncle Luppertz. He is a brother of Elisabeth, her dead mother. For a number of years he has run an inn in the lower village. First, Maria sees the manure heap in the yard, and behind it the small stone house with the inn. A hall has been added to it, but dances are not held there anymore. German soldiers sit in front of the hall with their guns. They are guarding Russian prisoners. Maria has had to get used to the sight of the prisoners with their padded jackets and overalls. The prisoners can move about quite freely in the village. They are friendly and good-natured. Whenever help is needed on the farms, because the men are at war or have fallen, the Russians readily lend a hand in the fields and in the stables.

Maria is very surprised to see that everyone uses gestures to communicate with the prisoners. She can understand everything they mean. When she asks, Grandmother says, "The prisoners have a different language." The Russian prisoners of war and the beggars from other towns have changed life in the village.

On Sunday mornings, Father drills the sixteen- and seventeen-year-old village youths in the meadows behind the Reech. They use a wooden stick in place of a rifle to practice "Shoulder arms!" They have to crawl on the ground and learn to shoot using a real rifle. Father sets up a large target. Once, Maria watched from a distance and saw the flash from the muzzle, followed by a puff of smoke. Father is very proud of the fact that he is giving the boys preliminary military training. "I am an old soldier," he tells Maria. *Has he already been to war?* she wonders.

Aunt Barbara tries to give her an answer and writes on a piece of paper: *Regiment Horn in Trier*. Father was there, before he went to America. Maria does not know what to make of *Regiment Horn*. But, she does not want to bother anyone with further questions.

The people of Freilingen go to work, looking more and more downhearted. Sixteen husbands and sons from the village have already been killed. The hunger increases. The throng of beggars and barterers seems endless. At midday, they now often eat turnips, which used to be cattle food. In late autumn, the turnips with their leaves and stalks are pickled in big stoneware jars much like sauerkraut or green beans. Dried and chopped potato leaves, mixed with hay and straw, are now fed to the animals.

Grandmother wants to live with her daughter Barbara. It is awful for Maria that her beloved Grandmother moves out, but she can't get along with Mother. Although she lives just around the corner, Maria cries and misses her. Klöss cries too. The house suddenly feels empty. As often as she can, Maria pops over to Aunt Barbara's to see Grandmother. She usually takes her brother Josef, her favorite, with her. Grandmother sometimes boils an egg for the two of them. How long has it been since they had an egg at home? How good it tastes! Grandmother sits with them and is pleased.

34

Late summer is drawing to an end. The swallows have flown away and gossamer glistens in the golden September sun. In the evening, long shadows cast the Giefers' house across the yard and into the street. Maria goes to fetch water from the well. Suddenly, she sees horses and carts full of German soldiers streaming into the village, then more of them, and still more. The soldiers are haggard and weary. The horses look even more wretched. Their ribs stand out in a curve under their thin hides. The soldiers stop when they get to the chapel. Their boots are worn out, their baggy uniforms dusty. The men are unshaven, bone thin, and they stare out of big eye sockets.

Just when Maria returns to the farm with her pails of slopping water, Setta arrives home from the pastures with the flock of sheep and the dog. Setta often has to tend to the flock on her own. The bleating sheep try to push through the blocked street to the stable. The girls see the soldiers just as they are sitting down on the Giefers' stone steps and on the bench in front of the house. In the front room and hallway, too, they crouch on steps, on chairs, on the floor. Some of them have a kind word for Maria, she can see it in their faces. But she is a bit shy and cannot answer them, even though she is afraid they might think she is an unfriendly girl. Father sends Maria and Setta to get straw from the barn and spread it out in the front room. The soldiers lie down on it, close together, and immediately fall asleep. All over the village, people take in soldiers for the night. They sleep in barns and stables as well as inside the houses. The next morning, Father examines the wretched horses. The leg of one is badly injured and walking causes him great pain. Father and a neighbor slaughter the horse in the yard. Mother makes soup from the horsemeat and roasts a great deal of it. At midday, the whole family and all the soldiers who were given shelter at the Giefers' can eat their fill. Maria sees Father bargaining with the soldiers for the other horses. He leads four of the skinny animals into the stable and gives the soldiers money for them. Maria thinks the horses belong to the emperor, but she doesn't ask. After the slaughtering, cooking, roasting, and eating, it takes Maria several hours to clean up. The soldiers stay the whole day, rest, wash themselves, and talk to the people in the village. In the evening, when Maria is going to bed, she sees the soldiers from her window, still crossing the yard and the street. Storm lanterns shine on their carts. Sometimes, she sees a sudden flare when someone lights a pipe. The next morning everything has disappeared. The mess of straw and cart tracks are the only signs of the nightmare of war.

Maria asks Grandmother, "Where the soldiers come from? What about war?"

Grandmother replies, "All the soldiers want to go home. Germany will lose the war. German soldiers are coming back from France. The war is very bad, soldiers said."

October 1918 is cold. Gone is the mild autumn. Rain sets in, and wind. Ragged clouds drift low across the Eifel hills. Maria is cold. The cold cuts to the marrow of her bones. She sneezes and coughs. She would just like to sleep. She steals away to her room and crawls into her straw bed, but she doesn't feel any warmer. Her teeth chatter and she shivers. It is not long before Father is standing at her bed. He orders: "Get up!"

"I ill. I not well," Maria says.

But Father is cross. "Go to pasture! Go to pasture! No time to be ill. Take Josef."

Maria and Josef drive the cows through the village, past the mill, and up a hill. Up there it is bare, except for a little copse where raspberries and blackberries grow. From here they can look beyond the Ahr valley out to the hills covered with dark fir trees. The ruins of a round tower that looks like a warning finger built on a soaring rock, point to the sky: They are the remains of Dollendorf Castle. Maria and her brother see birds of prey circling above the copse. They are both very cold. They are wearing old, long men's coats that do not provide much warmth. They have sticks with them to herd the cattle. In a little hollow with moss-covered stones, elder and hazel bushes grow, with a few creepers in between, yellow and thorny, and a tough gorse bush. Maria and Josef squat in the hollow, huddling close together, trying to find some shelter from the wind. The brown cows graze peacefully in the wet grass.

Maria knows the weather; she can forecast it for days ahead. For many years she has observed the winds, the sky, and the light. She points to the sky and tells Josef, "If wind comes from east, will be very cold and dry, if wind comes from south, will be warm. If wind comes from west, rain soon. If wind comes from north, cold and raw. If chickens always clean feathers, will rain. If cows graze downhill, rain. If you can see far, very clear—rain."

Maria can no longer speak in complete sentences. She has long forgotten how. She cannot write correct sentences any more, either. When was the last time she wrote? And what about reading? When she goes to see Aunt Barbara and Grandmother, she reads sometimes, if there is a newspaper lying around. But she can't understand everything any more, as she could when she was at school. The sentences confuse her and are difficult to understand. This makes her feel sad. So much effort at school, and for what?

Josef is miserably cold, and his eyes are strangely bright. Although Maria is shivering herself, she puts her arm around him and feels sorry for him. He is so delicate. Mother died giving birth to him. Maria does not know if that is why she is particularly fond of him. Josef leans against her arm, trembling. *He should go home,* Maria thinks to herself. But she is afraid that Father might be cross, so she keeps him with her and tells him whatever comes into her head. Then she decides it would be better to move around a bit and walk. But Josef doesn't want to and begs her to stay sitting there. At dusk, Maria gathers the cows, and they go home in the murky, gray light. They both feel stiff, clammy, and damp. They long for warmth and sleep.

During the following days, Maria and the other Giefer children are all ill. But not only they. An influenza epidemic breaks out and rages all over the country. The Giefer children lie in their cold small rooms, feverish and with headaches, sore throats, runny noses, and coughs, until they finally get over it. One of them does not get better. He lies in his bed, wasting away; he is very weak and sleeps most of the time. Mother Helene has no time to look after him. Maria, still weak from the illness, sees neglected work everywhere. The little ones whine and are not yet fully themselves. Shivering, Maria goes upstairs to make the beds and tidy up. In the boys' room, Mother is standing by Josef's bed with a piece of bread and a cup of milk. Maria can see Mother asking Josef to sit up and eat something, but the little boy is too weak to raise his head. Mother just stands there at the bed with the bread and milk. Maria is suddenly seized by panic.

With quaking knees she runs downstairs, races across the yard, and around the house to Grandmother and cries, "Grandmother, you come, please you come, immediately! With Josef not good, I afraid! Come now! Please!"

Grandmother has not set foot in her son's house since she moved out, but she sees Maria is afraid. She quickly grabs a scarf, ties it round her head on the way, and rushes up to the room with Maria. But Josef's bed is empty. Frightened, they run down to the front room. Mother Helene has wrapped Josef up in a blanket and pillows and laid him on the wooden bench. Grandmother, deeply worried, leans over the pale boy. No, he waves weakly, nothing to eat or drink. Shortly after midnight, his life comes to an end. He is eleven years old. Grandmother takes the bitterly weeping Maria into her arms.

November comes in, cold and damp. The people tell Maria to pray for the poor souls who have passed on. The war has killed so many people—and from April to November 1918, 21,600,000 people, all over Europe, died in the influenza epidemic. Where have their souls gone? Maria learned at school that souls must first do penance for their sins in purgatory before they can go to Heaven. Maria has pity on the poor souls, and fear of God. But reverence, too.

Aunt Barbara tells her a few days later that the war is over, that Germany has lost the war. "Thank God!" Maria says "now it gets better."

She has a thousand questions: What has been 'lost' now, what the emperor and his family are doing now, what it was all about, and why? But she does not ask. She senses that it is difficult to explain a lot of things to her. She shies away from asking questions and does not want to be a nuisance.

One February night in 1919, the Giefers are all sound asleep. The whole day long they had been threshing stored grain. Willi has to stand in front of the Giefer house for a long time, shouting "Father! Father!" and must bang on the door until he is finally heard. He has returned home from captivity in France.

35

"You to Neuwied, to sew!" Father says to Maria.

"Where Neuwied?" She is very surprised.

"On the Rhine."

Maria later learns from Aunt Barbara that one of the soldiers who guarded the Russian prisoners was from Neuwied. This soldier's wife is a master dressmaker. Father has received a letter from her saying that Maria can work there. Maria is glad. She tells everyone she knows. She packs her clothes and waits. Shortly after Christmas, Father and Maria take the train from Ahrdorf, transfer in Remagen and travel on toward the little town of Neuwied. They sit alone in a compartment on wooden seats. Father holds his walking stick between his knees. He has not said a single word the whole journey. Suddenly he turns to Maria and says, "Never marry a farmer! Too hard work for you, and not good. You not marry farmer!"

Surprised and startled Maria replies, "Oh—I not think of marriage!" Father remains silent for the rest of the journey. They look out at the countryside flying past. Maria can think only of Father's words.

Mrs. Raschke, the dressmaker, lives with her husband in a small house. Maria is given a room all to herself. Apart from her, four other girls work for Mrs. Raschke, who sets great store by order and punctuality. The sewing room is also the living room. Mrs. Raschke has two sewing machines, both with a treadle. The girls clean the machines every week with rags and brushes, and oil the nipples from a little oilcan. When working, they wear dark dresses and white aprons with lace and frills. The girls are friendly to Maria. From the very first day, she feels at ease. A lot of ladies come, choose things from magazines, get changed behind a curtain, try things on, and turn around in front of a large mirror.

One day, Maria asks Mrs. Raschke where the other girls come from and what their names are. "They all come from Neuwied, and one is a Jewish girl." Maria is puzzled. Why does Mrs. Raschke mention that especially? While she is sewing, Maria keeps looking at the Jewish girl, watching how she moves and works. A Jewish girl? Maria cannot find anything remarkable. For the others, she and the Jewish girl are different. She, because she is deaf, but why the Jewish girl? Maria thinks of the cattle dealer who comes to Father. He is a Jew, too; Grandmother told her that with a grim face. Deaf people sign a hooked nose with their forefinger when they mean a Jew, and it is always done with disdain. She does not know why. Is it bad to be a Jew? Why is it bad? Which is worse—to be a Jew or to be deaf?

The winter of 1920 arrives with a terrible, severe cold. Maria goes out only on Sundays, walking quickly to church with Mr. and Mrs. Raschke through the snow-bound streets. In this icy weather it is almost impossible to breathe, and the cold bites the face. Mrs. Raschke keeps the iron stove filled up with coal and briquettes. It is Maria's task to take the ashes out every day. Apart from sewing she also helps around the house. Mrs. Raschke has put rolled up blankets in front of the cracks below the door and hung large woolen cloths in front of the windowsills. She tells Maria that the Rhine has frozen over. Maria asks if she can go to the Rhine on Sunday and have a look. Mrs. Raschke lends Maria her fur muff. When Maria catches sight of the river, it lies there, glistening and glittering in the morning sun. From bank to bank there is solid ice. Ice floes, strangely shaped, are piled up in terraces. Gulls are strutting on the ice or flying across the frozen river. A man is feeding the gulls. They swoop down to snatch the breadcrumbs in midflight or peck at them in the hard snow. Maria watches for a while. Then the cold drives her home. She has really not seen any water at all, only solid ice!

One day she wants to clean the windows. She prepares hot water in the kitchen and tries to wash the windowpanes very quickly. But no matter how fast she wipes, the cloth almost freezes to the glass. All the water on the windows turns straight into ice. Mrs. Raschke shakes her head. No, windows aren't cleaned in this cold weather! That is foolish! Throughout the winter, all the windows in the unheated rooms stay opaque. Even in the heated rooms the ice never melts at the edge of the panes. Only in the middle is there a little hole to look through.

Maria is content, although a little bit sad at times. The girls chat and laugh with each other. Maria sits there and cannot join in. And she can't keep asking, "What you talk about?" or "Why laugh?" all the time. And besides, the girls can talk and work at the same time; but if they talk to her, they have to stop sewing for that moment. Nor does she always understand them right away. The girls find it a nuisance to repeat themselves. They prefer to chat among themselves. It often saddens Maria that she has to be with them, so deaf and left out.

At last, spring arrives!—Maria looks up from her sewing and sees Father standing in the room. Maria leaps up, she is glad to see him. He says, "Pack things! You home." Mrs. Raschke nods and shrugs her shoulders to indicate there is nothing she can do. Father stays for the midday meal, then Maria says goodbye to the girls and Mrs. Raschke. She takes a photograph with her as a souvenir—Maria and the girls, with Mrs. Raschke in the middle.

On the train, Maria asks her silent Father, "Why I must go home?"

"We save money if you stay at home." Maria considers what that might mean. Save money if she stays at home? Money? She has never had any money, apart from the pennies from Papa Bunden. Mrs. Raschke didn't give her any. She had free room and board there. Or did Father have to pay something?

From Ahrdorf, the two walk through Lommersdorf to Freilingen. They carry a travel basket, slung on a stick, between them. In Neuwied on the Rhine, it was springtime, mild and warm. Here in the Eifel, the buds are hardly opening. There is not a single fruit tree in blossom yet.

Maria is glad to see her family again. But she sees her home through different eyes; the roads are rutted and neglected, the houses and huts shabby. So many children! Cattle, stables, and fields are crying out for care.

Maria takes off her lace-up boots and puts on her stout shoes. She hangs her good dress away. She ties on her white headscarf and sets about doing the work that is familiar to her.

Father ploughs and harrows. Maria plants potatoes and turnips. The garden is waiting for her digging and sowing. The stable is cleaned out twice a day, clothes have to be mended. Five-year-old Toni, the youngest of the children, follows Maria around all the time. It does Maria good to know that Toni is fond of her.

Maria knows how the year goes: Thin out turnip plants, hill up potatoes, hoe root vegetables, harvest hay, bring in the grain, lift turnips and potatoes, spread manure from the stable on the stubble fields, plough.

In spring, sow oats and clover, in autumn grain and some wheat, plant vegetables in the fields—it is an eternal rhythm, determined by the weather and nature.

Toward the end of autumn, Father sends Maria to Mrs. Gossen in Lommersdorf to learn how to cut out material. She has never tried cutting new material before. Her friend Traudchen is also learning with Mrs. Gossen. They meet in the mornings and walk together.

Maria has cut out a blouse on her own and sewn in tucks and lace. Mrs. Gossen is so enthusiastic about her fine work, she lets Maria take the blouse to the customer herself. Mrs. Gossen hangs it carefully over her arm and says, "You must say: I sewed the blouse myself." Maria is proud and happy. She takes the blouse to the farmer's wife and says loudly that she made the blouse all by herself. But the woman takes the blouse from her without a smile and without a glance at her, puts it away and goes on with her work. Maria is disappointed. Perhaps the farmer's wife has not understood her? Perhaps she cannot find pleasure in anything anymore because her husband died in Russia in the war? *Poor woman,* Maria thinks.

All winter long, she trudges up to Lommersdorf early in the morning. At midday, her sister Setta brings her something to eat in two small billy cans. When she returns home in the evening, she helps Mother, looks after her brothers and sisters, and goes to see Grandmother and Aunt Barbara. What a good thing she does not have to spend the whole day on the Giefers' farm! By the time spring comes and Maria is needed in the fields, she has mastered the art of cutting out material.

36

Father must be a clever man. In spite of the hard times, he owns two farm horses. The older boys clean and groom the horses. Their coats have to shine, their manes are combed and trimmed, and the tails, too, are clean and trim. It is a pleasure to look at them. Every morning before the horses are harnessed, they stand at the front door of the stable and wait. Then Mother or Maria gives them a slice of bread. Maria likes doing that. She likes the feel of the horses' soft, warm lips on the palm of her flat hand. Her brothers often ride the horses out to the fields. They are very proud; they know the other people in the village have to hitch a cow or an ox to their carts and plows. But they have got two horses! And two pigs and a piglet as well! There aren't any sows with piglets in Freilingen. Whoever has the money buys a piglet at the market, brings it home in a sack, and fattens it up. Father bought his piglet when it was six weeks old, two hands long, and rosy pink. Because Father has two sows, Setta has to drive them all the way to the other side of the Ahr so they can breed with the boar at Vellerhof manorial farm.

In the stable next to the threshing machine, Father has over a hundred sheep. He bought most of them at the livestock market in Mayen. He and Maria's brother Mäthes traveled to Mayen and drove them back to Freilingen in two days, a ninety-mile roundtrip. Father bought the other sheep in the surrounding villages. Now the undemanding animals are thriving particularly well on the barren Freilingen land, as the limestone soil yields richer feed than farther out in the Eifel. Father has a knack for buying emaciated sheep cheaply and selling them again, strengthened, for a substantially higher price. Klöss has to tend the flock, much to his annoyance. It is too lonely for him out there. Like a dense cloud, the flock sets out from the Giefers' farm early in the morning—white sheep with black legs, black tails, black ears, and black mouths. The lambs squeeze in between the larger sheep; they are afraid of the two dogs Klöss takes along. The flock leaves a wide trail of round black droppings behind.

May and June is sheep shearing time. Father takes his eldest sons and Maria along to help him wash the sheep's woolly coats in the shallow water of the Ahr River. The sheep are unwilling to go into the water, and it takes all one's strength to shove them in and hold them tight. Afterwards, the sheep stand in the meadow, wet and bleating. On the way back from the river to the village, their clean wool dries in the sun. Father has hired a shepherd, and he is in the yard waiting for the flock. First, the animals are put in the stable and then brought back out one at a time. Father and the shepherd sit on low stools in the yard. Each of them takes a sheep between his knees. In a flash, the animal is turned on its back. Maria helps to hold and tie together the sheep's legs. Swiftly and skillfully, the two men run the shears over the woolly coats, and the fleece drops off in strips. When they are finished, the naked sheep scurry nervously back to the stable.

Villagers passing by stop to watch the sheep shearing for a while. The air smells of spring, of animals, and of wool. The hens and cock strut around unruffled, pecking. The baby chicks run with flapping wings behind the mother hen. The wool piles up in the sun to form a soft, warm mountain. How the children would love to sink into it!

Father's and the shepherd's hands are clean but greasy when the shearing is finished. The wool is packed into sacks and taken to the wool market in Mayen where it is purchased by the buyers from the spinning mills. Whatever wool the Giefers need for themselves, for stockings and cardigans, Father gets spun at the spinning mill in Schönau. In winter, Mother will sit at a quilting frame with a double layer of cloth stretched across it. She will stuff it evenly with sheep's wool, and then she will stitch the cloth into little squares to make warm quilts for winter.

Twice a year, in spring and autumn, the shoemaker Heinrich Heinrichs comes to the farm and brings the tools of his trade. Maria's sewing machine is taken up to her parents' bedroom so the shoemaker can set up his bench in the front room, below the windows. He lays out wooden lasts, knives, hammers, all kinds of small nails, and the pincers that he later clamps between his knees to hold the leather in place while he is sewing. On the right of the door frame hangs the leather loop through which the shoemaker pulls his hemp threads. He uses pitch to rub and roll hemp fibers on his apron across his knees, and then pulls them through his fingers until the pitch-covered hemp becomes tightly rolled thread. He twists the bristle of a wild boar into one end so he can thread the needle more easily.

With an awl, the shoemaker punches a hole in the leather and sticks the needle through the hole. Father has bought the leather from the tanner Zinzius in Hillesheim. The sole leather is made of tough ox or bull hide, the upper leather from a two-year-old cow. In Freilingen, there is no one else who buys such fine quality leather. For a whole week, the shoemaker repairs shoes and makes each member of the Giefer family a new pair of hobnail boots. Each shoe of the pair is made on the same wooden last (form) so it can be worn on either foot. Each night, the shoes are placed the other way around below the bed, the left shoe exchanged with the right one, so they wear evenly. Father makes sure it is done.

Maria's brothers, Hubert, Toni, and especially Mäthes, swipe the coveted small nails from the shoemaker and hammer them with abandon into any piece of wood outside. At midday, the shoemaker sits down at the meal table with the family; the children, as always, are strictly forbidden to say anything without being spoken to first. The shoemaker lines up the new shoes for the whole family in rows. No one is allowed to touch them, even if it means going barefoot. He wants to see the finished result of his work before leaving the farm. For his work, the shoemaker receives some money from Father and also the promise of help from Father's sons to work in the shoemaker's fields, with draft animals, tools, and carts.

It seems as if things are looking up on the Giefer farm, but Maria learns from Aunt Barbara that Germany has lost the war. Father, like all the farmers, has to keep handing over cattle to the French because their country has been devastated by the war. It is hard for the farmers, and those who are not as clever as Maria's Father have a difficult time making ends meet.

Early one morning, Father instructs Maria to go to Münstereifel with Willi. Setta has been living in this little old town since she left school. She works in the household of a Jewish cattle dealer who is a business partner of Father's.

Willi and Maria make their way across the Luck, a wooded hilltop, along a stretch of the Roman road to Rohr, and on through Tondorf; it is half a day's journey on foot. For hours on end, they do not meet a soul. They see people only when they pass through villages. They are both carrying meat and bacon fat, butter and bread. They are bringing this food to Setta's employers as a gift and to let them know that the Giefer farm takes care of Setta.

Willi walks beside Maria in silence, looking here and there but never at her. She tries to talk to him now and then, but he does not reply. She is used to her brothers and sisters hardly speaking to her, but it is so lonely with only the two of them, and it is such a long way to Münstereifel. The farther they walk, the sadder her thoughts become, the lonelier she feels. In Münstereifel, the lady of the house opens the door with a smile. Maria is horrified to see that all the woman's teeth are made of gold; a set of golden teeth! She is suddenly beside herself. In her misery and fright she starts to cry. In tears, she unpacks the food she has brought.

Setta stands there not knowing what to make of her sister. She has always regarded her eldest sister as strange, but she has always put up with her, even when she seems reserved or indifferent. Setta thinks it is because Maria is deaf. She does not understand why Maria is crying now.

The head of the house invites Maria and Willi to stay for the midday meal. Maria sits at the table, sunk into her lonely misery, while the others talk. No one addresses her, and she cannot bring herself to make the effort to talk to them. Setta will work in this household for two and a half years, milking the many cows in the pasture and in the stable, and carrying the washing water every day up the twenty-nine steep steps behind the house to water the berry bushes. Setta receives no pay, no soap to wash with, not even a few pennies for a stamp to write home if she feels homesick. Nevertheless, Setta respects her employers.

Poor Setta, Maria thinks, as she and Willi set off on their long, lonely walk back. By now, Maria has calmed down. She does not even try to start talking. She has to bear her fate alone. It is already late in the evening when they arrive home. The whole long day, the whole long way there and back, Willi has not spoken a single word to her.

37

Maria asks Father to hang green window boxes for flowers in front of the windows of the Giefer house. Father shakes his head: "Not necessary!" *What is that, "necessary?"* Maria thinks about the word. She is sad that she can't make the house pretty. It looks so nice and friendly when red flowers bloom in green boxes against the whitewashed walls. "Not necessary." What is *necessary?*

Late one evening Maria sees Klöss and Willi secretly climbing out of the window and down a ladder into the dark green, strong smelling nettles behind the house. She sees them going off with other boys from the village. Surely, they are going to enjoy themselves. Maybe they do it often? For their strict Father, the children's enjoyment is not necessary, only their work on the farm. *Father is very strict,* Maria thinks, *but yet good.* Is it enough to have only what is necessary?

The little ones, Hubert and Toni, make their own fun. They sit behind the manure heap, playing with green pine cones and arranging them into a village. Pine cones are cows and horses, carts and trains. Maria walks past and Toni explains to her what they are playing. He is the only one who likes talking to her. He is always friendly when he comes to Maria to ask for a slice of bread, for a patch for his torn trousers, for this and that. He is affectionate and lets himself be hugged and caressed. *What is "not necessary?"* Flower boxes on the house? Having fun? Playing? Showing affection?

In some gardens bright nasturtiums grow along the fence, and hollyhocks bloom right up to the gutters. In the Giefers' garden the phlox, which blooms in three colors, smells sweet in midsummer. Is that *necessary?* What is *necessary?* What makes a need *necessary? Necessary* is what is needed, isn't it? Maria thinks that everyone has his or her own needs. Joy? Is that *necessary?* And is what is not needed, *necessary* all the same?

38

In summer and autumn, barn and cellar fill up. Dry potatoes lie sorted out beneath the dark vaults; there they cannot sprout. The heaps of grain in the attic get smaller and smaller. The new grain won't be threshed until winter.

The Eifel winter is hard and cold. The bedroom windows frost over. Gaps and holes in the stables are stuffed with sacks and straw. Snow starts at the end of November. How good it is to have electric light in winter. Electricity did not come to Lommersdorf and Freilingen until the summer of 1921, only after long resistance by the farmers because the country people thought it unnecessary.

Father's sheep stay outside for as long as possible. Unflaggingly, they scrape in the snow and search for food. In the evening, Klöss brings the flock home to the stable.

On one of the early January mornings in 1922, when the sheep are already a long way out, it begins to snow steadily. Maria looks outside and sees the snow pelting down incessantly in dense showers. Higher and higher it piles up on the roads, yards, and land. A bitter wind is blowing. Maria is worried about the sheep and wonders how they will find food in this blizzard.

In the yard, Father shovels a path all the way to the stables and barn. Willi is kept busy clearing the path to the street over and over again. It gets dark early. Father takes the lantern and stick and leaves the house. Maria asks her sister Anna, "What is wrong? Where Father go?" Maria can easily read the reply from Anna's mouth. She speaks slowly and forms her words well, "See where Klöss is."

It is not long before Father comes back and speaks very agitatedly to Mother. Something must have happened! Father goes off again. "What is wrong?" Maria wants to know.

"Father is going to the communal servant," Anna explains to her. "Sheep are snowed in!"

The communal servant trudges through the village street. He rings a bell to call the people out of their houses, summoning them to come to the Giefers' farm with shovels and lanterns. Soon all the men from the lower village have assembled; their wives, wrapped in woolen shawls, carry the storm lanterns. Father leads the way out of the village to the Stein. It is hard, strenuous work to plod through the knee-deep snow. The last ones in the long row are lucky to have a beaten, if narrow, trackpath. Maria and Toni trudge after them. Outside the village, the wind whips freely from the northeast. It drives the snow from the Stein down into the valley of Grindel Creek, where the snowdrift is higher than a man. Here, Klöss and the sheep are stuck. The men begin to dig a way through. The glow from the lanterns hardly gives them enough light. Maria can see that the people enjoy working together. She takes little Toni under her shawl; only his head peeps out. They stand and wait. When Toni taps Maria on the arm, she bends down to him, turns his face toward the light of a lantern, and reads from his lips, "I hear sheep coming!"

Then Maria sees the leader of the flock push her way out and up, and directly behind it another one, with its black mouth on the back of the first. One behind the other, they emerge from the narrow gorge of snow. More than a hundred animals are glad to be free, and they hasten homewards. Maria suddenly has a strange feeling. She would like to cry. She wonders why she feels like that.

Klöss keeps hold of the dogs till last. The men with the shovels, the women with the lanterns, and the cheerful children all trudge their way to the Giefers' farm. Father brings out a bottle of schnapps, and the glass is passed around. Not until the bottle is empty do the helpers head home, through the heavily falling snow.

39

At the end of January 1923, Grandmother dies.

With her go love and warmth; a person who was good to Maria, who talked to her. Gone forever. Maria is very sad and quiet. *Why do people die? Where do they go?*

A few days later, Maria helps a cousin sew a dress. When she gets home in the evening, Father says: "You have got a letter!" Maria tries to grasp what he has said.

She repeats Father's words: *You have got a letter.*—"Letter? For me? I don't believe!" she exclaims. Father points to the window bench. The letter is lying there. Who would write to her? She has never received a letter! And yet, there on the envelope is written "Miss Maria Giefer, Freilingen, Eifel, Post Office Blankenheim Land." Maria turns the envelope to read who it is from: Professor Heumann, Aachen, Hasselholz 16. She has no idea who that is. Bewildered, she opens the envelope and reads the letter. She hands it to Father. Has she understood the letter properly? And what will Father say to it? She sees from Father's lips that he is reading the letter aloud.

Dear Miss Giefer,

I have been given your address by Master Wirtz, your former teacher at the Deaf and Dumb School. I am looking for a household help. Master Wirtz has recommended you. Can you start on February 15th? I would be grateful for a prompt reply.

Yours Sincerely,
Mrs. Heumann

Father turns to Maria and says, "You write immediately. Yes! You can go on February 14th."

Maria shouts for joy. "Thank you! I love to go to Aachen, very much!" She is beside herself with delight. To see Aachen again! After ten years! She gets paper and ink and writes a reply. She writes it three times before she is satisfied. Father says the letter is good, and he gives her some money for the stamp. She takes the letter to Aunt Barbara at the post office. Maria has written

Dear Mrs. Heumann,

I will leave here on February 14th. I am glad to get the post in your household.

Yours Sincerely,
Maria Giefer

She writes a second letter to the Rögert ladies, asking to be met at the train.

From Aunt Barbara, Maria learns that Father had written a letter to her former teacher Master Wirtz first, asking him if he could find work for his daughter in Aachen. Maria is very surprised and grateful that Father does so much for her.

She starts with her preparations straightaway. She alters Grandmother's clothes to fit herself, and it occurs to her that she has had only one new dress since she left school ten years ago.

During the first few days of February, Father tells her that she may not be able to go after all. "Why not?" Maria asks in dismay.

"Train not running; resistance!" is his reply. She asks Aunt Barbara what that means.

"The men from the railway are not working, as a protest against French troops marching into the Ruhr area." Maria cannot make much out of this information. Every day now, she goes to her aunt to inquire nervously if the train is running again, and she is consoled when the answer is finally yes. She breathes a sigh of relief. Now she can go after all!

A man from the village has to travel to Cologne on February 14th. Father has asked him to accompany Maria as far as Euskirchen. She carries her things tied up in a cardboard box. She also has the same basket that her mother took along when they first went to Aachen together—in 1905, eighteen years ago. She brings slices of bread, two hardboiled eggs, two pounds of butter, and a dozen fresh eggs. Father wanted her to take the things for the Rögert ladies.

Her traveling companion does not speak a word on the journey to Euskirchen. From there she continues on alone. She pays attention to the names of the railway stations and is glad to recognize the countryside again. Elated, she sees the town, spread out below Lousberg. Woods, churches and steeples, hills and streets—she recognizes them all. The train crosses the high viaduct and enters the familiar town. Aachen!

40

Hasselholz is up on the edge of town, near the Aachen Woods. Hasselholz Weg, with its splendid houses with carved wooden gables and balcony balustrades, oriel windows, and well-tended front gardens branches off the main road that leads to Liège. Old trees spread above laburnums, lilacs, and roses. It is a quiet street, ending in a path into the woods. Professor Heumann lives in one of these stately houses. He teaches at the University of Technology in Aachen. In spite of complaints about his bad stomach, he is a friendly man. Maria rarely sees him. The professor's wife dresses very simply. She combs her hair back smoothly and severely into a bun. She makes an effort to move her mouth slowly and distinctly when talking to Maria. Master Wirtz probably has explained to her why this is necessary. Mrs. Heumann and Maria can soon understand each other very well. Maria learns from her that she grew up on a large estate near Tilsit. She and her husband lived first in Berlin, then in Metz, and again in Berlin, before they came to Aachen. "Aachen is the most beautiful. We like it here best. Aachen is a very beautiful town!"

Maria confirms that with shining eyes. "Yes, true. Aachen is very beautiful town!"

The Heumanns have three sons: Hermann, Heiko, and Wolfram. They approve of Maria. She is always afraid of meeting new people. She worries whether they will understand her, whether she will understand them. Will they be disconcerted, repelled, contemptuous, or embarrassed by her voice? How will the new people she meets react when she starts to talk?

The kitchen where Maria works is in the basement. When Maria goes down there for the first time she thinks, *Pity! Kitchen in cellar. Is not nice.* The kitchen has a big window, but it is very high up, and Maria has to press her nose against the windowsill when she wants to look out at the garden bordered all around by an old hedge. Enough light, though, falls through the window on the stone floor, on the blue and white tiled walls, the kitchen equipment, and the bed in the alcove where Maria will sleep.

At half past six in the morning, Mrs. Heumann wakes Maria. She cannot hear the alarm clock. Every morning Maria cooks porridge with water, salt, and rolled oats. That is breakfast for the whole family. She sends it up to the dining room by a dumbwaiter. Maria eats a slice of bread in the kitchen, as she does not like porridge for breakfast. In the mornings, she tidies up the house. In the living room, she dusts the piano, having no idea what it is used for. Sometimes Mrs. Heumann sits at it and runs her fingers quickly over the black and white keys. Maria cannot imagine why anyone would want to do that; nothing seems to happen. Afterwards nothing has been accomplished, except that the keys have moved. Maria makes the beds in the main bedroom and in the boys' rooms and wipes the three high desks where the boys do their homework in the afternoon.

When Maria goes back down to the kitchen, Mrs. Heumann has returned from her daily shopping. They begin preparing the midday meal. Mrs. Heumann is a very thrifty and efficient housewife. In her household, everything is plain but good. She keeps chickens behind a fence in the garden, and there are fresh eggs every day. For the midday meal, even on Sundays, they always boil potatoes in their jackets. Maria has to get used to the bland, unsalted taste. At home they never eat jacketed potatoes, they are only for the pigs. Maria learns to be very economical. Mrs. Heumann shows her how to clean vegetables without the slightest waste. Even the leftovers are used, nothing must be wasted. At home on the farm that is no problem, all the leftovers go into the feed bucket for the animals.

Every year, Mrs. Heumann receives a whole pig from her parents' estate near Tilsit. It is packed in tins and made into sausages; even the bones are sent, and Mrs. Heumann pickles them in an earthenware pot. Vegetables, fruit, and berries are filled into jugs, stoneware pots, and jars. There is nothing that cannot be bottled, pickled, or dried. Everything goes into the store cellar.

At mealtimes, Maria sits by herself in the kitchen; it is lonelier than at home, where the whole family sits together at the table and somebody or other always drops in to say hello. But she is not homesick.

Every evening while Maria is washing up, the Heumann couple go for a walk; whatever the weather, whatever the season. They walk toward the woods, through a valley where three scattered farms are surrounded by grassy hills. Ducks bob up and down on the ponds, and the willows stretch their branches into the evening sky. At the ponds, the Heumanns turn back and leisurely stroll home. Sometimes Maria sees them leaving or coming back arm in arm. She finds that lovely. She has never seen her parents doing that.

One morning, when passing the bedroom, Maria happens to see the professor and his three sons doing exercises naked in front of an open window. It gives her a terrible fright. Never has she seen a grownup naked. Shaken and amazed, she wonders how it is possible that these four men can move around naked so naturally. The only conclusion she can come up with is that they must be Protestants. Catholics would never do such a thing. She is certain of that.

On Sunday afternoons, Maria has a few hours free. Then she goes to see the Rögert ladies where she also meets her sister Christina. Christina works and lives very withdrawn in a secluded villa in the woods. At the Rögerts' there is coffee with rice or fruit flans, and they chat, do needlework or go for a short walk together. Christina was seventeen when she left school. Her shoulder still slumps, some of her wounds are still open. Christina's face is soft and lacks the alertness, the fire in the eyes that Maria has.

Everything is well and fine with Maria. Only one thing troubles her. The Rögert ladies tell her that she no longer speaks in proper sentences, as she did in her last year at school. Maria does not know how to do it better. "I can't any more, forgotten. Pity, perhaps come back if I talk more."

Weeks pass. Mrs. Heumann says to her, "You are to visit the deaf-and-dumb teacher Master Wirtz on Thursday afternoon."

"Oh?" says Maria, very surprised. "Why?"

"You are to visit him."

On Thursday afternoon, Maria is in Hubertusstrasse at Master Wirtz's house. He is sitting in the kitchen with his wife. After the welcome, Maria is invited to sit down. Gertrud, the oldest of the fourteen Wirtz children, serves coffee and cake. Master Wirtz says to Maria: "You have become a beautiful girl," and he asks how she likes it at Professor Heumann's. Maria thanks and tells him. After coffee, Master Wirtz takes off his jacket the sleeve of which is torn. "Please mend this jacket for me. Do it well," he says, handing it to the astonished girl. Gertrud brings patching material, needle and thread, and Maria quietly begins to work. When she has finished, the teacher examines the mended sleeve and says: "Thank you, it is good" and puts his jacket back on. *Strange*, thinks Maria *I come for that? Or Master Wirtz wants to see what I can do?* How old are you now?" he asks the girl. "I twenty-four now. In August twenty-five."

"Have you already been to the Deaf Club?"

"No, I have never heard of it."

"Then you must go, once a month."

"Where is it?"

"Do you know where Seilgraben is?"

"No, I don't know. I forgotten."

"Then come here on Sunday afternoon. I go with you to the Deaf and Dumb Club. It starts at five o'clock."

"Thank you. Yes, I come! I very glad! I great joy!" Maria counts the days until Sunday. She can hardly wait. A club for deaf-mute people! Will she meet anyone there from her schooldays?

On Sunday, she goes with Master Wirtz to an inn on Seilgraben, next to the guild house. They go through the inn and then upstairs to a small hall. The first thing Maria sees, are long rows of tables laid with white cloths. At the end of the small hall is a platform. Many people are sitting at the tables, and a waiter is carrying cups of coffee and glasses around. Everyone is talking to each other in sign language. The waiter hears only a few strange, unmodulated sounds now and then. Maria sees the confusing hand movements, sees many mouths moving in an exaggerated way. To catch someone's attention they stamp on the floor or bang a hand on the table. It is an excited and exciting scene. Maria is not used to it.

The teacher has hung up her coat. "Come," he says to her, and he leads her past the rows of tables to introduce her at the head table. But they do not get that far because Maria has been recognized. A few people jump up, nudge each other, and point to the new guest: "Maria Giefer! Maria Giefer!" In no time, Maria is surrounded. Hands reach out to her. She is being embraced. Many people talk to her at once, and she has to try to watch ten or more mouths at the same time. So many gestures and gesticulations! Maria is bewildered. She laughs and cannot say anything. She had not expected all this! They separated as children and now, as adults, they are meeting again.

She remembers, recognizes, discovers—it is a great reunion. Adelheid is there, and Gertrud, and Juliane. They have tears of joy in their eyes. She is bombarded with questions. Everyone wants to know where she has been for so long, if she will stay in Aachen, where she lives, what she is doing. "Have you got a sweetheart? Here is a sweetheart for you!" Maria laughs and cannot answer. She cannot keep up with everything that is happening so quickly. It takes a long time before she has greeted the club committee, and the teachers, and is seated somewhere on a chair. On the left is someone who wants to talk to her, and on the right somebody else, and opposite her two or three more, who all want to say something, at the same time. She is brought coffee and has no idea who ordered it. New people come in. She has to shake hands, say hello, and remember their names. She begins to feel so happy, so glad that she belongs here, to people like herself, that she has a home here. Yet she also experiences an almost sad kind of wonder that she hasn't been part of this in all the years that have gone before.

Someone gets up on the platform and waves *Quiet!* It takes a long time for all the members to tell each other they have to look toward the platform. Someone says to Maria, "That is the chairman," and points to the man who now wants to speak to them all. She does not know what "the chairman" is. He waits for a long time, until all eyes are on him.

"Dear ladies and gentlemen, dear friends! We are astounded! Today we have a guest here from the Eifel: Maria Giefer. We have not seen her for ten years. We would all like to welcome her!" Maria's neighbors indicate to her that she should stand up. She does so. Many hands clap and wave to her, and she can read her name on their mouths: "Maria Giefer!" She is happy and shows it; she waves toward everyone all around and nods her head. Then she sits down again with a pounding heart. It is all so exciting. The speech continues, but she cannot understand very well what it is about. It is all much too fast for her. Something is put to a vote. Then two men act out a little play without words on the platform and everyone laughs a lot. But Maria is paying such close attention that she cannot laugh. When the play is over, everyone begins to chatter and walk around from one table to another.

Toward evening, a young man sits down next to Maria. He tells her his name is Josef Sistermann. He is younger than Maria; she can hardly remember him. He begins a lively conversation with her, and she watches him quietly and attentively. He tries to make her laugh, and sometimes he succeeds. His thin face is nervous, his eyes keep darting about the room, and his nostrils quiver. A young girl joins them. She is wearing a white blouse with black dots and a large black velvet bow. A similar bow at the back of her head holds up her curly hair. She is a pretty girl, and the earrings and the bracelet on her slim wrist suit her well. She begins to chat endlessly and so fast that Maria has to keep saying, "Please speak slower."

"My name is Luise Sistermann, I am Josef's sister. You are Maria Giefer. I know you. I still know—I remember you wore a sailor hat to school with a long ribbon. You were always serious and very proud. You always walked so erect and straight." At the same time, she indicates with her hands the round hat and the ribbon and imitates Maria's walk. It all goes so fast, the talking, the gesticulating.

Maria can remember Luise. She is younger and was not in her class. Luise has twinkling eyes. "My brother will take you home. But you must be careful. My brother likes girls. We live in Eilendorf. Do you know where Eilendorf is?"

"No, I don't know," Maria says. It has become too much for her, all of it. She is getting a strong headache and cannot follow the confusing gestures any more. It is time to go home, anyway. She says goodbye and has to promise to come again next month. She does that gladly. Josef accompanies her. Beneath the lanterns he wants to stop and talk to her but she presses on home. Then he takes her arm and puts it through his. Maria finds that nice. They walk along like this until they reach the Heumanns' house.

"I come for you Sunday. We go for a walk," Josef says. He turns his face to the light so Maria can see what he is saying. "What time shall I come?" She tells him. To say goodbye the young man puts his arm round Maria and kisses her. That night, in her bed, she lies awake for a while. There is so much to think about. She is filled with joy about the afternoon at the club and that she will now belong to it. She is expected to become a member and pay dues. And Josef? Has she got a sweetheart now? And the kiss? Did she like it? She found the kiss strange, but she guesses you have to kiss if you have a sweetheart.

41

Maria meets a girl named Finchen at the club. She lives near Hasselholz. The two girls become friends. On Sundays, Maria, Finchen, Christina, and Josef Sistermann all go for a walk together. Maria realizes again and again that she has forgotten the sign language they used at school. Often she cannot follow what they are talking about. She has to learn again how to sign with deaf people. So, usually she walks silently beside them and is simply happy. When other people approach, Josef stops signing. He says to the girls, "Not talk when people pass by. People always stare, I don't like." Maria thinks *Josef is ashamed.* He says, "I am not deaf and dumb. I went to school for hearing children for one year. I can hear when doors go 'bang.' I can hear if you shout 'Jupp.' I can hear well. I can speak well. All people understand me."

"But you were at Deaf and Dumb Institution," Maria says thoughtfully.

But Josef retorts fiercely, "I not deaf and dumb. I hard of hearing." Maria thinks to herself that Josef does not want to be deaf and dumb.

After a month, the Sunday arrives when the Deaf and Dumb Club meets again. Maria puts on a hat, a present from one of the Rögert ladies. It is the first hat she has ever owned and she finds it pretty, with its colored feathers. Finchen comes to fetch her, and Maria is so happy that she goes down into town with a skip in her walk, hand in hand with her friend. Life is wonderful! In the little hall on Seilgraben, Josef has saved seats for her and Finchen. Josef's sister Luise joins them again. Her face is always so cheerful, as if she could never be angry or sad. Maria, who is wearing the same simple dress as on the Sunday a month before, notices that Luise has a new dress. Her hair is done differently, too; little curls are combed down her forehead and held back by a wide horn barrette. Luise chats vivaciously, faster than any of the others.

Maria drinks her lemonade, greets the newcomers who shake hands across the tables, and answers questions. Teachers arrive, the chairman signs from the platform again, and everyone claps. Anyone, who has a word to say and gets up on the platform, begins: "My dear ladies and gentlemen." Maria likes that very much. When the speeches have finished, they all chat with one another.

Maria's eyes fall on a young man. He is sitting alone at the end of the rows of tables. His chair is placed at an angle, his legs are crossed. She has not seen him before. Perhaps he arrived late? She does not know him, she cannot remember seeing him before. Maria can't help but stare. Why is he sitting there on his own? The young man is well dressed. There are sharp creases in his trousers. His shoes and spats are like new. A gold watch chain hangs on his waistcoat, and his collar and cuffs are very correct. Maria notices the attractive cufflinks, the pin on his fashionable tie, and the handkerchief in his breast pocket. She has never really paid attention to such things before. But the manner and appearance of the young man make such a fine impression, she cannot keep her eyes from him. He sits upright, the part in his dark hair is perfectly straight. His hands are calmly folded. His gaze, too, is calm and peaceful. His build is delicate, almost boyishly slight, the features of his youthful face soft and well defined. Maria likes the look of him very much, and suddenly she knows. It is quite simple: He is the one! She loves him at once. She taps Luise on the shoulder and directs her eyes at the young man. "Who is that? Alone, at the table?" she asks.

Luise looks. "Oh! Oh!" She claps her hands. "Don't you know? That is my oldest brother Wilhelm!" Maria looks at him. Strong feelings of tenderness and affection well up in her. So suddenly it happens! In the joy of this moment, whatever she does is all good. She stands up, and is not at all shy. She goes over to the young man, touches his shoulder, and looks into a pair of surprised eyes, a wonderful blue.

"Why alone?" Maria asks. "Come!" She takes his hand and points to her table where Luise and Josef are sitting, beckoning him to come. He smiles. Maria sees the smile. Never before has a face seemed so dear to her. Wilhelm stands up and, holding on to Maria's hand, joins his brother and sister. They move their chairs to the side, and the young man sits down next to Maria. He soon learns from his sister who Maria is, where she comes from, when and with whom she was at school, and that she now works for Professor Heumann.

Gradually, he remembers. "Maria Giefer?" Wasn't she one of the cleverest and most hardworking girls, a class below him? Couldn't she speak very well, and isn't she a year younger than he? Yes, she was always very proud, with an upright walk and sharp-looking eyes. That is how Wilhelm remembers her. Maria has to laugh. Proud? No, she has never been proud!

"Yes, yes" the others insist. Maria can only wonder why they think this.

She is glad to learn what Luise signs about Wilhelm. "Wilhelm is my dear, good brother. We never fight. Wilhelm can't quarrel. He is very hardworking." Wilhelm notices and is surprised that Maria has difficulty in following the conversation. Has she become stupid? Can Maria not speak the deaf language fluently? Wilhelm sees this as a shortcoming, and he doesn't like it.

When Maria has to think about going home, she asks Wilhelm to accompany her. He agrees politely and pleasantly. His younger brother Josef shrugs his shoulders, grins a little, and signs, "I go home with Finchen." Luise approves readily.

Silently, the two couples walk, one behind the other, up to Hasselholz. Maria hopes that Wilhelm will kiss her goodnight. That would be wonderful! Josef and Finchen go on alone, past gardens and beneath overhanging bushes along Morillenweg. In front of Maria's door, Wilhelm says goodbye and promises to come and take her for a walk next Sunday. As he turns to leave, Maria cannot help but put her arms around him and kiss him tenderly on his mouth. Wilhelm, in shock, leaves quickly.

That evening, she lies awake for a long time. Will he come again? On Sunday? Was that kiss a mistake? She is afraid, and then again happy. She is in love and spellbound. Yes, he must have cast a spell on her, for the next day, she can think of nothing else but him.

She is blithe and brisk in her work, and in her heart there is something she has never known before—exultation, tenderness, warmth, happiness! There are no words to express love! Maria counts the days until Sunday. They crawl by. But the closer it gets to Sunday, the more often her heart suddenly begins to race and she feels she can't breathe properly. There is always a little trepidation: Will he come again? Does he like her? Can he love her a little bit? Does he think of her? She really longs for a reunion.

On Sunday, she quickly finishes all her duties around the house. She is on tenterhooks. Mrs. Heumann knows that Maria is expecting someone, and she can also tell that Maria is in love. It is plain for the whole

Wilhelm Sistermann as a young man.

world to see. When the doorbell rings, she tells Maria, who rushes to the door. Wilhelm is standing there, his hat in his hand and a smile on his face. Happiness and relief overwhelm Maria. She gives him her hand and invites him in so she can introduce him to Mrs. Heumann. "My deaf friend Wilhelm Sistermann from Eilendorf," says Maria, beaming. Mrs. Heumann wants to talk to him and she asks how old he is and what his job is. But he cannot understand Mrs. Heumann and looks at her somewhat helplessly. Maria puts her hand gently on his shoulder and indicates that he should turn toward her so that she can mouth the words for him. He understands Maria immediately and answers Mrs. Heumann.

"I painter and decorator, self-employed. I twenty-seven years old," he says, but Mrs. Heumann has not understood a single word.

Maria asks Wilhelm what he has said, and then she repeats it to Mrs. Heumann. Maria puts on her coat and hat and goes out with Wilhelm: He, the smart gentleman, with her, the country girl. They walk toward the woods. Maria is happy to walk beside the person she cannot help but love so passionately. And it has only been one week since they first met!

As they walk, Maria and Wilhelm sign to each other. "How much money you earn from professor?" Wilhelm asks her.

"A lot!" replies Maria with conviction. "I earn 25 Marks a month. But now I get more and more. Mrs. Heumann says everything getting more expensive. My pay always stays worth 25 Marks."

"Yes," Wilhelm signs. "Inflation now."

Maria continues, "I never earned money before. First time now." She is quite proud.

"You buy new things to wear," says Wilhelm. "You must look like town girl."

Maria looks at him in astonishment. "Coat is good, dress is good, shoes too; everything good. Not ruined yet, I must wear out." She tells him that in Freilingen, she had only one new dress in ten years. Wilhelm can hardly believe it. He stares at her incredulously. Then he urges her not to save money, it will only lose value through inflation. All her hard-earned money will soon be worth nothing. She should use it to buy new clothes for spring and make herself look pretty. Maria is sad as she senses he does not like her the way she is. But she wants him to like her. Why is she not well dressed?

Nevertheless, he must like something about her for he enjoys talking to her. Maria is eager to learn more about him and she says to Wilhelm, "I want to hear many new things from you." "Hear," she says, although she cannot hear anything at all but only read everything from his silent lips and from his signs. Maria wants to know everything about Wilhelm's life. She wants to get to know him. Wilhelm never gets tired of answering all of her questions.

Alone that evening, she thinks about everything he has told her, and she knows that she loves him more and more. She also thinks about what Mrs. Heumann said to her so insistently just before she went to bed: "Wilhelm is no man for you. You are too good for him. You can marry a better man."

Maria looked at her in horror. How could anyone say such a thing? "Why?" she asked angrily.

"He cannot speak well. Nobody can understand him. He speaks terribly! His voice is ugly. He is not the man for you!"

"Is all?" Maria asked. And when Mrs. Heumann answered yes, Maria tossed her head.

Love shone unshakably in her eyes. "Don't care if Wilhelm speak badly. I love Wilhelm!" If nobody understands him, she can speak clearly! She will be his voice!

But—will he come to like her?

42

In the days between Sunday and Sunday, when Maria will see Wilhelm again, Maria is surprised at herself. She flies through her work; it is as if she has not done it at all. She rolls out noodle dough, makes the beds, cleans the shoes in the yard, dusts, sweeps the garden path—all the while, her thoughts are only with Wilhelm. She longs for him. She wants to be with him, close to him, wants to stroke his face, hold his hand, or just be beside him and look at him. It is so wonderful, to no longer feel alone.

How is it possible that Wilhelm could have existed for so long without her knowing him? That she knew nothing about him? Where did he come from? Who was he?

The whole day long, she thinks about his life, the things he has told her. She imagines him small, with tiny hands wrapped in bandages so he can't scratch the rash all over his body and face. The rash itches and torments him in his early years.

His mother, Alexandrine, is serious and remote. She never laughs; Wilhelm couldn't even imagine her smiling. Every day Wilhelm climbs up the many winding steps of the church bell tower with his father, Josef. In the round room at the top, there are high windows in the thick walls, and dangling through the ceiling are four strong ropes. One of the ropes is split into two ends; two men have to pull it to move the huge Severinus bell. Here, his father has to ring the bells that hang above the tower in a wooden frame. He pulls on the ropes, stretching and then bending his knees again and again. From here, Wilhelm only has to climb up the narrow wooden steps to see how Father moves one of the four bells in the bell tower. The handrail of the steps trembles. The whole tower vibrates. If he hadn't been used to them already, Wilhelm would have been frightened by these tremors. When Wilhelm watches the bell swinging to and fro, his head moves from side to side as well. Not the slightest bit of sound from the booming bells finds its way into his consciousness.

Josef Sistermann is slim, and he is shorter than most men. He is friendly, and when he talks to other people, his kind eyes narrow, little wrinkles appear at their sides, and his mouth smiles under his moustache. He works hard at the church. He is responsible for ringing the bells, treading the bellows of the organ so that enough air gushes into the pipes, and winding up the huge church clock. He also makes all the coffins for the village, plus the crosses and wooden tablets, and he paints and inscribes them, digs the graves, and drapes and buries the dead. He tends to the paths and squares around the church, as well as the grotto in the churchyard to honor the Virgin Mary, which he built from large stones. Wilhelm is allowed to accompany his father everywhere, even to the gallery on Sundays, which vibrates so pleasantly while Father treads the bellows and the organist plays. From up here, Wilhelm can look down at the people below.

Father is never cross with Wilhelm or the other children, he is never strict. The Sistermanns live in a little old house near the church. In the carpentry workshop behind the house, Wilhelm watches his father working and plays with pieces of timber.

A few days before Easter, they take a basket and go to the farmers' houses, some of them far out, others right in the village. Wilhelm's father is collecting fresh eggs for the pastor; each farmer can give as many as he likes. In the end, the pastor gets quite a few. On the way to the farmers' houses, when they are alone, Father takes an egg from the basket, pricks a hole with a pin, and sucks out the yolk. Wilhelm wonders how a whole yolk can slip through such a tiny hole. Father gives him an egg, but Wilhelm shudders. He doesn't want to do the same. Father puts his finger on his mouth. Wilhelm understands: *Don't tell!* Is it wrong to suck one of the pastor's raw eggs? Even if Wilhelm is a small, quiet boy who can hear nothing, say nothing, smell nothing, and not, as Maria, detect every vibration, but he can certainly see! With one good eye and one almost blind eye, the shapes and colors of things in his environment are rich experiences for Wilhelm. To be happy, he only needs paper, a pencil, a small paintbrush, and watercolors. He can re-create everything he sees on sheets of white paper.

One day, Wilhelm finds himself in Aachen, in a house with strangers. Father is not there, nor are his brothers and sisters or the neighbors.

Neither is the butcher from next door, who sometimes passes a sausage over the wall to Wilhelm on a long stick. Now, he lives with foster parents, and during the day he goes to the Institute for the Deaf. For Maria Giefer, the hard work of learning is exciting and stimulating, but for Wilhelm it is an almost insoluble task, a torture. Why must a human being be able to talk? Why must Wilhelm learn to lipread? What trouble it is having to learn that! Wilhelm is obedient and obliging. He does everything he can. Why is he punished then? Why is he beaten? Why does the teacher pull his earlobes in a rage, so hard that they bleed? Why? He has said "i" when he was supposed to! But the teacher shows him that he keeps saying "e." He wants to do it right! It is hard, going to school and learning to speak.

But how nice it is when the teacher praises him for something he has drawn or painted. Nobody can do it as well as he, not even the teacher. Every year it says on his reports,

speech—unsatisfactory
drawing and painting—excellent

Maria, searching in her memory, remembers a walk with all the other school classes to the Bismarck Tower in Aachen woods. The headmaster gave a delicate, quiet boy a sheet of paper and pointed to the tower. The children stood around the boy and watched in amazement as he sketched the Bismarck Tower with a few swift strokes. A teacher asked him to draw her. In no time, the drawing was finished, and she gave Wilhelm a Mark for it. But the Mark got lost and the headmaster ordered all the children to help look for it. Maria is so glad to have this memory of Wilhelm!

Although it is only half an hour by tram from Aachen to Eilendorf, Wilhelm is only at home during the school holidays. He lives with foster parents on Karlsgraben for a year, and then with another family for five years in Franzstrasse near Marschiertor. In the last two years at school, he lives in Junkerstrasse with his younger brother Josef. The foster parents there are nasty and mean. The two brothers are always hungry. Usually they only get a slice of dry black bread for breakfast and not much more at midday. Josef asks for more because he is hungry. Then he gets a beating. When Father and Mother visit the boys occasionally, they bring money or a bag of sweets. The foster parents take it away from them and never give it back. Josef is furious, and he rebels against such injustice. He does not want to suffer. He is at odds with his fate. He wants to live like people who can hear, and he is bitter and dissatisfied. Wilhelm endures without complaining. Patience and endurance are part of his life. Injustice and anguish make him sad but do not embitter him. Disregard and humiliation hurt him deeply. And yet, in some miraculous way, his quiet, cheerful nature is invulnerable.

At home on holidays, Wilhelm has a great time constructing things. He makes a model of an Aachen tram. He boils up glue and sticks thin strips of wood together; he puts in a driver's cab and seats and makes windows out of scraps of glass. Father shows him how to cast lead wheels in clay molds, so the tram can actually roll. He hammers axles out of strips of iron. An installed battery and some bulbs provide lighting. Finally, Wilhelm paints his model tram just like the real Aachen trams. He takes the weighty thing to school where it is admired by one and all.

Using plasticine clay, he once sculpted a replica of the bronze statue of the monument in Jakobstrasse. The blacksmith stands in his leather apron with a heavy hammer in his hand, ready to slay the Count of Jülich and his sons, who led an attack on Aachen.

Sometimes the teacher is indulgent toward Wilhelm. While the others are learning, Wilhelm is allowed to draw and paint. Quietly and happily, he sits at his work.

Wilhelm has a large portfolio. He puts all of his pictures into it. On some Sundays, Father tells him to bring his portfolio, and they go to see the mayor, Pastor Hansmann, and other people. Then Wilhelm spreads out his portfolio on the table, and whoever is in the house comes to look at his pictures. Father tells him to say his name, and they all look at him kindly and praise his pictures by nodding their heads. The pastor has Wilhelm draw his portrait and gives him five Marks for it. That is a lot of money. Other people, too, give him money for his drawings.

During the autumn holidays, he stays in Cologne with Aunt Maria, his father's sister. She lives alone in the center of the big city. She spoils her nephew. Aunt Maria is pretty and fun and—something Wilhelm has never seen a woman do—she smokes cigarettes. It is wonderful to have all that love to himself! On one of the very first days, she takes him to a beautiful shop and buys him a new suit with a broad, white, shoulder cape. A big bow decorates his chest. His aunt also buys him patent leather shoes and a golden watch on a chain, which he puts in his waistcoat pocket. Wilhelm likes to be well dressed. The older he gets, the more attention he pays to it. If people are startled when they hear his voice, he at least wants to give them something nice to look at. He wants people to show him a friendly face when he greets them. Unfriendliness hurts his sensitive heart and causes him pain.

Wilhelm wants to learn at school, to make progress, to know more. But throughout his years at school, he has the feeling that he is not learning enough. He thinks that perhaps it is his own fault because he can't speak clearly or lipread quickly enough. Perhaps it is also because, for eight years, he has had the same teacher, day in, day out. Wilhelm learns only basic arithmetic: addition, subtraction, multiplication, and division. Even in his final year at school, the lazy teacher spends a whole arithmetic lesson making his pupils work on basic addition problems, while the other children at school do arithmetic that is much more advanced. Leaving school is a relief for Wilhelm. But what is he to do now? His art teacher goes with him to Master Johannes Küpper in Aachen. Master Küpper has twenty-five journeymen and does not only undertake painting work but has also a Studio for Interior Decorating and a Special Department for Church Painting. He takes Wilhelm on as an apprentice. Master Küpper writes in Wilhelm's contract that "as the apprentice is deaf and dumb, there is a period of probation of one year." Wilhelm thinks that now he will be able to paint all day long.

On the first morning, equipped with a packet of sandwiches, he takes the tram from Eilendorf to Aachen. In the workshop, Master Küpper assigns the day's work to his journeymen and apprentices. Wilhelm puts on his overalls, stiff and new and yellowish. As his first job, he spends the whole day cleaning the rusted iron railing of a front garden with a steel brush. It is hard and unpleasant work. During his first year, he is given such preliminary work: washing off old paint, scraping off wallpaper, sanding down doors and windows, and so on. He earns 2 Marks a week and is grateful for it. All the journeymen are good to him and leave him in peace. In his three and a half years as an apprentice, Wilhelm learns how to mix paints, hang wallpaper straight, varnish marble and woodgrain, stencil, and strip and burn off paint, plaster, and gild—everything a competent painter and decorator should know. Through his work, he enters the houses of well-to-do Aacheners and marvels at what he sees.

Every week, Wilhelm gets a large worksheet on which he has to write down where and and how long he has worked and what he has done. On the back of each of these worksheets, printed in large letters, are the work regulations, which read as follows:

- *Hours of work are from 7.30 a.m.–12.00 p.m. and 12.30–7 p.m. in the summer months; in the winter months according to hours of daylight.*
- *Breakfast or afternoon breaks are not permitted; each employee may, however, partake of food at his place of work, but under no circumstances may the break exceed 10 minutes in length.*
- *Smoking, drinking schnapps, and idle chatter or conversation are strictly prohibited.*
- *Each employee is responsible for the correct care and protection of materials and tools.*
- *The employee may resign without notice at any time, and each employee may be dismissed by me at any time.*
- *The instructions of the foreman are always to be complied with obligingly in the interest of the business and successful cooperation.*
- *These work regulations will, without a signature, be taken as acknowledged by the employee as soon as he has received the same and is in my employment.*

This ***worksheet is to be filled in accurately every day*** *and is open to inspection.*

Johannes Küpper

Once a week, Wilhelm goes to the School of Further Education, but nobody can communicate with him. While the other pupils are studying theoretical subjects, he is allowed to design stencils, draw perspectives, and copy from originals. His reports from this school only testify that Wilhelm is *excellent* in conduct, technical drawing, and lesson participation, and that his attendance is *regular*. For all the other subjects there is a dash instead of an assessment. The remark, *The pupil is deaf and dumb!* serves as an explanation.

On finishing his apprenticeship, Wilhelm receives his certificate.

The apprentice Wilhelm Sistermann of Eilendorf, born in Eilendorf on 16th January 1896, has, under the instruction of the undersigned Master, duly learned the trade of painter and decorator for the period of 3½ years, and at the request of the same on this day, this certificate has been drawn up after verification of his abilities. We declare him herewith a journeyman and wish him good luck and God's blessing for the future.

Aachen, 6th November 1914
Johannes Küpper

Master Küpper has added in handwriting, *In the practical examination, the holder received the grade excellent and due to deaf-dumbness was exempted from the theoretical examination.* At home everyone congratulates him, and he is proud.

Now Wilhelm works as a journeyman for Master Küpper and earns 25 Marks a week. The master takes him along to Düren where he has to paint the vaulted ceiling of the church of a Carmelite convent. They lie on their backs on a scaffold for hours on end, and Wilhelm has to paint what the master has drafted. On the weekends, he tells his father how very much he enjoys this particular work.

In 1913, Josef Sistermann bought a plot of land in Steinstrasse, together with a small farmhouse built of natural stone. In front of the old building, he erects a big new house on the street, with a shop and an entrance gate. Wilhelm's father uses the rooms, sheds, barn, and stables of the small farmhouse for his carpentry work, and Wilhelm gets a workshop for himself. Behind the old house and the yard there is a long garden, enclosed by hawthorn bushes and fruit trees. It is a marvelous domain, with lots of space for the large family.

Originally, there were nine siblings, and six of them were unable to hear. Two of the deaf children died in childhood. The people in the village would whisper amongst themselves, "How terrible!"

Wilhelm's parents are devout and Godfearing. They wonder why God has dealt them such misfortune. Nobody can understand it. Wilhelm's mother, who has never been seen to smile, has buried her dreams. She has a lovely voice, and she wanted to be a singer . She wanted to live surrounded by beautiful things. But now, she has deaf children. Why she, of all people? It is hard to live with a stigma. She is deeply perturbed and locked into herself. There is no key anymore. Mechanically she sees to the physical needs of her children.

Of all his brothers and sisters, Wilhelm loves little Maria best. She is like him: quiet, patient, grateful, and sensitive. But she is even more helpless than Wilhelm. She cannot stay at the school in Aachen. She has

Wilhelm's parents—Josef and Alexandrine (née Ortmanns) Sistermann.

to go to the institution in Euskirchen for children who require more assistance than other children. When the World War breaks out in 1914, the institution is turned into a military hospital for wounded soldiers, and Maria has to go to school in Trier. During the holidays, the Sistermann children are all at home together. Again and again, Wilhelm draws his little sister's gentle face, her wavy hair tied back with a bow. Her eyes stare into space. From his pay, Wilhelm buys his little sister what clothing she needs—dresses with sailor collars, pinafores with frilly shoulders, and, once, a wide Florentine hat with long ribbons that cost 40 Marks, a small fortune. He paints her in oil on canvas, wearing that hat. She sits for him patiently. Wilhelm is always trying to think of different ways to make her laugh. He knows no greater happiness than when his little sister is happy. He loves no one as much as his youngest sister Maria.

Of course, he is fond of the others, too. There is his eldest brother Johann, who can hear. Johann has a lot of friends whom he brings home. He is kind to his brothers and sisters. Johann is a hard worker; he gets up early to ring the church bell for Father. Then he goes to Rothe Erde in Aachen, where he operates a crane at the iron and steel works, moving pieces of iron. When he gets home from work, he helps his father build coffins in the workshop, planing, hammering, and sawing, and he works in the garden as well. Father can talk to him about anything that has to do with the business and the house, and Johann looks after all of Father's needs. He is Father's only mainstay and hope. Wilhelm is proud of his older brother Johann.

Josef and Luise, in spite of being deaf, can speak so clearly that almost everyone can understand them. They have to interpret for Wilhelm. The two youngest are Lisa and Heinrich; they can both hear. They grow up so close to their deaf brothers and sisters that a stranger watching them talking together would not realize that they can hear. Lisa and Heinrich are shy of people who can hear; they would rather be with deaf people. Early on in life, Wilhelm makes a surprising discovery. Although Lisa and Heinrich have the sense of hearing and are thus far better equipped for the struggle of existence than he is, Wilhelm feels that he has more strength and potential than these siblings have. He also knows that Lisa and Heinrich can experience more of the world than he can, yet he feels superior to them in spite of his perceived inferiority. If he had their good ears and a normal voice, he would outstrip them both by far. This realization is hard for him to bear. To possess mental powers and a good intellect, to be aware of manifold possibilities within himself, to take pleasure in his own development and be dealt such a fate torments him. The incomplete organs of his body restrict him from assimilating and expressing himself as he would like to, and could do. He suffers—but he does not grow bitter.

In Eilendorf, many people ask Father for Wilhelm's help. More and more often, he does a painting job in the village after work; he starts to receive more commissions. He has again asked Master Küpper for a few days off before All Saints' Day. Every year, the master allows Wilhelm to help his father inscribe the crosses. Wilhelm has learned from his Father to write beautifully flowing letters with a fine paint brush. Sometimes, the gold of the names carved on the tombstones in the cemetery has to be renewed. He takes over this work from his father, for it is cold in November, especially when working without moving. At home, though, inscribing crosses indoors is cozy work. Father and Wilhelm sit side by side and take turns dipping their fine brushes into a little pot, dabbing them off a bit on the rim, and writing with a steady hand *Here rests in the Lord . . .*

The other children sit in the middle of the big kitchen among fir branches Father has gathered from the woods. They make wreaths and bouquets from them. Lisa deftly makes tissue paper flowers, which she threads on wire and puts into the wreaths and bouquets. The whole house is filled with the tang of fir and paint, and everyone enjoys keeping busy. On one such evening, Father tells Wilhelm he should no longer go to work for Master Küpper in Aachen; instead, he should set up his own business in Eilendorf. Father says there would be enough work. Without further ado, Wilhelm becomes self-employed in April 1917. Master Küpper is sorry to lose his silent, hardworking, and reliable journeyman. In 1910, Wilhelm had started his apprenticeship with a wage of 2 Marks per week; his latest wage as a journeyman was 25 Marks per week. Now his master wishes him all the best.

Maria reflects on everything Wilhelm tells her about his life. She is looking forward to meeting him again and is eager to get to know more and more about him.

43

Spring is twice as enchanting when one is in love! The reawakening of nature, the unfolding of new life all around corresponds exactly with Maria's feelings of being alive and in love. They are like the expression of her new emotions. It is wonderful to sit with Wilhelm and drink coffee at the Rögerts' house on Sundays. It is as if she has invited him to her own house. She serves him coffee, passes him milk and sugar, puts a piece of fruit flan on his plate, and enjoys him watching her clean up afterwards. When there is a spring shower, they place their chairs next to the window and sign silently to each other. The Rögert sisters leave the two young people in peace. In good weather, they walk along all the routes Maria remembers from her school days.

Wilhelm shows Maria what has changed in Aachen since she was in school. For instance, the Kaiser Friedrich Park is new to her. They like going to the valley below the wooded hills, into which the park with its little artificial pond is located. On the pond, there are rowboats for hire. But Maria never goes boating; she is afraid of water. She would rather watch the swans and ducks from the safety of a bench. The couple walk out of the park, past fields and a grassy slope, where the Kannegiesser Brook winds through the meadows. Hay meadows and patches of clover have been mown. The trunks of the little fruit trees bear a fresh white chalk covering to protect them from the sun; cut-off branches and twigs lie piled up next to them.

Maria and Wilhelm come to the Grundhaus Inn on the main Liège road. The inn lies secluded at the edge of the forest. Here, they drink coffee at garden tables beneath the trees, or they cross the road and take a path through the fields along the woods to van Halfern Park. The broad, well-kept lawns are dotted with white daisies. Many little paths crisscross the grassy hillocks, and strange trees from foreign countries grow singly or in groups. On a bench among blossoming shrubs, they can talk undisturbed. The sun warms them, and the earth at their feet smells of spring.

Wilhelm has a lot to tell and is glad to have found an attentive observer in Maria. Maria realizes that Wilhelm has not mastered the German language as well as most deaf people. His vocabulary is much smaller, yet his signing is very clear. He tells whole stories in just a few words using signs, facial expressions, and movements. He even describes some events only with gestures. Can she not express herself much better than he, even though her speech is not as good as it used to be? Still, Maria can understand Wilhelm well and is surprised at how much he knows.

Maria asks question after question. She wants to know what happened during the ten years she was living in her village. Wilhelm is constantly surprised by Maria's questions. Is she so stupid? No, she is not stupid, but in a way, she is. All she knows is that the war is over and the emperor is gone. She does not know that there was a revolution in Germany on 9 November 1918, just before the armistice. Germany had lost the war; the soldiers were tired of fighting, the emperor fled to Holland, and a new republic was established. Toward the end of the war, many people in Germany suffered from lack of food. Wilhelm would eat rutabaga without potatoes at home. Mother cut one slice of bread for each child every day, and all the children stood around her, making sure that every slice was the same size.

During the Allied occupation, there was a curfew at night. Wilhelm's father carried a permit when he went to the small powerhouse next door to switch off the street lighting. Rashly, Wilhelm followed him once. The military patrol stopped him. Father in his wooden clogs and Wilhelm in his slippers were taken in and locked up in the mayor's office overnight.

For two weeks, Wilhelm worked for distant relatives of his mother in Krauthausen near Jülich. His youngest brother Heinrich helped him paint their house. They were fed well and, after finishing work, given eggs and ham to take home with them. Wilhelm rode his bicycle and Heinrich sat on the crossbar in front of him. Once, on the long ride home, the bicycle broke down and, as they were still not home by curfew time, they spent the night outside huddled among heaps of stones. Wilhelm kept saying to hearing Heinrich, "You listen out!" But all Heinrich heard, was the eerie screeching of the crows.

When Father is very busy, Wilhelm occasionally helps him with burials. He and his brother Heinrich push the high-wheeled cart with the empty coffin to the house of the dead; they pick up the corpse, and bring it to the small mortuary on Eilendorf churchyard.

For a time, the French occupation soldiers had their canteen in the emptied Sistermann coffin workshop. Later, when the Belgian troops moved in, they set up their office there, and to the amazement of the children, they had a real telephone!

"Why was war?" Maria asks.

"You don't know about Sarajevo? Don't you know about the Austrian heir apparent? He was shot in Sarajevo." Wilhelm explains where Sarajevo is. "Don't you know about the *Treaty of Versailles?*"

"What is that?"

"Don't you know who the government is now?"

"No," says Maria. "I don't know."

"We have Weimar Republic now. We have a democracy now. President of the Reich, Mr. Ebert, was elected in 1919. Don't you know that? The Rhineland is occupied by foreign soldiers. We have to pay a lot of money to other countries. Don't you know?" Maria knows some details, but has no idea how they are connected. Wilhelm can't believe it. Every week since 1914, he bought the *Wochenschau*, a weekly magazine with brown print and a lot of pictures. He carefully read and collected everything. The pictures help him understand the text. After 1918, he regularly bought *Das Illustrirte Blatt* and discussed the contents with his friends. Wilhelm always wanted to know what was going on in world politics. He bought maps and an atlas. He pinned a map to the wall and, with little flags on pins, he followed the campaigns during the war.

Every Sunday, Wilhelm explains everything to Maria. He brings magazines, and they look at the pictures together. Wilhelm gets excited when he is telling her things. Their faces bend over a picture, then they look at each other so they can converse about it. Maria wants to know everything exactly. She is amazed by what she is learning. With Wilhelm's help, the past becomes clear. Now she realizes the significance of the foreign soldiers in town. Now she understands why Mrs. Heumann is so extremely thrifty with coal. There is none to be had because every month, Germany has to hand over more than two million tons of coal to the victorious powers.

Wilhelm knows how it all connects. Because the coal deliveries are in arrears, the Ruhr area has been occupied since 11 January 1923 by 40,000 French soldiers who came with arms, tanks, and airplanes.

In the Ruhr area, there is now passive resistance. All the shops and houses are closed. The workers have left the factories and coal mines, the fires in the big plants have gone out. No German trains will transport French military troops, no post is delivered, and no German officials work for the French. All economic life has been paralyzed in the Ruhr area. New French troops arrive—87,000 soldiers are now occupying the Ruhr area. No coal is allowed to be brought in to the unoccupied part of Germany. Maria's heart starts to pound. "That is bad, everything," she says. Now she understands why prices for food and everything else keep rising.

Wilhelm can explain the reason: Because Germany lost the war, it must pay billions of Goldmarks in reparations to the Allied countries—France, Great Britain, Italy, Belgium, Southern Slavia, and the United States. There is less and less money in Germany. New money has to be printed, but it is worth even less than before.

Maria learns to her surprise that Germany has no more colonies; they have been taken over by the Allied Powers. But the worst is unthinkable. The war cost the lives of 8.5 million soldiers in Europe, 2 million of them German. Because of epidemics and the blockade of food into Germany, 750,000 civilians died. Maria is deeply distressed. So many deaths in Europe. She hadn't known how bad it was.

Wilhelm tells Maria what happened to his hearing brother Johann. In 1915, he received his call-up orders. The letter arrived in the morning, while Johann was working in Rothe Erde. Wilhelm's mother gave the letter to the man who collected the lunch pots filled with food for the men in the iron and steel works, and he took the letter to Johann. Josef Sistermann had tried his best to keep his hearing son at home, to exempt him from military service, but all the entreaties to the authorities had been to no avail. He had even written a letter to the emperor himself, but received no reply.

His brothers and sisters and friends went with Johann to the railway station. He left on one of the packed trains. Soon he returned for a visit in his new uniform. Wilhelm admired his brother and was sad that he himself couldn't be a soldier. If only he had been able to hear! Or so he thought at the time. Johann was deployed to Russia, and he wrote a letter

Wilhelm (*back row, far left*) with his parents and siblings, minus his hearing brother Johann, who was killed in World War I.

home. During the fighting he was wounded in the knee, sent to a military hospital near Hannover, and later was placed on convalescent leave. Johann had a limp, but his Father was glad to have him home again. Father needed Johann's help to enlarge his business, pay for the nice house they had been living in for a year, and make his life with the deaf children easier. With Johann, he would be able to calculate, plan, and work. Johann was hardworking, ambitious, kindhearted, and strong; he would stand by his younger siblings, he is Father's comfort and hope for the future.

After his convalescent leave, Johann had to return to the front. His friends and family accompanied him to the station again. Wilhelm and the others waved for a long time, until the train disappeared into the dark hole of the Nirmer Tunnel. Later that year, Johann was killed by a shot to the head in Russia. He was twenty-one years old. Wilhelm saw his father pacing up and down in the room, tearing his hair out in despair. Wilhelm read the terrible letter: *He died a hero's death for the Fatherland!* But nobody was proud of it. For a long time, no friends dared to come to the house.

Wilhelm tells all of this to Maria, and he has to wipe his eyes and blow his nose. After his brother's death, he didn't want to be a soldier anymore.

He can still remember the beginning of the war. He was with his father in Wilhelmstrasse in Aachen, a wide, tree-lined street leading up from Kaiserplatz to Burtscheid and on to Eupen and deeper into Belgium. Crowds of people stood in the street to cheer on the departing German soldiers. The girls and women ran up to the marching soldiers and stuck posies into their gun barrels and on their jackets. Gray cloth caps were pulled over their shiny spiked helmets as camouflage. Waving and smiling and singing, regiment after regiment marched toward Belgium and France. At that time, Wilhelm had watched the soldiers with longing; how he would have loved to go to war!

Only a few days later, he hurried with Father to the inn in the forests on Lütticherstrasse. The inn had been declared a military hospital. Wilhelm saw many Red Cross trucks, saw stretchers with wounded men. They had been wounded in a short fight with the Belgians, who had defended themselves against the invading troops.

Wilhelm asks Maria if she knows that Aachen town has lost its region known as the *Butterländchen* (Butterland). Since 1920, the towns of Eupen and Malmedy are no longer part of Germany, they belong to Belgium. The Belgian border has now moved closer to Aachen. Wilhelm tells her how, with a group of other young men from Eilendorf, he had tried to smuggle things across the border in the Aachen woods. But the customs officers caught him, and he had to empty his rucksack of the tins of apple syrup, coffee, chocolate, and cigarettes. Because he is deaf, smuggling was really too dangerous. He could not hear the customs officers cry "Stop!" After he was caught, he decided he wouldn't try to smuggle again.

Wilhelm also relates the fate of his sister Maria. When the revolution broke out in 1918, Father and Wilhelm went to Trier on the Moselle River to pick her up. The train they traveled in was full of German soldiers on their way home from France. The soldiers had sausage, ham, bread, and sweets. The three Sistermanns were dying of hunger, and Father asked the soldiers to give his deaf children something to eat. After much convincing, all three were able to eat their fill. At home, Wilhelm and his gentle little sister were inseparable. But this happiness lasted only for a few weeks. Maria began to complain of headaches, and she died soon after. She was just fourteen, and Wilhelm was sick with grief. He had loved his sister so much. She may have seemed helpless and useless, yet for him she had meant happiness and joy. Wilhelm put a plaque on her gravestone that included her name and dates of birth and death. Above it, he fixed an oval photograph of her behind glass. On the high, narrow pedestal stands a white marble angel with wings spread, ready to fly. Wilhelm chose the tombstone and paid for it. He tends the grave and visits it often. His pain and grief lasted for many years.

Maria watches Wilhelm as he tells his stories. She sees not only his mouth, his "talking" hands, his face, but also his heart. It is good and soft. Too good, too soft. She will have to take care of him. She will have to watch over him, over his tender soul. She is there to make sure nothing bad happens to him. She is more robust than he is, she realizes that more and more. Her strength is growing like her love, and she prays, *Dear God, please, I want to marry Wilhelm, please!*

44

"I go to Tilsit! For a few weeks," Mrs. Heumann says to Maria. It is the beginning of summer. Maria is dismayed.

"I must stay here alone?"

"Yes, you have learned, you are hardworking, you can manage alone."

Maria starts to cry: "No, no, no! I can't manage alone. I can't. I can't work out the money when I go shopping. I don't understand money because inflation. Please not leave me alone!" Professor Heumann assures her that he will not cause any problems, and he will be satisfied with her work.

Mrs. Heumann says, "On a big list, I will write what you are to cook every day. When I come back, you can have a six-week holiday. Then you can go to Freilingen." Right now Maria is not at all interested in holidays in Freilingen. She is full of trepidation that she alone shall be responsible for four men, hens, cats, the household, washing, shopping, and all the rest. Mrs. Heumann says as she leaves, "You can do everything!"

So, Maria begins. She has no choice, and she tells herself, "Must be! Must be!" Soon, she is proud that everything is going well. She conscientiously carries out her work.

Every Sunday, she tells Wilhelm how things are going and her growing self-confidence shows. She always goes home on time to prepare the evening meal. Wilhelm does not like that one little bit because for him, the evening is just beginning then. He has a lot of friends whom he meets in Aachen or, as usually happens, they come to his house and stay up late, talking and enjoying themselves.

At the Deaf club, Maria gets to know a farmer's son named Clemens, and he can talk well. His parents have a farm near the Dutch border. Clemens is a pleasant, strong man. Maria sees straightaway that he can do his share of hard work. Clemens joins Maria and Wilhelm on Sundays; he looks at Maria with great interest. He begins to court Maria seriously.

He tells her she is the right woman for him. Then he asks Wilhelm, "Do you want to marry Maria?" Wilhelm stares at him, baffled.

"No," he signs, "I not thought." Then Clemens asks Wilhelm to give up Maria. He would like to go walking alone with her on Sundays, he would like her to be his girl, and he would like to marry her soon; she is after all a farmer's daughter and would be a good match for him. Maria stands there, and is not asked for her opinion. Wilhelm is somewhat surprised, but he realizes that Clemens is right and, out of good-naturedness, he agrees. Maria is so shocked that she doesn't know what to do. Does this mean Wilhelm has not lost his heart to her? He doesn't love her; otherwise, how could he give her up so easily? She is very, very sad.

The next Sunday, Clemens comes for her. Wilhelm stays away. She walks silently beside Clemens through the summer day. Through fields and pastures, and on through vegetable gardens, they walk along from Hanbruch across Vaalser Landstrasse to the Hörn, a long hill stretching from Lousberg to Holland. Clemens points out the land belonging to his parents and talks about his work on the farm. He is nice to her and sincere. She would become mistress of the farm one day, which is not at all small or poor. Maria is sorry she has to disappoint him. How could she say yes to someone when her whole being is filled with thoughts of another man? She would cry, cry all the time for Wilhelm. Why did he let her go so easily?

For several Sundays, Clemens comes to visit Maria and waits to see if there is any hope for him.

When Mrs. Heumann comes back from her long trip to East Prussia, she is full of praise for Maria. The girl has taken care of everything to her satisfaction. She has really done well. The professor praises Maria in front of his wife. On Sunday at the Deaf club, Master Wirtz comes up to her and says, "The Professor told me you can't cook. Your food does not taste good. You always put too much salt in the food." Maria grins at him and does not believe a word of it. Clemens is sitting at the table with her and orders her a drink. He is very attentive toward her. Wilhelm is with his friends and siblings. He looks quiet and lost, and Maria feels sorrier for him than for herself. Such a silly man, doesn't he realize how much she loves him? Sometimes he looks, as if by chance, in her direction, then Maria looks away to make Wilhelm think she hadn't noticed. Toward evening he apparently can't take it any longer and comes to Maria and Clemens' table. They sit together like good friends and talk. Soon Maria has to go.

Wilhelm says to Clemens, "I take Maria home. I have funny feeling when Maria with you. Don't like it. Maria better my girl." Maria is so glad. In a friendly manner and with a plea for indulgence in her smile she says to Clemens, "Don't be angry, please! I like being with Wilhelm more."

Clemens shrugs his shoulders and his hands make a gesture of resignation. Then he signs, "There is nothing I can do. Maria must know herself. Wilhelm is very lucky, very lucky." They shake hands and part as friends.

The summer evening is still bright and warm. Groups of walkers are coming back down into town from the woods. Families with many children, prams, and dogs. The people, a little dusty and disheveled from play and the heat of the day, are carrying thick bunches of flowers, empty baskets, and limp bags; they make their way home, tired but content. Some of them turn around to look at the young deaf couple walking arm in arm, stopping, letting go of each other to use their hands to speak, linking arms again, and walking on a bit further until they want to talk again. Wilhelm says that he will pick Maria up on Sunday and take her to Eilendorf; he wants to introduce her to his parents. Maria's eyes shine with happiness. Now, everything is good again.

The next Sunday, Wilhelm comes for her. She is wearing a new outfit. Mrs. Heumann went with her to buy it. Mrs. Heumann had to give her some money in advance, as the money Maria had saved had lost value and was not worth much anymore. She decides she will not go on saving. For Wilhelm's sake, she will buy nice shoes and silk stockings and some other new things. Radiantly, she now stands in front of Wilhelm, searching his eyes for approval. He does not seem to be all that impressed. Her bag, shoes, and woolen stockings, do not go any longer with the new clothes. Maria consoles him, "Main thing, new outfit." They go to the tram. Wilhelm is wearing his flat straw boater and is carrying a light, black cane with a silver handle.

45

The chimneys of the iron and steel works in Rothe Erde on the east side of Aachen no longer emit smoke. Due to a lack of iron ore from Luxemburg, the plant has become unprofitable. The high, lifeless chimneys loom in the sky. Just behind them lies the countryside of Eilendorf.

Wilhelm swings his cane smartly in the air with every step. Maria walks happily beside him. He has not linked arms with her, as he usually does. They pass the church, a splendid building surrounded by meadows. Cows rest beneath an old pear tree that later will bear hard Münster pears. The cows and hens on a farm are the only living creatures they encounter on this early Sunday afternoon. When they turn the corner around Pannhaus, the oldest house in the village, Wilhelm's parents' house is there in front of them on Steinstrasse. The roof rises to form a cupola in the middle. The full midday light falls on the gray slabbed plinth and the dark red brick walls. Stone scrolls and bows frame the windows. Each one has a railed ledge, painted green, for flowerpots. Maria is impressed. In the workshop window, she sees dark coffins with gleaming metal fittings. She glances at Wilhelm and thinks, *Coffins, corpses! Dreadful. Doesn't he always think of death if he has to live with things for dead people every day?* But Wilhelm gives her a cheerful smile and asks, "Isn't it a beautiful house?" "Yes, yes, very beautiful house," she replies quickly and eagerly.

The main door, with its two heavy wooden wings, is closed. One side of the house slopes into sunken gardens where, between rambling hop plants and elder bushes, the Clover Brook flows.

Wilhelm unlatches the front door and lets Maria in. In the hall, she stops, waiting. Wilhelm points out that he did all the painting, and he explains that he designed the light-colored oil paint on the ceiling and walls, the green wainscot, and its frieze of colorful, fancy stencils. The steps of the wooden staircase and the turned banister posts are painted in a shiny gloss paint. Nothing is worn or scuffed. Maria's face shows her appreciation of Wilhelm's fine work. They go into the large, combination kitchen and living room. Wilhelm's mother is sitting at the stove and has nodded off. She looks up sleepily. His father is smoking a pipe and reading the newspaper. Wilhelm introduces Maria to his parents. Maria shakes hands with his mother. Her indifference makes Maria feel shy. His father stands up and greats her warmly. He has deep furrows in his forehead and a moustache like her father in Freilingen.

While Wilhelm helps Maria out of her jacket, his mother sees to the stove fire and puts water on for coffee. Maria admires the kitchen walls, which Wilhelm has also painted, especially the funny figures all around the molding that Wilhelm created himself. "Everything in house I painted new, everything," he tells her. He is very proud of his work. Wilhelm leads Maria into the living room. There are pictures hanging on all the walls, beside each other and above each other, in wide frames and in narrow ones. There are paintings of landscapes and people, in addition to many, many photographs. "I made all myself," Wilhelm says.

"Photographs, too?" Maria asks in surprise.

"Yes." Wilhelm tells her that he has a camera and a darkroom where he develops the photographs himself. In the old farmhouse, there is a cupboard full of nothing but exposed plates. When he sees Maria's expression of disbelief, he takes a number of big photo albums and cardboard boxes full of pictures out of a little cupboard. He spreads everything out on the table.

"Where you learn?" Maria asks him. Wilhelm tells her that only two people in Eilendorf owned cameras—the young teacher Heinrich Schmitz and his hearing friend and merchant Josef Woopen. They were the first in Eilendorf who understood photography. Wilhelm is the third person in the whole village who has his own camera. He bought it in 1915, and the other two men taught him how to use it and how to develop photographs. Now Wilhelm takes photographs with a real passion.

When the war came to an end, the occupation authorities ordered that everyone had to have an identity card with a photograph. This gave Wilhelm a lot of work. The people of Eilendorf also ask him to take a family portrait. He visits their homes with his camera, tripod, and black cloth, and finds the large, excited family waiting for him, dressed in their Sunday best.

Wilhelm and Maria sit together at the table, and Maria looks at one picture after another. Wilhelm's head is very close to her face, she can almost feel his skin. She likes that. When Wilhelm wants to explain a picture to her, their heads separate so they can look at each other to talk. Then, they bend down again for the next picture. Maria can only marvel. How exciting it had been for her to own a single photograph of herself! But Wilhelm has captured whole stories and events in photographs. He himself can be seen in almost all the pictures. They are never boring, all the pictures are alive. They tell of the games played with brothers and sisters; Wilhelm's little sister Maria and his brother Johann are there, too. In one photograph little Maria is wearing wooden clogs and a big fringed shawl, and she is pulling lazy Heinrich in a little cart, his clogged feet up in the air. There is one of Josef hanging onto the bell rope in the high church tower, swinging from one window ledge to the other. The pictures tell of Wilhelm's deaf friends, who, during the war, dug trenches crisscross through the garden and played at being soldiers with homemade cannons, helmets, and wooden rifles. Maria looks at Wilhelm and asks, "Are you allowed to dig and play like that in the garden? What do Father and Mother say?"

"Never scold," Wilhelm replies. The pictures show Wilhelm's father helping load the church bells onto a cart because they had to be handed over during the war to be melted down for weapons. Since 1915 Wilhelm has captured the lives of his family and friends in the funniest poses and costumes and up to all kinds of pranks, on walks, climbing trips, tobogganing, dashing through cloudbursts, and at work. Maria sees the streets and squares of Eilendorf, too, and the surrounding countryside. And again and again, there is Wilhelm himself: painting, driving coffins in a high-wheeled cart, digging graves, riding his bicycle, walking with his rucksack on, or dressing up in borrowed soldier's and student's uniforms. Maria sees him in the photographs, sees his dear face, but she is never there with him. But now she is with him, and she knows that she does not want to be without him ever again.

When his mother wants to set the table for coffee, Wilhelm gathers his photos and puts them back in the cupboard. The peace and quiet disappears as his sisters and brothers come in, bringing friends with them. In no time at all, everything is in turmoil. There is a cheerful hustle and bustle. Luise causes the greatest commotion, and her gaiety is catching. She embraces Maria and is pleased that Wilhelm has brought her home with him.

Wilhelm's sister Lisa and brother Heinrich are there as well. Maria has never seen them before. She is surprised to learn that they are able to hear. She doesn't notice any difference between the hearing and deaf children. Lisa has a fiancé called Engelbert who cannot hear.

Maria helps set the table. Soon she realizes that everything in the Sistermann household is different from the Giefers'. Here it is the deaf family members and their friends who determine the lifestyle in the house. The parents are barely noticeable. In the course of the afternoon, a few deaf friends arrive from Aachen and Stolberg; among them is Josef, a goldsmith, and Wilhelm's favorite partner for the exchange of political opinions. They all seem to be at home here. The two younger children, who can hear, sign with this group and participate in it. They have no hearing friends. "Why so many visitors?" Maria asks Luise.

"Many visitors?" Luise asks, surprised. "Every Sunday like this, often many more, when no club," she explains.

Luise says that they often perform a play together. At the old house, they built a stage in the former barn. There was a real curtain and colorful painted scenery with funny drawings, all done by Wilhelm. When they perform plays in sign language and mime, they invite their friends and neighbors. They think up the plays themselves. They like dressing up. Luise talks about Wilhelm's workshop, where there is a strong smell of paint. On the floor and hanging on the walls, there are windmills, farmhouses, cribs, zeppelins, and airplanes that Wilhelm has made himself. A biplane is there too, with an engine to turn the propeller; it is so big, it hardly fits in a room. When the French Occupation came, and the foreign soldiers heard about it, they could hardly wait to see the plane.

"We play ball a lot in the yard, and we like playing hide-and-seek!" Luise relates to Maria what happens when they play hide-and-seek with a new friend. He goes searching in all corners of the house and has to crawl around in the stables and the barn. He climbs up to the loft on swaying wooden ladders. It is gloomy under the long roof, and the wind blows through the cracks. The junk in the dark corners looks eerie, and the floorboards are so rotten and full of gaps that one is afraid of falling through. If the new playmate goes into Father's workshop, he smells wood and glue, and he searches among the rough coffins leaning against the walls or lying on the sawdust-strewn floor. All of a sudden, one of the coffins will open all by itself, and a figure, swathed in white, will rise up with outstretched arms. Terrified, the new friend flees, and the others laugh until the tears run down their cheeks. Maria looks at Luise wide-eyed. What a good time they have! They can play and work on whatever they enjoy. Whoever doesn't feel like working stays at home and helps the parents, but only if he or she wants to.

Luise works as a carpet darner in Aachen. She goes into rich people's houses to darn their valuable carpets. She only does it when she feels like it or needs money for her clothes. But she is industrious. "Come, I show you my hats!" Luise says as she drags Maria by the hand up to the bedroom she shares with her sister Lisa.

Luise stands in front of her wardrobe and asks "Can you whistle?" But before Maria can reply, Luise puckers up her mouth like Maria's brothers do at home when they call the dog. "I can whistle well. A lot of deaf people can't whistle." Luise is very proud of her single-toned whistle, which she has been practicing for a long time. Hearing people have told her she whistles well. "Can you speak Aachen dialect?" Luise continues. Maria shakes her head. "But I can! A few words!" Luise says excitedly and then asks, "Can you speak French?" Because Aachen is close to Belgium, the Aachen dialect includes many French words. Now, Luise says something Maria cannot understand. "Was French," Luise explains. Maria wonders why on earth she should speak Aachen dialect, or whistle, or speak French.

Luise takes one hat after another from her wardrobe. "I have made myself. I can do everything." In front of the mirror, she puts each hat on, twists and turns and arranges her hair and asks for Maria's opinion. Maria can't tell any difference, all the hats look equally pretty on Luise. But she cannot imagine why anyone would need so many hats. Maria finds it boring looking at the hats, she would rather be with Wilhelm and the others.

"Come, we go downstairs!" Maria requests.

"Wait, I show my clothes quickly. One moment! Quick!" With a flourish, Luise takes a row of clothes from the wardrobe and lays them on the bed quilts. Then she picks up each dress, skirt, and blouse and holds it in front of her. Maria has to say how she likes them. "I have sewn everything myself!" Luise repeats. All the clothes are pretty; there is something stylish about them. But Maria inspects the seams, fastenings, and linings of the clothes, and does not approve of Luise's handiwork.

"But you not work neatly," she says to Luise. "Badly sewn!" Luise shrugs. She is not at all offended.

"Oh," she laughs, "doesn't matter. Main thing, pretty!" Maria cannot understand how something can be pretty if it has not been made properly and with care.

Suddenly, the young men come charging into the girls' bedroom. They have missed Maria and Luise and gone in search of them. They take Luise's clothes, hold them up against themselves, put the hats on, start to dance around in them, fall on the bed, and in no time there is chaos. Luise protests and pounds her fists on her friends in vain. Maria rescues what she can and hangs the clothes in the wardrobe. The young men laugh, get even wilder, and start a pillow fight. Luise scrambles over the beds to chase after her clothes. Maria is horrified. She does not find it at all funny. What if the parents come in now? A chase through the other bedrooms starts, then everything goes topsy-turvy. Wilhelm tries to restore the peace, grabbing his friends and dragging them out of the bedrooms. He tells them to go back downstairs. Laughing, they finally do so. Maria shakes the pillows and tidies the beds. Grumbling, Luise gathers up her crushed hats. "Gone crazy! Gone crazy!" she signs and taps her forehead with her finger, angrily.

Maria asks, "Your father scolds when everyone wild, and everything in a mess?"

Luise responds reproachfully, almost insulted. "Papa never scold! Never! Good Papa!"

In the meantime, Lisa has helped her mother clean up. Lisa is a quiet, shy girl. Her hair is fair, her face round and gentle. She prefers to stay near her mother. She is not clever, and she is afraid of the world. Anything rough, violent, or loud she cannot bear. Shyly, but in a friendly way, she looks at Maria. *Can Lisa really hear?* Maria wonders, but then she notices that Lisa talks to her mother without gestures, without having to lipread. *Strange*, thinks Maria, and although she herself is deaf, she feels superior to Lisa right from the start.

Toward evening, the friends, together with Josef and Heinrich, fetch a basket full of beer bottles from the Am Pümpchen Inn. Mother has already made a large pan of fried potatoes. Maria jumps up and signs, "I must go home!" Wilhelm is annoyed, and the others feel the same. How can she go home now? Before supper, even, and when the evening is only just beginning? The Sistermanns always sit together until late at night, all of them. It is only natural that she stays, too. Now that Wilhelm has a sweetheart, is he to spend the evening alone with his friends? But, sorry as Maria is to see him sad, she is used to being punctual and obedient. "No! No! I must go!" Maria has already fetched her jacket and cannot be persuaded to stay. Wilhelm asks her one more time to stay; after supper he wants to take a photograph so that they have a souvenir of her first visit to Eilendorf. But Maria is unrelenting. She must go home. She says goodbye to everyone and thanks Wilhelm's parents in the kitchen. Wilhelm takes her back to Aachen, troubled. He is not at all pleased with her.

How different the world has become for Maria, since she has known Wilhelm! In the morning, when she wakes up, she feels full of strength and joy. The whole day long her face radiates happiness. She is friendlier than ever before to the people around her. Even if someone is in a bad mood, they are soon infected with Maria's cheerfulness.

How wonderful it is to be alive! She feels like running, jumping, or shouting for joy. Is it the same for people who can hear? Is that why they sing? Maria doesn't know, but she feels that she has to do something like that. Sing! Somehow one ought to set that abundance of emotion free from the confines of one's soul and simply tell it to the world, or shout it, or—sing? Her heart is so full, it is overflowing. What is one to do with it? She would like to embrace the whole world. The whole world is Wilhelm! That's the way love is.

But in the world around her, times are troubled. Unemployment and unrest are increasing. Whoever still has work is afraid of losing it. Dissatisfied, unemployed men hang around in the streets of Aachen. They discuss the hard times among themselves. Mrs. Heumann carries thick bundles of paper money when she goes shopping; she has to stand with many other women in long lines at the shops. She pays for goods with millions of Marks. Maria is amazed at how carefully and sensibly Mrs. Heumann budgets and prepares the food so that the family has enough to eat every day.

Wilhelm, too, is now sometimes without commissions. Fewer people are concerned with redecorating their homes. The money people have saved is only worthless paper now. Many people are poverty-stricken. Rich people are close to destitution. Plans for the future are dashed. The factories pay daily wages because the money can be worthless by the next day. Wilhelm can hardly wait until Sunday to tell Maria what has happened in the days before. He spreads out newspapers in front of her, and then they try to understand all that they read. Since Maria has returned to Aachen, her vocabulary has grown larger than Wilhelm's, but he can understand the meaning of the information in the papers much better then she, although he can convey it with only a few words; mainly he explains the news through signs.

Starvation, inflation, unemployment, and a new word—*separatism*—come up again and again in the newspapers. Wilhelm has asked his friends at the Deaf Club about this word; they explained that the Rhineland is about to separate from Germany and become an independent Rhineland Republic. What troubled times! Aachen is patrolled by Belgian soldiers. At night the town is plunged into darkness. Because of the coal shortage, no electric lights burn, no gas lamps are lit. The people feel that they cannot go on. With the money that Maria earns in a month, she cannot even buy a bread roll.

Because Wilhelm has no work, Mrs. Heumann tells Maria to ask Wilhelm if he could paint her cupboard and the small corridor leading to the kitchen. So one day he comes to the Heumanns' in his white overalls. He washes down the ceiling and walls and paints everything new and fresh. Maria cleans up after him. She is glad not to have to eat her midday meal alone in the kitchen since Wilhelm is with her. It is a wonderful day for Maria, even though she has more work than usual.

Mrs. Heumann talks to her in the evening and warns her again, "You must not marry Wilhelm. Wilhelm speaks terribly. He has an ugly voice. If you could hear, you wouldn't want him anymore. You can have a husband who speaks well. You are a clever girl." Mrs. Heumann means well, but Maria is angry with her. After such a lovely day, after Wilhelm has helped her make the house look so nice, Maria finds Mrs. Heumann's warning doubly unfair. Without saying goodnight she goes to bed. There she cries for a long time.

46

The day after Mrs. Heumann's scolding, Maria is ready to take her holiday. Mrs. Heumann urged her to do so in the previous weeks, but Maria did not want to leave. Now, she cannot stand Mrs. Heumann anymore. If Mrs. Heumann disapproves of Wilhelm so much, how can she stay with her any longer? Mrs. Heumann suggests that she take three weeks now, at the beginning of summer, and three weeks in autumn. On Sunday, she talks it over with Wilhelm. She is a little afraid of the journey. The trains run irregularly. Most of the trains are run by the Belgian occupiers; a "respectable German" does not travel by train now. Fearing sabotage, Belgian soldiers guard the bridges and tunnels. So Maria is very glad when Wilhelm offers to accompany her as far as Düren.

As the train rolls along the tracks, Maria and Wilhelm sit at the window, facing each other. They do not look very happy. Wilhelm is not in a good mood. How nice this trip could have been! But already at the station they have argued. Maria is unhappy and also a bit sulky. Why is Wilhelm not pleased with her? He arrived well-dressed in the station hall at the arranged time. When he saw her, his face changed. Maria was taken aback and asked, "Why you change face? You not friendly."

"Hat off, please," he signed.

"Hat? Why? Hat is pretty and still good. Miss Rögert has given me."

"Terrible! Long, colored feather! Terrible hat!" But Maria did not take it off and is still wearing it. Now and then they speak, but they are both disgruntled.

Just before Düren, Maria says, wanting to clear up the matter of the hat: "My hat I like. Miss Rögert has also said hat is nice. I am proud of fine hat. My first hat."

Wilhelm replies, "I am ashamed because travel with you. You have old fashion on your head!"

Maria becomes sulky again. "Don't care. Hat I like. I leave on!"

Wilhelm is offended. "I not walk with you in Aachen like that!" Wilhelm only says the word *Aachen* with his lips, he has signed everything else. Maria leaves the hat on and holds her head up high. Everyone should see her hat. But her heart is weeping. Why are they quarreling now, just before their long separation? In Düren, they wait for the connecting train. They hardly talk. When the train to Euskirchen finally arrives, they barely shake hands to say goodbye. They only wave their hands, briefly, and then Wilhelm goes to the other platform. She watches him walking away, on his own; immediately, she wants to run after him. Her love wrestles with her pride. But her train is leaving, and, unhappily, she sits down in a corner. Toward evening, she arrives at her family's farm. She feels miserable and tired, from worry, from the journey, the long wait times, and the walk home. Father is standing at the front door. She is glad to see him.

"Father! Father!" she calls, and lifts and moves her bag. Father looks at her in astonishment. Then his face breaks into a wide grin. He slaps himself on the thigh and shakes with laughter. The others come running from the stables and the house to see what is making him laugh so loud. Father points to Maria's hat, and the children gape. For a moment, Maria stands there confused and shocked, then she pushes past Father and the others without a word and rushes up to the bedroom. She takes several steps at a time, flings the doors open and slams them shut, throws her bag on the bed, tears the hat from her head, and hurls it furiously to the floor. Then she quickly picks it up again, opens her parents' wardrobe, and slings the hat into the farthest, darkest corner of the top shelf. She slams the door shut. She never wants to see it again! She throws herself on the bed, buries her face in the pillow, and weeps. With her tears she washes away all her anger at this incomprehensible world.

When, after a long time, she has calmed down, she goes downstairs to greet her family pleasantly. In the following days, everything seems as if she has never been away. The hat no longer exists in her mind, but Wilhelm does. When she is back in Aachen, she will have to make peace with him at all costs, and never again will she wear anything he doesn't like. But three weeks can be a very long time. She tells nobody about her love for Wilhelm. It is her secret. She is afraid to talk about it. In Freilingen she is not really at home any more. Her thoughts are in Aachen and Eilendorf; in fact, she feels lonelier here than ever before.

After a week, a letter arrives from Aachen for Miss Maria Giefer. Only Aunt Barbara knows about it, and she does not ask who it is from. Maria puts the letter in her apron pocket and reads it later in secret, with trembling hands. The letter is from Wilhelm. He is sad because they have quarreled, and announces his visit. He wants to visit her! Next Sunday! Maria is dismayed. She cannot allow that, it is impossible. What would Father say? She secretly writes a letter back asking him not to come, for it is still too soon. She cannot tell her Father that she has a boyfriend. Father would certainly not permit him to visit.

Only a few days later, a reply arrives. Nervously, she opens the letter, again in secret. The photograph of herself that she had given Wilhelm falls out first. Wilhelm has sent it back to her. He writes that he is now deeply hurt by her asking him not to come to Freilingen, and he wants to break off their relationship. He does not want her to be his fiancée; it is all over. Frightened to death, Maria lets the words of the letter sink in. How it hurts that Wilhelm wants nothing more to do with her!

Suddenly, everything is empty and dismal. She is hopelessly alone now. She feels her stomach cramping, her chest tighten, and her heart becoming as heavy as a stone. Slowly she goes up to the attic unnoticed; she wants to be alone, undisturbed by any people. Wilhelm's letter has hurt her so deeply, she cannot even cry.

Maria sits down amid the junk in the attic. She cannot think clearly. Wilhelm was her world. Now this world does not exist anymore. What is she to do, where is she to go? Rigidly, relentlessly, her thoughts revolve around the same thing. They revolve around Wilhelm, around the end. They hurt!

For a long time, Maria sits in the attic. A ray of sunlight has wandered across the floor. Maria's heartbreak is still just as painful as when she came up here. It does not change. With all her will power, she forces herself to get up and go on with her work. She tells no one about the letter. Wilhelm has asked for his photographs; obediently, she sends them back to him without enclosing a single word. Now she does not even have a photograph of him. She has nothing anymore!

She works as usual, but she scarcely eats or sleeps, and she avoids everyone. Even though Maria is working out in the hay field and getting some color in her face, Father sometimes scrutinizes her. After a few days, he lifts up her chin and asks sternly, "What is wrong?" Maria looks at him with joyless eyes. "What is it about?" Father wants to know, asking even more sternly.

"I feel homesick for Aachen." Father makes no comment and leaves.

How wondrous the world seemed until just a short while ago. How intensely Maria has lived, and now how pointless it all seems. Why should she work? Why bother with the harvest? Why bother with anything? How hard the work is when one is so tired. Without Wilhelm, life passes her by. Toni cuddles up in her arms, seeking tenderness. She shows him affection, but feels nothing. She feels only the anguish of her love, the despair that will not even let her pray.

For the first time in her life, she wishes that she could die. She would like to leave this world where there is no Wilhelm, and where she has no home.

Father leaves her in peace. After three weeks, she departs quietly, almost unnoticed because everyone has his or her own work to do.

Apprehensively, Maria approaches Aachen. Fear and agitation seize her. Can she live here—so close to Wilhelm? How will she bear her sorrow? She is afraid of seeing him, and yet she longs for it, unable to think of anything else.

47

Mrs. Heumann is alarmed when she sees Maria. The girl has lost weight, her face has become stern and care-worn. Even though Maria knows that Mrs. Heumann cannot understand her love for Wilhelm, she tells her of her misery, and suddenly she feels she can cry. It is the first time since Wilhelm's letter of farewell. Now, she can't stop crying; it is as if she had been damming up a sea of tears. Mrs. Heumann tries to console her, telling her there are so many decent and industrious men in the world, and some of them deaf. Why should she run after the very one who does not deserve her love? He certainly has not loved her, otherwise he could not have rejected her the way he did. And what is all this anyway? No woman should cry for a man, nor run after one. Men are far too stupid when in love! But Maria cries. She cries while peeling potatoes, while cleaning, feeding the chickens, darning the stockings, and while mending; she just keeps crying. It is very awkward for her when the professor and his sons look at her. She knows what a pitiable sight she is, with a puffy face and dripping nose. But she can't help it.

When the day for going to the Deaf club comes, Mrs. Heumann orders her to go. She does not have the courage to go alone, so Finchen picks her up, and Maria goes along, dreading it. It will be hard to see her deaf friends again. They are always cheerful and happy. Maria arrives at the club and looks at them as if they were distant and odd.

Clemens sits down next to Maria, and her sister Christina joins them. Luise is full of sympathy when she sees Maria looking so small and sad, barely able to bring a smile to her lips. Then she waves to her brother Wilhelm. Maria noticed him when she first arrived; it hurts to see him. When Wilhelm comes over, joy and pain build up inside of her, and she gives him her hand, gravely. Wilhelm is as friendly as ever toward her, as if nothing had happened. He says, "We friendship, you and I. Just friendship." But Maria cannot understand. *Is everything to be the same as before, or how?*

So she asks, "What is that—*friendship?*"

Wilhelm is surprised. *Is she stupid?* "We not think of marriage, no engaged couple, only friends." Maria nods. Then he sits down next to her and begins chatting.

Like someone seriously ill who finally has been relieved from the worst of pains, she begins to hope again.

Clemens takes her home that evening, but she can only think of Wilhelm and everything he has said. Her heart is profoundly moved, filled with longing and tenderness for Wilhelm. Clemens comes to take her for walks on the following Sundays. Mrs. Heumann recommends this man to her.

"He is also respectable, hardworking, and comes from a good family," she says. "Everyone can understand him well, and he speaks in complete sentences. And he values you. That is important!"

Maria keeps silent. She knows that the professor's wife means well. Maria spends three Sundays with Clemens, but she does not let him believe he has a chance.

After four weeks, Maria sees Wilhelm again at the club. He brings his chair with him when he comes to where she is sitting, and he gently but firmly pushes it between Clemens and Maria, so they are forced to move apart. As soon as Wilhelm is sitting next to Maria, he turns to Clemens and signs, "Maria my bride!" He takes both her hands in his and holds them tightly for a while until he has to use them to talk. But as often as he can, he takes her left hand in his right and holds it firmly. Maria has to summon up all her strength not to cave in. She is battling against an overwhelming weakness. Only gradually can she believe it: She has got Wilhelm back! Slowly she finds faith again. The anguish of the last few weeks, when she was so utterly alone, is over. Wilhelm has come back! He loves her after all!

Wilhelm reads the *Volksfreund* every day; it is the newspaper of the *Zentrum,* which is a Christian political party. Sometimes he also buys the papers of other parties, of which there are so many in Germany now. On 13 August 1923, Gustav Stresemann becomes the Chancellor of Germany.

He establishes the Grand Coalition. Wilhelm does not know this term, so he asks his hearing friend Josef Hahnengress, who works in Eilendorf in his father's print shop, what it means. Josef often visits Wilhelm and teaches him how to prepare invoices and estimates and how to deal with insurance and tax matters. He is patient and understands his deaf friend. Wilhelm underlines all the unknown expressions in the newspapers and shows them to Josef. With gratitude and attention, Wilhelm follows Josef's explanations.

On Sundays, Wilhelm spreads out the week's newspapers and magazines in front of Maria. Everything he knows, he passes on to her. Nobody "listens" to him more attentively than Maria. The Grand Coalition includes the Social Democratic Party, the Catholic Centre Party, and the liberal German Democratic Party and German People's Party; Mr. Stresemann has brought them all together. The coalition members discuss whether they should give up passive resistance, how to prevent Germany from disintegrating into several smaller states, and how to put an end to postwar poverty. The Separatists are still pressing for the Rhineland to become an independent country. Maria can't imagine not belonging to Germany any more. Maria and Wilhelm read about thousands of people being expelled by the occupying powers, of people killed in street fights and starving in the cities, executions of rebels, imprisonment, and fines. In Aachen, 15 people were killed and about 100 injured during demonstrations on 15 August 1923. When will things get better?

At the end of September, the government declares a state of emergency. Mrs. Heumann says to Maria, "It is best you go home. You still have three weeks of holiday. Times are troubled. I don't know if you can get home later on. It may even get worse. Perhaps you would like to stay in Freilingen for the time being? I do not have enough food for you. It is best, you go straightaway." But Maria would rather stay in Aachen. She discusses Mrs. Heumann's suggestion with Wilhelm, who advises her to go home and says he will go with her. She ought to introduce him to her Father at last. Maria agrees with Wilhelm and writes a letter home.

Dear Father!

I will come to Freilingen on Saturday. I will stay for three weeks. I have a fiancé. His name is Wilhelm Sistermann and he is also deaf. I will bring him with me. He will leave again on Monday. I want to introduce Wilhelm. I am well. I am looking forward to seeing you again. Give my love to everyone.

Your daughter Maria.

They set off early one morning in September. The Belgians still control the railway system in the Rhineland. The train Wilhelm and Maria board is guarded by Belgian soldiers. Six German hostages are on the train to protect it from attacks. In Düren, Wilhelm and Maria wait for the train to Euskirchen, but they cannot travel any further. A few people are standing around nervously; the station officials raise their arms in frustration. *What is wrong?* Maria wants to know. She takes Wilhelm's hand, goes up to the officials, and asks them why the trains aren't leaving the station. She only understands the word *resistance*. But that is enough for Maria and Wilhelm to realize that the German railway workers are practicing passive resistance against the occupation. They refuse to work. So the young couple stands there on the platform, not knowing what to do. The official advises her to try to get to Ahrdorf via Cologne and Remagen. Maria finds it laborious to communicate with the station official.

They have to wait a long time before a train arrives from Aachen, which they then take as far as Cologne. There they try to find the train to Remagen. Everything is so bewildering. In such situations, Wilhelm depends totally on Maria. Hearing people can't seem to understand him. Finally, they board the right train and are on their way to Remagen. But before long, the train comes to a halt at the station in Brühl. Again, the passengers look out of the windows, get off impatiently, and talk among themselves. In the end, everyone gets out; the train is going no further because the railway workers are on strike. What to do? Maria and Wilhelm are at a loss. Suddenly, Wilhelm nudges Maria. He has an idea. One of the teachers from Aachen has become headmaster of the Institute for the Deaf in Brühl. His name is Mr. Radermacher; they can go to see him. Maria thinks it is a good idea. She asks someone for the way to the Institute, and there they find the headmaster. Maria tells him who they are, where they have come from, and what their misfortune is. The headmaster advises them to go back to the station, that there is bound to be another train in the course of the day. That would be the only sensible thing to do. Maria tells the headmaster that she is taking her friend home for the first time to introduce him to her father. Wilhelm has remained silent the whole time; sometimes Maria interprets for him what she lipreads from the headmaster. She knows Wilhelm cannot lipread as fast or as well as she can. When the headmaster asks Wilhelm if he wants to marry Maria, he nods eagerly and tells him about his work, his family, and his home where there will be enough room for the two of them to live. Maria has taken Wilhelm's hand and is standing there with shining eyes. The headmaster says nothing for a while, then he turns to Maria and says, "I don't think your father will let you marry Wilhelm. I really don't think so."

Astounded and perplexed, Maria asks, "Why not?"

"Your fiancé cannot speak well. No one can understand him. Your father won't approve of that at all. Wilhelm speaks too badly. That is not good for marrying. Life is very hard, it is better to have a husband people can understand. Your father will not want him as a son-in-law." He shakes his head doubtfully, the corners of his mouth pulled down.

Maria is alarmed; she hadn't thought of that. Suddenly she starts to cry. She is afraid, very afraid that the headmaster may be right. He is embarrassed when he sees how much his words have affected her, and he tries to console her. But it is too late. She cries, and Wilhelm is upset and wants to know why she is crying. She tells him, sobbing. And now he, too, is sad and helpless. Life has suddenly become so difficult again.

They quickly take their leave of the headmaster. Maria does not want to stay there a minute longer. They go back to the railway station without talking to each other: Wilhelm depressed, Maria in tears. They silently huddle together on the platform and wait with the other passengers until finally, hours later, the train does go on to Remagen. Here they change trains to go to Ahrdorf. By now it is night; they cannot sign to each other in the dark train. It is well past midnight by the time they get to Ahrdorf. They are both very tired. Maria can smell the village and the water and plants of the Ahr River. She takes Wilhelm's hand, and they leave the Ahr road and walk up the long winding track past thick woodlands to Lommersdorf. Up there, on a hill, beneath lime trees, stands an octagonal Baroque chapel dedicated to St. Jodocus. Here, Wilhelm stops to say something to Maria. She crouches down a little, and Wilhelm raises his face and hands toward the starlight, so that Maria can see his movements silhouetted against the night sky. Maria sees him sign, "Father not want me, we two separate—you peace." Maria shakes her head vehemently.

She becomes calmer the closer they get to Freilingen. Maria links arms with Wilhelm. In front of them lies Lommersdorf with its white church. Maria takes Wilhelm's hand, taps with it on her chest, and points it down to a valley. "I live there" is what Wilhelm is to understand. He realizes that they have to go down to the valley, and that this is Freilingen. In Lommersdorf, they walk past the church. They do not hear the barking of a dog, the animals pushing against the stable doors, the rattle of a cow chain, or the rustle of straw when an animal moves. For them, everyone and everything is fast asleep.

They walk quickly on the road down into Freilingen. Maria is eager to get home. She has to convince Father that Wilhelm, and only Wilhelm, can be her partner for life. She has to tell him how wonderful he is for her, and how much she loves him. Wilhelm can sense Maria's confidence growing. She holds his arm in hers, presses it now and then, and feels his reply in the slight pressure he returns. At last, they come to the Giefer farm. Here is her parental home, and she has brought Wilhelm with her. They walk around the manure heap; the big dog comes toward them, wagging his tail. Maria bends down and pats him quickly, then she tries in vain to open the door. "Father! Father!" she shouts up to the window. Her voice sounds shrill in the silence of the night. Mother Helene's head pokes out of the window. The light goes on and shines through the fanlight of the door. Mother opens the door, and Father is behind her. He is still buttoning his shirt and combing his fingers through his sleep-tousled hair. Maria takes Wilhelm into the front room.

"This is my fiancé Wilhelm," she says, and Wilhelm shakes hands with her parents. He says nothing, only bows politely, for he is afraid to speak. When they have sat down, Maria tells them about the troublesome journey from Aachen to Freilingen. She says that they are both very hungry. Mother fans the fire, makes fresh coffee, and puts bread and butter on the table. Father watches while they eat, and then he asks Wilhelm about his work. Wilhelm is nervous, but he tries to speak as clearly as possible. Father hears only strange, incomprehensible, discordant sounds. He cannot understand a single word Wilhelm says. Maria does not let any anxiety or panic mount up inside her. She watches Wilhelm's mouth while he is speaking, then turns to Father and repeats what Wilhelm has said. At the same time, she lays her hand gently but firmly on Wilhelm's.

Father nods and says gravely but pleasantly, "A trade is good!"

Maria breathes a sigh of relief and quickly assures Father that Wilhelm is very hardworking and good, he earns good money and is never lazy. "Wilhelm is good husband for me. I want no other husband," she tells him.

Father looks at them for a long time. Then he says to his daughter, "Marriage is not easy."

Maria looks at him, not understanding: "Why you say?"

"Marriage is not easy," Father repeats. Maria does not question him further, but the words are imprinted on her mind. "You were born deaf, and Wilhelm too?" asks Father.

"Yes," she replies.

"If you have a child, the child will be deaf, too."

Maria reacts quite fiercely. "Oh no! Oh no!" she says loudly and uses her hands for emphasis. "I certainly believe our child can hear!"

Father is silent for a while, then he says, "One child is enough. It is too difficult for you to have more children."

"Yes," says Maria, and interprets her conversation with Father for Wilhelm.

"Yes," Wilhelm repeats.

The two young people are cheerful. Maria senses that Father approves of Wilhelm and likes him. Everything is good.

Before she falls asleep, her thoughts revolve around Father's words: "Marriage is not easy." She now understands what Father means: Being married means not only happiness, but also effort.

The next day is Sunday. The warm sun makes the world even more delightful. Maria and Wilhelm go to the church in Lommersdorf, where he kneels quietly beside her. Some people in church turn around to look at the fine stranger. On the way back home, Maria has to introduce him many times. When they are back home, Wilhelm walks around the yard, and Maria's youngest siblings and the neighborhood children surround and follow him.

His slim appearance is elegant and well-groomed; no, he is no farmer's son. Wilhelm entertains the children. From his knotted white handkerchief, he has conjured up a mouse with pointed ears and a little tail. He lets the mouse jump out of his hand and hop down his arms or, with a quick leap, up into the children's fascinated faces. He sits down on the bench in front of the house, takes slips of papers from his wallet, and draws merry little figures on them. He distributes them among the delighted children.

In between her household chores, Maria keeps darting outside to make sure Wilhelm is all right and is not bored. She has already led him around the house, yard, barn, shed, stables, and garden. Wherever he goes, he takes care not to get dirty. Maria even wipes the chair before Wilhelm sits down.

In the afternoon, Maria asks her large family to come out to the garden. She has brought out chairs for her parents. Wilhelm takes a picture of the Giefer family. Using the self-timer he takes a picture of himself and Maria on their own. With his watch chain across his waistcoat, a flower in his buttonhole, a cigarette in one hand, and his free hand on the back of the chair, he stands next to Maria, who is seated. No one in the village has a camera, and most of them have never seen one. So, all of the neighbors stand and stare while Wilhelm takes his photographs, and then, carefully and quietly, places the exposed plates in the plate holder and folds up his apparatus.

What Father does then is so unexpected that Maria would never have dreamt of it—he goes for a walk with her and Wilhelm through the entire village! He has never done that before, with her or with Mother. People are sitting in front of their houses enjoying the peace of a quiet Sunday afternoon, and they stop to look at the young, handsome couple. They call out something to Father, who says something in return, and they nod or wave to Maria, who keeps saying as they pass by, "This is my fiancé." Some come up and shake hands with Maria and Wilhelm, and everyone notices her radiant face filled with happiness. She looks at Wilhelm and wonders what he is thinking right now. In Aachen no one has taken any notice of Maria. But here everyone greets her warmly and shares her happiness. Here she is, the daughter from the Giefer house, and Father is proud of her.

Monday morning is gray, the sky heavily overcast. It is pouring rain. The house is clammy, cold, and uncomfortable. Maria has overslept and hurries downstairs. The family is sitting cheerfully at the breakfast table. Maria gets suspicious and is worried about Wilhelm, who had wanted to leave at five o'clock in the morning. She senses uneasily that the family's good mood must have something to do with Wilhelm. "What is wrong, Father?" she asks. Father tells her that Klöss had Wilhelm sit on the crossbar of his bicycle, to bring him as far as Ahrdorf. Wilhelm had lifted his legs up high so that his trousers wouldn't get splashed. Because it was raining so hard, he opened up his umbrella. But just before they got to the Ahr road, the bicycle skidded on the slippery path and Klöss and Wilhelm toppled into

Maria (*back row, center*) with her father, Mother Helene, and her siblings.

the mud. Maria sees that Klöss is dirty from head to toe. She is horrified. Tears of compassion for Wilhelm and of anger at her family's laughter well up in her eyes. "Father! Not nice, you laugh. Poor Wilhelm!"

Father calms her by saying, "Ask Nikolaus. Wilhelm laughed a lot, too." Kloss nods and grins.

"Really?" Maria asks in surprise.

"Yes, yes, yes, Wilhelm laughed a lot," Klöss says.

Maria sighs with relief and breaks into a smile. She is quite touched by her family's acceptance of Wilhelm and by knowing he must have enjoyed the visit to Freilingen if he did not even get annoyed about a soiled suit!

In the middle of the following week, Wilhelm returns to Freilingen with his deaf friend. They come all the way through the Eifel hills on their bicycles. The two young men look nice in their smart-looking knickerbockers and peaked caps. Wilhelm brings with him the photograph of the Giefer family. Everyone admires it, and Father puts it behind the glass front of the cupboard in the living room. This time, Wilhelm takes photographs of the family as they go about their daily lives; for instance, how they set off for their work in the fields. Mäthes makes sure that Father's three horses and the foal are in the photograph. Aunt Barbara watches from the window.

The next day, Wilhelm and his friend cycle back to Aachen. Wilhelm writes to Maria that, on his way back, a herd of pigs caused him to crash his bicycle. He tells her he is going to give her a fretwork piece he made and painted colorfully when he got home. He has drawn a picture of it in the letter. The piece depicts a pig farmer driving his swine and Wilhelm carrying his damaged bicycle on his back, the two of them marching in opposite directions. Under the fellow who had crashed he has written *To Eilendorf* in fine handwriting, and under the pig farmer *To Freilingen*. The piece will be a calendar holder for their future home. Maria laughs and is glad that Wilhelm can make something funny out of a mishap.

Three weeks in Freilingen is all that Maria can bear, not a day longer. It is too quiet for her there, where everyone goes about their daily work as if nothing were happening in the outside world.

48

In Aachen, things are much different than in Freilingen. At midnight on 20–21 October 1923, the armed Separatists declare the creation of the Rhineland Republic in the Imperial Room of the Aachen town hall. But the populace is outraged, and the local police and fire brigade retake the town hall and attempt to drive out the Separatists.

On November 2nd Wilhelm walks from Eilendorf to Aachen because no trams are running. His father has told him that there is fighting in Aachen, and Wilhelm wants to see it for himself. When he reaches Adalbertstrasse, he sees many people running toward the city center, some of them armed with clubs and stones. The Separatists have returned to Aachen to take over the town hall and the government buildings of the Rhineland Province. The town is in turmoil. The Separatists race through the streets in cars and trucks, firing off random shots, but the Belgian occupation soldiers mounted on horses and on foot remain neutral. Because of pressure from the British government, the Belgian occupation authorities, who have had their headquarters in Aachen since the end of the war, do not interfere on that November day. Wilhelm, seeing this dangerous unrest, decides to return home to Eilendorf. Later, he learns that the Separatists have finally been driven out.

The German economy suffers from hyperinflation, and the money that Maria earns is practically worthless. The factories now pay only daily wages. The gray fall, with its gloomy, foggy days, and the onset of winter increase the misery. Everyone in the Heumann house wears a coat all day long. Freezing cold, Maria sits at the sewing machine in the kitchen making shirts for the professor's sons. Her fingers are numb. There is no coal for the oven or stove. Mrs. Heumann has set up a sort of mini-stove on top of the cold main one; this is where she cooks dinner now, using single pieces of coal or wood. Even more meticulous than usual, she divides up what little there is to eat. Sometimes, the Heumann family and Maria go hungry. Large numbers of Belgian soldiers are patrolling the town. A quiet and meager Christmas passes. Maria spends one day at Wilhelm's house. At the Deaf Club Master Wirtz asks her, "Do you want a change? Do you want to work for other people? Do you want to get to know something new?" Maria likes the idea, and Mrs. Heumann would certainly be glad to have one less mouth to feed in these bitter times.

On 24 February 1924, Maria receives her last monthly pay from Professor Heumann—16,666 billion Marks! It is a thick bundle of colorful, large notes with very little value. Maria says her goodbyes and thank-yous, and then goes with her few belongings to the address that Master Wirtz has given her.

Maria now lives with the teacher Master Kau and his wife in a block of flats on the Schanz. Mrs. Kau is a plump woman who treats Maria as if she were her own daughter. Maria has a nice room all to herself, and she is allowed to join the couple at mealtimes. She feels at home right from the start. On 31 March, Mrs. Kau pays her the first wages: 25 Rentenmarks! The Rentenmark is a new currency first circulated on 15 November 1923. Now 4.2 trillion Marks are equal to 4.3 Rentenmarks and worth about the same as one American dollar. For the first time, Maria has earned stable, valuable money, and she can plan, spend, and save!

On Whitsunday, she is due to be engaged to Wilhelm. Now she has to think about her dowry and her future household. She goes shopping with Wilhelm the day before Whitsunday. Wilhelm wants her to buy a completely new outfit. They go to Appelrath am Dom, the shop with a broad, white marble staircase, where Maria explains what she wants. Then Wilhelm, with a critical and careful eye, selects the clothes. Trying them on, Maria looks at herself in the mirror. She feels strange. Is she still the girl from the poor Eifel? Isn't Wilhelm right? Doesn't she now look much more attractive? But she learned in school that vanity is not good, and that the devil sits in the mirror. She has never seen the devil. Wilhelm wants her to be vain, to believe that the mirror is her friend. When she looks at the beloved man, all her doubts fade. She wants to please him. When he looks at her with pleasure, it feels good. And how he likes her! He discovers her all over again—how lovely she is! Has he never noticed her fresh face and lively, bright eyes before? Why has he never seen her soft hair and tender, gentle mouth? She is slim, with pretty legs. Was he blind? She really is a lovely girl, with a nice figure. Proudly he walks with her arm-in-arm through Eilendorf.

For their engagement, Wilhelm gives her a little silver chain. The pendant on it is an oval onyx set in a wreath of silver tendrils. On the black stone there is a delicate silver flower with a tiny, sparkling diamond. As is the custom, Maria now wears a gold ring on her left hand, which will be transferred to her right hand when she marries. Their initials, *MG-WS*, are engraved inside the ring. Wilhelm also wears a gold ring. In front of the guests gathered in Eilendorf, the couple declare their engagement and seal their commitment with an engagement kiss.

For the time being, they do not want to go to the Deaf Club. They do not like the crude jokes some of their friends make when they tease lovers. Maria and Wilhelm find the allusions to their love coarse and nasty, doubly unpleasant because the friends accompany their words with the corresponding signs and gestures. Their love is tender, considerate, and gentle. It is precious. It belongs to them alone.

49

A wonderful summer is drawing to an end. Maria is perfectly happy. All her free time has been spent preparing for her future household. On Sundays, she has sewn bedlinens on Luise's sewing machine in Eilendorf. She has made sheets, pillowcases, and quilt covers and trimmed them with lace she crocheted herself. She has sewn loops on towels and tea towels. Maria buys a thick notebook and writes down in it all the recipes she has learned from Mrs. Heumann and Mrs. Kau. With the money she has earned, she buys cooking pots and other kitchen utensils. She can hardly wait to be a housewife herself.

It is Sunday, and she is waiting for Wilhelm to come and pick her up at the Kau's. The whole morning, the sun has been shining on the brightly polished kitchen floor. The aroma of the Sunday meal cooking fills the house. After the meal, Maria clears the table. Now she is trying to wash the dishes quietly so as not to disturb Mr. and Mrs. Kau, who are resting in the living room. She must be careful not to knock the dishes together as that is noisy, according to hearing people. If only she could be with Wilhelm all the time! The time until the wedding seems to be dragging on.

She keeps an eye on the window to watch for Wilhelm. Because she cannot hear the doorbell, she has arranged with Wilhelm to wait down on the street until she notices him. When she sees him, she waves to him and throws the key down. Then she quickly puts away the last dishes, puts the cloth on the table, and takes off her apron. Smiling, she waits for him at the door. Almost before he can take off his hat, she puts her arms around him and presses her face to his, tenderly, longingly. But this time he is different. His small, slim figure is stiff, as if she were holding a lifeless object in her arms. She kisses him, but Wilhelm's mouth is unyielding. She presses her face to his again, expecting and seeking his response to her affection.

But she feels nothing. Dismayed, she lets go of him and takes a step back. What is the matter with him? Why doesn't he kiss her? Wilhelm looks very serious and a little embarrassed.

"Why you different face?" Maria asks him. Wilhelm shakes his head. Maria is now alarmed. "What is wrong? You please tell me!" she urges. She pulls a chair out from under the kitchen table and asks Wilhelm to sit down. She remains standing at the table, her hands gripping the edge. Wilhelm keeps silent and looks down at his folded hands. Maria knocks on the table to make him look at her. "Why you strange? Please tell me!" she begs. Her question troubles him, but his face appears cool and distant. Fear begins to well up in Maria, and when she reads from his lips, "I finish with you! Not marry!" she stares at him as if she had not understood. She cannot understand it. Then she sees that he is not wearing the gold ring. She feels wretched. Her face turns white.

Then she just says, "Why?"

It is embarrassing for Wilhelm to say what he has to say. He has promised his mother to break it off with Maria today. She has wanted him to end the relationship for a long time. His mother thinks he still has plenty of time to marry and that he can find another girl from town who is more suited to him. Also, the last time Maria visited his parents' house, she said she did not like the wallpaper border Wilhelm had put up below the kitchen ceiling. That was a bad sign, his mother said, because in marriage, Maria would certainly always want her own way, and that would be bad for him. Finally, Wilhelm mentions his mother is sad because he does not hand his money over to her like he did before, but instead puts most of it aside for Maria. His mother needs his money for her living expenses, as his brothers and sisters make no financial contribution toward the household. He sits there, dejectedly, and helplessly shrugs his shoulders. Maria has understood everything Wilhelm said; her face is paralyzed with horror. Then she jumps up and rushes into the living room to Mrs. Kau who is sitting in a chair, reading. Maria throws herself at her feet, buries her face in her lap, and sobs loudly. Startled, Mrs. Kau lays her book aside. Tears stream from Maria's eyes and she cries, "Wilhelm wants to finish! Wilhelm not love me!" She sobs heartrendingly.

Mrs. Kau takes Maria by the shoulders, lifts up her face, and says kindly: "Don't cry! Don't cry!" Then, holding her hand, she goes to the kitchen with her, where Wilhelm stands up to greet them. Mrs. Kau knows him and likes him, this quiet, friendly man, with the fine-drawn features. She moves her mouth slowly to make sure he really understands her. "Why do you want to leave Maria?" she asks him sternly. Wilhelm shrugs his shoulders helplessly. Amid tears, Maria tells her the reasons he has stated. Mrs. Kau shakes her head reproachfully. "You are a stupid man! Maria Giefer is a very hardworking, clean, good girl."

"Yes," says Wilhelm. He turns pale. The motherly woman stands in front of him resolutely and is not as friendly as she usually is when he picks Maria up or brings her home. He turns his hat around and around in his hands and feels terribly uncomfortable. He is ashamed because he feels stupid. Just before he came here, his mother was so convincing, and now he knows Mrs. Kau is right.

"Maria can do everything in the house," she says. "She can cook, wash, and sew very well! Maria is worth a lot. She is healthy, a lovely girl, clever, hardworking and loyal. She can speak well." Wilhelm, stares at Mrs. Kau's mouth and nods in agreement with everything she says.

"Maria loves you very, very much! You are a stupid man! You should be glad for such great love from Maria. Do not leave Maria! Maria loves you!" Maria has stood next to her the whole time and read everything from her lips. Agreeing with everything Mrs. Kau has said, Maria nods and then sobs into her handkerchief. "Have you understood me?" Mrs. Kau asks gravely.

"Yes, I understood," Wilhelm says. Then he looks at Maria, goes to her shamefacedly, stands in front of her, and timidly touches her arm. She looks at him with tearful eyes. "I stupid—Not be angry—I good again," he says. Maria sighs with relief.

"Where ring?" she asks. Wilhelm takes it out of his breast pocket and slips it on his finger.

"I stupid," he says again, and taps his finger against his forehead. Maria leans her face on his shoulder, and he strokes her hair for a long time, until she has calmed down.

Mrs. Kau asks them to stay there for the rest of day and invites them for coffee and supper. The whole time, Maria is very quiet and still pale. Pain has marked her face. The day's events have affected her very deeply. When he leaves, Wilhelm kisses her affectionately. "Everything good again, please." Maria nods. Being separated from him hurts. She cannot stand it much longer.

Shaken to the core, she turns over in her mind the events of that Sunday. How could Wilhelm have parted with her so quickly, so easily? Has he not understood anything about her? He is her world. Without him, her life is unimportant and worthless. Does he not sense that? Does Wilhelm not feel the same about her? The love she feels for him is so strong it must leap over, infect him, and suffuse him. She broods. Her concern for the man she loves increases. No, she cannot leave him alone in this world. He is too innocent, too sensitive, too obliging; he can be taken advantage of, he is defenseless. He knows no lies, no cunning, and no falseness. He is at the mercy of and dependent on the decency of other people. She has to take care of him and protect him. She feels strong enough to do that.

The wedding is to take place on Whitsunday 1925. It is all arranged. Wilhelm is determined. Maria writes a letter to her father telling him of their plans. Now Father wants her to spend the last few months before the wedding at home.

In Freilingen, nuts are ripening on the yellowing hazel bushes on the Stein. The plums behind the Giefer house are showing a purple gleam; fallen fruit lies in the grass, and in the fields the potatoes are ready to be harvested. Fragrant clouds of smoke from burning potato plants drift across the land. For the Feast of St. Barbara, the house has to be scrubbed and the cupboard shelves lined with fresh paper and new paper lace trimmings.

Wilhelm comes to visit once with his sister Luise. Luise does not feel at home on the farm and is afraid of Father's strictness. She finds it incredible that he sends them all to bed at half past ten in the evening and that they have to obey.

Letters go back and forth from Aachen to Freilingen. Wilhelm writes about his work to prepare for their life together. He is saving money and painting and wallpapering their future flat on the second floor of his parents' house. He has done the electric wiring himself. With his father, he chooses the bedroom furniture and pays for it with his own money. He orders the kitchen furniture from the cabinetmaker whose products he has been graining and varnishing for some time. The furniture arrives at the old house in rough condition, and Wilhelm adds the finishing touches with enthusiasm. Maria often thinks about all these preparations; she doesn't really mind what Wilhelm does, as long as it is to his liking.

Two weeks before the wedding, Maria travels back to Aachen to spend the rest of the time at the Rögerts'. With her, she brings all the good wishes of the people of Freilingen.

On her wedding day, Maria wears a black dress, with a white veil hanging over it. In the midst of the merry hubbub of the celebrations, she is a quiet bride. The bride and groom and their families from Eilendorf and Freilingen ride in carriages to the wedding ceremony. In the Rock Church of St. Adalbert in Aachen, the priest for the deaf community joins Maria's and Wilhelm's hands, blesses them, and says slowly and clearly to them that they are now husband and wife, "till death do thee part."

Maria knows that only death can separate her from Wilhelm—only death.

50

One clothespin and one more clothespin, and the last pair of trousers is hanging on the line. Two pairs of painter's trousers and two painter's jackets are nice and white and clean again. Maria has boiled the clothes twice on the kitchen stove and rubbed them on the washboard. There are hardly any more paint stains to be seen, and now a neat patch sits on the knee of one pair of trousers.

The early morning sun is shining on the garden and the wash on the line. It will bleach it even whiter. The old tree nearby casts its shadow across part of the lawn. Yellow plums are lying in the grass. Maria gathers them up into her empty laundry basket. When she bends down, she can feel her belly, which bulges a little below her apron. She lays her hand protectively on it. She feels both joy and disquiet. Every time she realizes that a baby is growing inside her, she feels this joyful anxiety.

Fresh air, a brook, meadows, gardens, hedges, trees, and bushes surround the young woman, and in the distance are the backs of houses. Maria has been given half of the large garden behind Wilhelm's parental home. Her part reaches from the rough wall of the old house up to the high hawthorn hedge. She tends the garden all on her own. Wilhelm doesn't know anything about gardening. He only carries heavy buckets of water and the watering can on warm summer evenings and helps with the watering.

The vegetable beds are planted in neat rows. The other half of the garden looks miserable in comparison. So many weeds are growing there! Maria walks slowly alongside her garden. How dense and tall the runner beans are growing! Soon she will be able to pick the long beans, snip them with the slicer, and fill them into stoneware pots. The heads of the savoy cabbage are crinkly and plump. Every day, she picks the caterpillars off the vegetables. It is the second year that Maria has been able to harvest all kinds of vegetables from her garden, even the sensitive cauliflowers that she carefully covers with leaves to keep them pleasantly white. Wilhelm's favorite berries, tangy and black, grow on the dark green blackcurrant bush in the middle of the garden. At the upper fringe of the garden, a thick peony bush grows, along with a round cushion of fragrant white carnations. That is all. Maria thinks those flowers are enough.

She fetches a head of savoy cabbage, two leeks, and three carrots from the garden. Then she picks a bunch of celery and puts everything on top of the yellow plums in the basket. She crosses the yard for the washhouse where the tub of soapy water, the washboard, the big tub for rinsing, and the bucket are. She pours out the soapy water, rinses the tubs with clean water, and wipes them with a cloth. She takes everything down to the dark cellar, where she lights a candle. Only a faint ray of light falls through the tiny cellar window onto the heap of coal sludge underneath. Briquettes are piled up in the corner, and pieces of wood from the coffin workshop lie stacked up. Wilhelm has put up wooden shelves on one of the walls, as high as the low ceiling. They are lined with canning jars filled with vegetables, fruit, jams and jellies, pickled gherkins, small onions, and beets. The heavy stoneware pots are still empty. Not until autumn will they hold the sour smelling beans and the home-shredded, pressed white cabbage for sauerkraut. Above the potato box hangs the meat safe with its dense green mesh. Here, Maria stores butter, meat, sausages, and bacon fat in summer. She now takes out the wrapped bacon fat and places it in the basket with the vegetables. While she is putting potatoes into an aluminum pot, she glances at the mousetrap, but the glow from the candle does not light up the dark corner where a piece of bacon fat is laid to lure the mouse. Maria has to go over to the corner with the candle. No mice have taken the bait. She is not sorry about that; otherwise she would have to bury the mouse. She has an aversion to that.

She carries the potatoes and the vegetables to the cellar steps, blows out the candle, and carefully locks the padlock in the dark passage. She has nailed a sack to the inside of the lattice door. She does not want people to shine a light in and see what she has in her cellar. She takes her things up to the top floor of the house, wipes her feet carefully on the mat, and unlocks the door. It leads directly into her kitchen. Every time she enters her small flat, she feels thoroughly at ease. She delights in having her own home.

Breathing heavily, she sets down the vegetables on the wash table. In the corner next to the stove, there is an iron stand with an enamel bowl on top and a soap dish below. Wilhelm has painted the stand a shiny green. A blue checkered hand towel hangs on a hook. Maria washes her hands and then tips the dirty water into a bucket. She refills the bowl with water from another bucket under the second wash table. Down in the dark cellar there is a water crane from where she must haul the water. But usually Wilhelm sees to that, if he remembers.

Maria takes the tablecloth off the table and folds it neatly. She prefers peeling potatoes and preparing vegetables at the large table in the center of the room, beneath the lamp. From there she can see her unlocked door; anyone who comes to visit has to walk straight in because she can't hear the knocking. Maria cleans the outer leaves of the vegetables, scrapes the carrots quickly, peels the potatoes, and washes everything in small buckets and big bowls. The sun streams through the wide open window and throws a bright rectangle on the polished, reddish-brown lacquered floorboards. Earlier, Maria had browned onions in suet, and later added water and pearl barley. When the greens are added, it will smell deliciously spicy. Maria is convinced that no young wife in the whole world could possibly have a better life than she!

She has a white stove with a lot of gleaming nickel, a wedding present from Father. After she has finished cooking, she will lay a briquette on the fire, close the ventilator and, after eating and washing up, she will clean the stove. When the top plate is still hot, the cleanser she applies smokes and stinks, and Maria sweats when she is scrubbing the top plate. The final step is to wipe the stove all over with a damp cloth and use a dry cloth to polish the nickel.

The stovepipe, painted silver, reaches up to the ceiling and then along the wall into the flue. It provides warmth in winter. Twice a year, Maria and Wilhelm work together to remove the pipe and dismantle it into several sections. They carry it carefully into the garden and sweep out the soot. They store wood and two flat irons in the oven of the stove. When Maria does the ironing in the summer, she has to stoke up a blazing fire in the stove, even if the sun is burning hot on the window and on the roof, to heat the iron on the hot plate. In winter, the damp wash is hung on the nickel bar around the stove, where it will quickly dry. On the rack above the stove, Maria spreads finely sliced leeks and celery leaves, and pear and apple rings, too, on greaseproof paper. When they have dried, she puts them into little cloth bags for the long winter.

Her sofa with straps and buttons is actually covered with brown oilcloth, but everyone calls it a leather sofa. It looks lovely with the embroidered cushions, and it is practical because it can be wiped clean. Two beautiful china cabinets stand facing each other below the sloping roof. They have little doors with glass panes and curtains, a lot of drawers with round knobs, and enough room on the shelves for rose-painted porcelain spice pots. Each pot has a lid, like a little hats. All the shelves are lined with brightly colored paper. The drawer for the sewing things is full of little boxes. One for silk thread, one for white buttons, another for dark buttons, one for belt buckles, another for snap fasteners and hooks and eyes, the next for ribbons, for loops, for needles, thimble and tailor's chalk, for darning wool and yarn; all sorted out separately into little tin boxes or cigarillo packets. There is a thin rubber band around each one of them and a label saying what is inside.

Behind one glass door is the first aid chest. In it there is boric ointment and glycerin, and bandages large and small for Wilhelm's frequently injured fingers; there are all kinds of herbal teas in little packets, headache tablets, and cough medicine. Maria has stoneware pottery for the midday meal and a set of rose-patterned porcelain for the coffee service, a wedding present from her hearing sister Setta. She has a set of cutlery with horn handles, plenty of pots and pans, all sorts of kitchen utensils, and glasses for wine, beer, and liqueurs, too.

Maria feels she is rich. She even owns a new foldaway sewing machine that is clearly visible as one enters the flat. It is covered with a pretty cloth and a flowerpot in the middle. Every Saturday, Maria carefully dusts the wheel, the stand, and the wrought-iron treadle. She is glad when she has something to mend or sew. Then she moves the sewing machine over to the window and can easily look down on the street while she is sewing.

Her linens are Maria's pride. When they are bleached and starched, it is a joy to see them hanging on the clothesline. Maria wants the neighbors to see that Wilhelm has a good wife. Nobody shall think that, just because she is deaf, she cannot be as efficient as a normal housewife. No one shall think she is stupid and incapable.

On the washstand in the corner of her kitchen hangs a towel rack with an embroidered cover. It has a shelf on which stand a crucifix, two candlesticks, and two blue vases. The pictures on the walls were painted by Wilhelm in years past. Maria never has seen him paint. He doesn't have the time anymore. Their bedroom is splendid; all the furniture is made of oak. The dressing table with its wide, practical drawers has a white marble top. On it, as is proper, stand a wash basin, ewer, comb tray, and soap dish, but they are never used; they are for decoration only. The dressing table has a large mirror, as does the middle door of the wardrobe. The beds are wide, and on the green quilts lie enthroned the throw pillows and eiderdowns, trimmed with lace.

By nine o'clock in the morning, Maria has aired and made the beds. Her little flat is clean and tidy. The light-colored tablecloth is spread on the kitchen table. If she did not have the big garden, she would certainly be bored. You can't just sit around and do nothing. Maria has put on the potatoes, boiled the vegetables, and browned flour in rendered bacon fat. Now she takes off her apron, fetches her drawstring bag and money, and walks a few steps up Steinstrasse to the butcher's. Wilhelm had previously done some work at the butcher shop. The butcher's wife is friendly to Maria; she is able to understand Maria well after a few weeks. Maria buys half a pound of frying sausages and some sliced sausage for sandwiches.

Maria is careful with money. She has to be. Even though Wilhelm always has work, he earns very little. The townspeople are poor. It looks as if unemployment will increase even more. Once, Wilhelm had to apply for unemployment benefits. Men stand waiting in lines in front of the town hall to pick up their unemployment checks. Most of them used to earn their living at the iron and steel works in Rothe Erde. What a good thing, Maria can get vegetables, potatoes, and berries from her garden! She is also given baskets of fruit in return for lending out the long painter's ladders to pick the fruit. This means the canning jars for winter are filled up for free.

The rose-adorned face of the porcelain clock in Maria's kitchen shows a few minutes before twelve. Maria compares the time with that on the pendulum clock in the bedroom, which was a wedding present from Wilhelm's father. The bedroom is pleasantly cool because Maria has drawn the white muslin curtains at the window. Soon, Wilhelm will come home for the midday meal. At twelve o'clock sharp, Maria has the table set and the meal ready.

Maria stands at the window in the sun waiting to see Wilhelm coming home. His first glance is always up to her window. The midday bell peals over the village. Flies buzz around the kitchen lamp, children come running noisily out of school, the languid midday grows loud. In her deep silence,

The Sistermann family home in Eilendorf. Wilhelm and Maria lived on the top floor.

Maria feels the warmth and the light, feels hunger, smells the good food, and sees children and adults going home to eat. She leans against the warm wood of the window frame, her hands on her belly, and waits.

From the window, she watches the life and activity of the street. No one in all of Eilendorf can have a more beautiful view than she has! On the opposite side of the broad street stands the solid Pannhaus. It was built in 1622 from rough stone with a half-timbered extension, and was originally the brewery for the Abbey of Cornelimünster. Later, the Pannhaus held the courtroom. The octagonal stone pillory built into the half-timbered part of the building is a reminder of the culprits who were publicly chained to it. Behind the Pannhaus looms the great gray church.

From her window, Maria can look down into Mrs. Woopen's garden next to the Pannhaus. There is a dark, dense box bush in it. On Palm Sunday morning, the women and children of the neighborhood ask Mrs. Woopen for small bunches from it to take to church, and she stands there at the bush, cutting and handing them out. Elder and snowball bushes, laburnums and lilacs hang abundantly over her fence, and the small garden gate is bowered by climbing roses. All through the summer, red poppies bloom on the crumbling parts of the thick, high wall that forms the boundary between Mrs. Woopen's garden and the Koch's farm.

This farm seems to have been made especially for Maria. It lies literally at her feet. It is not like the farms in Freilingen, it is much bigger and richer. The house, stables, barns, and sheds are built of whitewashed rough stone and surround a large cobbled yard. Maria can look straight into it, but it is shielded from the street by a high wall; passersby can only see into the yard through a trellised gate. The huge manure heap, housed in a stone pit, is in a separate small yard next to the stables. It can't be seen from the yard. From her window, Maria can see the pigs rolling in it while the sties are being cleaned. In the mornings, the black and white cows go out to the pasture as a veritable herd and come back in the evenings with full, heavily swaying udders. Horses are harnessed; carts and machines are driven in and out to work the land or bring in the fodder.

Maria watches everything with great interest. In spring and autumn, when she needs fertilizer for her garden, she makes sure she goes out to the street to collect fresh horse dung before the neighbors get to it. There is a long row of shiny milk churns in front of the vaulted milking parlor. Every day, she buys milk from the farm. The cow shed is as big as a hall, and the rooms of the house are as stylish as a town residence. She likes talking to the Kochs' four daughters. Maria inquires and admires and expresses surprise or approval with natural warmth and great interest. She is popular. Even so, there are some neighbors who pass her by with hardly a greeting, if at all. At first, she is hurt, but she sees how Wilhelm suffers when people they know are heedless or unkind toward him or her. Maria knows his sensitive nature. Disregard affects him deeply and painfully. He himself then says in surprise, "I quick pain—don't know why," placing his hand on his chest. Why is his soul so delicate? Maria overcomes her own hurt and comforts him by saying, "Stupid people!" Then she, too, walks past those people with her head held high.

Maria waits at the window knowing any moment now, Wilhelm will come around the corner of the Pannhaus. She looks at the weather vane on the nearby steeple, which shows her the wind direction; this allows her to predict what the weather will be like every day.

At last, she sees Wilhelm. He waves to her, a cheerful man in a white suit, riding his bicycle. She watches him until he has pushed his bicycle through the gate into the yard. Then she opens the door and waits for her husband. Swiftly, nimbly, he comes running up the stairs to her and smiles. His face is spattered with white paint. She takes him in her arms and kisses him. He smells of turpentine. She serves the soup while Wilhelm washes his hands. When they are seated opposite each other they make the sign of the cross and begin to eat. At each meal, Wilhelm demonstrates how good it tastes by patting his stomach and rolling his eyes in rapture. It is wonderful for Maria to be able to take care of him. If only they were undisturbed at such moments! But there is hardly a midday meal when they are alone. One of Wilhelm's siblings is almost always there, watching them, chatting with them. If customers come, knowing that Wilhelm is at home at lunchtime, they stop eating, ask the customer to sit down, and Wilhelm takes out his calendar and notebook. Maria talks to the customers, finds out what they want, and interprets for her husband. Wilhelm arranges to visit them on a Sunday morning to see what kind of work is required.

Sometimes, a stranger joins them at the table because Maria invites peddlers, beggars, gypsies, or musicians who happen to call at midday to join them at their meal. From the peddlers, she buys something for a few pennies. If she happens to see musicians from the window, she throws a few pennies down. Many of these traveling people who wander through the Eifel return year after year. Maria welcomes them as warmly as if they were old friends. Once a week, at midday, the mustard lady brings her can and refills Maria's small mustard pot for five pennies.

At regular intervals, Maria and Wilhelm are visited at midday by one of the brothers who own the Beissel Paint Factory in Aachen. They spread out catalogs, and Wilhelm can order materials and tools. They are glad to accept Maria's invitation to eat with her and Wilhelm. But today, the young couple is alone. Wilhelm gives Maria a detailed account of all the work he has done that morning. In between he makes jokes that make her laugh until her shoulders shake. As soon as they have finished eating, she clears the table and Wilhelm spreads out the newspaper. They stand, side by side, bent over the table, and read together. Often, Maria gets out the atlas to look up the places mentioned. Before Wilhelm says goodbye, he lights a cigarillo. When he has left the house, the smell of tobacco smoke lingers in the room for a while. Maria likes the smell because it comes from Wilhelm. She stands at the window, waves to him, and thinks *Wilhelm fine man! I must honor Wilhelm!*

It is satisfying to know that each of them works for the other. Just before four o'clock in the afternoon, in summer and in winter, Maria takes fresh coffee and bread to her husband at work, no matter how far away he is in the large village. Wilhelm leaves his bicycle in front of the house where he is working, so she can always find him. The places where Wilhelm works are usually untidy and uncomfortable. If he has to hang wallpaper, the furniture is pushed together and covered with old cloths, scraps of scraped off damp wallpaper lie in a heap, and the floors are smeared white and gray from the washing and painting of the ceiling. Pots of paint, ladders, wallpapering planks, buckets, and all sorts of tools lie scattered around, and the rooms smell of paste and damp walls, of paint, varnish, and turpentine. But when Wilhelm is finished, the clean rooms gleam with freshness.

Wilhelm sits on the floor with his back to a wall. He gets a chair for Maria; if it is dirty, he covers it with clean paper. She watches her husband eating his bread with paint-spattered fingers, though he holds it wrapped in the greaseproof paper. He drinks the steaming coffee from a thermos. Maria leaves him the thermos, and he puts it in a corner or on the window ledge to have a sip now and then until the evening. He shows Maria what he has been doing and what is still left to do. Usually the lady of the house or the whole family joins them and watches with astonishment at how they speak soundlessly to each other. The little children hide, frightened yet curious; the older children smile with embarrassment; the voices and gestures of these two deaf people seem so strange. Maria lipreads a lot of praise for Wilhelm's quiet, quick, and clean work. She senses the respect shown to him. She is proud of her husband. He always shows her to the door and they wave to each other when she leaves.

It will be late by the time Wilhelm comes home. He never finishes work before eight o'clock. Frequently, it is much later. But he is used to it, and when customers ask him to work late because they want the redecorating finished more quickly, Wilhelm just can't say no.

When his work is completely finished at one place, he pushes his gray cart home. He has written his name on the sides of the cart in large letters. Piled up on the cart are the wallpapering planks and their trestles; the ladder; the buckets; the bag of paintbrushes, spatulas, sponges and chamois leather; and all of his supplies. After he arrives home, he spends a long time in his workshop cleaning brushes and preparing the next day's work. Only then can he enjoy his fried potatoes with fresh salad from the garden, or pickled gherkins with onions. They must have fried potatoes, otherwise it just isn't supper. Maria fries them crispy and brown for him.

Again, they are rarely alone at supper. This was a great adjustment for Maria, as every evening it is late before brothers, sisters, and friends take their leave.

On the nights when they are alone, Maria can help Wilhelm draw up invoices and estimates in peace. Wilhelm writes down the hours he has worked every day and determines how much material he has used. Maria does not have to help him calculate, she just checks his work. Josef Hahnengress has shown her how to do the accounts. Maria has bought notebooks to neatly enter income and expenditures. She collects the receipts and does all the paperwork for the tax office. Wilhelm has nothing to do with that.

When Wilhelm runs out of daylight on long winter evenings, or when he finishes sooner or has not got much work to do, Maria is glad to have him home early. Before All Saints' Day, there are numerous grave crosses and tombstones to be inscribed, and before Christmas, Wilhelm repairs and repaints battered toys: old rocking horses, farmhouses, horses and carts, and doll's furniture. He does all that in the warm kitchen with Maria. She pushes the sewing machine nearer to the kitchen light and sews, or she does darning or needlework. Now and then, she watches Wilhelm working. She likes being alone with him like this. Sometimes he gilds darkened, old gold picture frames. He sands them down one evening with fine sandpaper, and he insulates them with shellac to prevent the oil he has applied from soaking in. The next night he checks with his finger to make sure the oil has the right adhesiveness. When he is satisfied, he builds three walls of stiff, greaseproof paper around a little suede pad. No breath of air must waft over the pad when the wafer-thin, genuine gold leaf is on it, otherwise it curls up and can't be used any more. The gold leaves lie individually between the transparent, pink pages of a little square folder. With his special gilding knife, Wilhelm lifts a gold leaf onto the pad and very, very carefully breathes on it to make it lie flat. Then he cuts it to size. Wilhelm dabs a special oil on his right cheek, which he touches with a flat sable brush. With the tips of the bristles, he gently lifts a piece of gold leaf and lays it on the frame. When doing this, he does not dare breathe. Piece by piece, he lays the gold leaf on the frame and dabs it into the grooves with a fine, round brush. Finally, he blows off any remaining gold dust from the gleaming frame. Maria carefully wipes up the glittering dust that flies in small clouds across the table.

On Sunday mornings, Wilhelm lights the fire and brings the big zinc bathtub up from the cellar. He places the tub on a large mat that Maria has sewn out of white floor cloths to protect the polished floor while they bathe. Maria has a bath and goes to church alone. When she comes home, it still smells of soap and steam. The bathtub is standing there full of dirty water, and a clean Wilhelm is sitting at the window with his shaving kit opened up on the window ledge. His chin is thickly lathered. He makes faces in the mirror so that he can shave in every crease with the long razor. His eyes welcome her warmly, he nods to her. Maria briskly gets to work; she empties the bathtub and Wilhelm takes it to the cellar. Maria clears away the rest of the bathing things and the dirty laundry, and, in next to no time, everything is tidy. She sees to the fire, puts the frying pan on the stove, and fries some lean bacon. Then she adds three eggs, whisked up with salt, flour, and milk. Now it really smells of Sunday morning.

Even if Wilhelm has managed to go the whole week without knocking over a cup of coffee while signing, it is bound to happen at the nicely laid Sunday morning breakfast table. It is simply a part of his life. The coffee spills across the table, Maria and Wilhelm jump up, and the brown stain soaks into the tablecloth and drips on the floor. They are lucky if it doesn't splash on her dress or his trousers. Maria fetches a cloth, quickly mops up the coffee, and wipes the floor dry. She is cross with him. Can't Wilhelm be careful for once?! She uses both hands to sign, and she has never knocked anything off the table! Ill-humored, she sits down at the spoiled breakfast table again to go on eating. Not a single glance she gives him. But he kneels down in front of her chair, wrings his hands, and beats his breast. With exaggerated remorse, he begs for forgiveness. Maria battles with herself:

Will she never manage to be seriously angry with him? No matter how clumsy or reckless he is, he is never afraid of her scolding. Now she has to laugh as well! Wilhelm leaps up, hugs her, kisses her hands, neck, and mouth; she has to gasp for breath, and the only thing she can do is pinch him hard. Then he lets her go and the two of them laugh like delighted children. Maria knows from experience she can't fight with Wilhelm. It is not possible to quarrel with him, even if it seems necessary. Does he really have to toss plates and cups in the air like a juggler? Of course, he is almost an acrobat, but there will be broken pottery in the end. But—even if there are shards lying on the floor—she always has to laugh. And his keys! He is forever losing and forgetting all kinds of keys! And what else is he not losing and forgetting? He wonders at himself, consoles Maria with amusing explanations, and remains cheerful. Wilhelm doesn't think it worthwhile to go on carrying a grudge about things that have gone wrong. If he is reckless, Maria is thrifty. If he is forgetful, Maria is watchful. If Maria gets angry, Wilhelm makes jokes. If she is furious, he calms her down. How easy it is to get along with an arrangement like this! They trust each other and know that even their faults and shortcomings are in the other's safekeeping. It is not that they don't quarrel—they do have their disagreements!

Sunday morning also means helping Wilhelm button his collar. Why on earth do they have to be so stiffly starched? She ties his tie for him, too, but how can she get it done quickly if he keeps making funny faces and she has to sit down and laugh? What a cheerful, lovable husband she has!

Later in the morning, Wilhelm goes to church for High Mass. He stops near the main portal; it is always full of men there, even if there is plenty of room at the front of the church. He makes the sign of the cross and, every Sunday, tries to say the Lord's Prayer. But he can't get any further than the first three sentences, although Maria has often practiced it with him. He just can't remember it. "Hail Mary, full of grace, the Lord is with thee" is as far as he can get with that too. So he stands still for a while, makes the semblance of a genuflection, makes the sign of the cross, and leaves. Once outside, the first thing he does is light a cigarillo.

After leaving the church, Wilhelm visits his customers who have asked him to come and see them. He never goes out without paper and pencil. Without these aids, he does not feel at ease and secure. By gesturing and writing things down, he manages to communicate with the people he knows. On Sundays, Maria, too, has to do some writing—she sets up appointments for Wilhelm's customers. Many customers pass their house on the way to church. Maria wears her fresh white apron, the best tablecloth is on the table, the flat is cozy and tidy, and the roast smells good. With a cheerful, attentive face she takes orders from the customers and reliably passes them on to Wilhelm.

On Sunday afternoons, Wilhelm devotes one and a half hour to the joys of soccer. He goes to the pitch with his brothers, and, afterwards, they drink coffee together and tell Maria every detail of the match. With patience and interest she watches them, although she knows nothing at all about soccer. The main thing is her Wilhelm enjoys himself. When the weather is fine, they go for a walk later in the afternoon through the large village, across the meadows, and sometimes up to the tall beech woods or up to the Maar-Au where rare yellow calamine violets blossom.

51

The days become gray, cold, and damp. The glow from the flickering fire in the stove filters through the little gaps of the cooking rings, throwing dancing darts of light on the kitchen ceiling. The water in the kettle is softly humming. In the cellar, the jars are full and the potatoes are stored. Vegetables in the stoneware pots are covered with a cloth, a plate of wood, and a heavy stone. Carrots are bedded in sand, and the coal sludge glistens below the cellar window; winter can come!

Maria sits at the window watching the gray world sink into dusk. In Mrs. Woopen's garden across the road, black, bare branches stand stiffly. Lights go on in the houses. Now and then, someone walks along the street. Maria cannot recognize who it is. She doesn't switch the light on yet.

She likes sitting quietly at the window on evenings like this. Every so often, she glances at the door to see if someone comes in. She does not always feel the draft when the door opens. When that happens, the visitor knocks on the table, stamps on the floor, switches the light on, or suddenly stands in front of her in the dim room like a black shadow. At first she is startled, but then she immediately welcomes the visitor.

This evening, nobody comes. Maria places her hands on her rounded belly. She can feel her child moving. She has so much to think about. She remembers lunchtime that day. After having finished his meal, Wilhelm pushed his plate to the middle of the table and played the piano on the table top. They had seen in the movies how that is done. He pounded out wild chords on imaginary keys, made his fingers fly furiously up and down in passages and runs, threw his hands up in the air, and crashed them down on the keys again. The upper part of his body swayed to and fro, and his hair fell over his forehead. At the end of this powerful musical performance, he rose to his feet with a smile and bowed low before Maria, who was applauding. Then he took a step back in order to conduct. He fixed his eyes sternly on the great orchestra, rapped his baton on the stand, raised his hand for the upbeat, and began to conduct the unknown music, softly and smoothly. He swayed to the rhythm. His hands brought in the individual instruments, checked the volume here, and drew out the sound there. Ever mightier, his arms swayed and his whole body shook as he turned and twisted with the rhythm. His hands coaxed and rejected. Wilhelm acted out every detail he had seen as a child, when he watched the choir conductor from the gallery in the church. His facial expressions went through the whole scale of emotions: sorrow, ecstasy, joy, tenderness, passion. He cocked his ear as if listening to the very softest tones. Then, with fire in his eyes, he drove the orchestra into a powerful, sweeping, magnificent finale. With dramatic dignity, as if exhausted, Wilhelm tossed back his hair and bowed to all sides.

Maria had watched this performance in amazement and laughter, admiring Wilhelm's magnificent authoritative gesture when he wiped his brow and neck with the paint-plastered, turpentine-laced handkerchief. Was he not just like a great conductor?

When Wilhelm sat at the table again, he told Maria that he would like his son to be famous, celebrated by all the people, a shining star. Everybody would be in awe, and the papers would write *What? Parents are deaf?!* How proud that would make the two of them!

Maria shook her head and laughed. She replied, "If a son, then painter like you, to help you!"

A son, a partner at work? Wilhelm can see that—that would be nice. But wouldn't it be much better to have a daughter? A daughter can be dressed up so prettily. He would buy her the finest dresses from the best shops in Aachen. He would go for walks with her and say, "My daughter!" Perhaps she will be able to sing beautifully! All the people in the whole world would listen to their daughter singing. Wilhelm was so excited, he stood up again and mimed a singer singing her heart out. Again, Maria laughed. *Wilhelm is so funny!* If her child is a girl, she will be able to sew her everything out of old clothes, and it won't cost anything. She will teach her daughter how to sew, too.

Such are Maria's thoughts in the dark room. Both Maria and Wilhelm always speak of a child who can hear. In their imagination the child is never deaf like them. And yet, Maria is afraid. Afraid of what?

Her deaf friends tell her she should be glad if her child cannot hear? She should be worried about having a hearing child! A hearing child is not good for deaf parents. Hearing children will disown, abandon, and be ashamed of deaf parents! They go away, they reject their parents! Their friends have given them numerous examples. If her child can hear, they say, Maria will shed many, many tears later. She will receive only ingratitude.

Maria sighs deeply. These examples are alarming. Can hearing children be so wicked to their deaf parents? Maybe she should wish for a deaf child. Such a child would be just like Wilhelm and herself. They would understand each other, get on well, and always stick together. They would love each other and be happy. Would that not be better?

Maria thinks of her father. Last time she visited Freilingen, the previous spring, Aunt Barbara told her something that distressed her very much—once Father wanted to move to America with all of his family. But Father was informed that America had a law that prevented him from taking his deaf children to the new country. People with a hereditary disease or defect, like Maria and Christina, were not permitted to become American citizens. So, Father stayed in Freilingen with his children. This story shocked Maria. Is it so terrible to be deaf? Is it so certain that such people will always have deaf children? Friends, teachers, and doctors tell her that if at least one parent was born hearing in a healthy family and became deaf later through illness or an accident, then there is hope that the child will hear. But she and Wilhelm were both born deaf and dumb and some of their siblings were, too.

Maria has a heavy heart. Deep down, she would prefer to give birth to a child who can hear. She wants her Father in Freilingen to have a hearing grandchild—how proud Maria would be! Oh yes, she wants her child to be like other children, not stared at with curiosity, pity, or even mockery. A hearing child! She hardly dares think of it, yet pictures what it would be like. Wilhelm would be proud, and everyone would congratulate him. When the child was older, she would be able to say "come in," if anyone knocked on the door. She would talk to people and interpret everything for Maria. On Sunday mornings, she would go visit customers with Wilhelm. And people would be amazed at how she could use sign language with her father and talk to hearing people, too. To offices, to the doctor, shopping—she would go everywhere with them and interpret, and they would never be without help. Life would be much better and easier for her and Wilhelm.

But what if the child is ashamed of her parents? What if she rejects them? No! No! She can't believe that! She will love her child, look after her, and spoil her like no other mother. She will protect her and never let her hear anything nasty. She will watch the child's mouth closely when she talks to hearing people and will try to understand what she is saying. The child will have to tell her everything she talked about with other people; Maria will have to watch everything, to know everything. But Maria is still afraid that a hearing child might reject her.

Reject! That terrible word has slipped unnoticed into the very depths of her subconscious, like poison. The poison of fear is in her soul. Maria does not realize this.

Her mood brightens when she thinks of the May Fair last year. She was in Freilingen with Wilhelm. Together they walked along the path from Stein down to Grindel Creek and followed the water toward its source, Weiler Creek. It was a sunny, warm May day. Mauve lady's smock was in bloom along the banks. Maria dragged Wilhelm past Am Stockebähne, Father's field, and into a little copse, also owned by Father. Springtime, home, freedom, her youth and good health, her love for Wilhelm—it all filled her with an overwhelming feeling of happiness. She was twenty-nine years old and had been married to Wilhelm for a year. In a spring forest in Freilingen, they made love for the very first time. Later Maria told Father about it, and she was proud and glad.

Maria stands up. In the dark, she gropes for the sink drawer and finds some matches. She lights the two candles on the towel rack with the bright flame. The room is lit by their soft glow. The Savior on the cross shimmers like silver in the candlelight. Maria looks at Him for a long time. If only she knew why, as they say, He had died for everyone. He is God, and is in Heaven, and knows Wilhelm and her? He can do everything, but he hangs on the cross? It is terrible, to hang on the cross. He can do everything, and yet He made her and Wilhelm deaf. Does He really know that she is praying now? Hearing people have told her she should pray. She stands near the stove at an angle to the crucifix, so that she can see the door if anyone comes in. She puts her hands together. *Dear God! I beg you. Please, you let my child hear. Please.* There are several long candles in the drawer. Every evening, Maria lights the candles near the crucifix. When she is alone with Wilhelm late at night, and the door has been locked, and the cloth hung over the large keyhole, she prays together with him. Maria's mouth moves soundlessly, slowly, and very distinctly. Wilhelm's hands are folded like hers, and he watches her lips. Reading them, he prays with her, and assumes that Maria knows the meaning of the *Our Father* and *Ave Maria*. They pray for a hearing child.

When they go to bed, their hands are clasped. When the lamp is switched off, they can no longer talk to each other. They do not hear the other's breathing in the darkness, but they feel each other. Maria does not want to hear. Not since she has known Wilhelm. She wants to be like him. He cannot hear, so it is good that she cannot hear either. Their child, though, soon to be born, should not be deaf.

52

The year 1927 has begun. Wilhelm has repainted and wallpapered the two rooms of the flat. A crib with soft pillows is standing ready. Maria is still carrying her baby. They are very close, although they do not know each other yet.

On 13 February, a Sunday morning, Maria gives birth to a daughter in the bedroom. With a pounding heart, Wilhelm gazes in wonder at the freshly bathed, naked child that Dr. Antoine places right in the middle of the kitchen table. As the weeks go by, Maria feels healthy and refreshed.

The winter sun filters through the net curtains into Maria's flat. In the bedroom, there is frost around the edges of the windowpanes. It is Sunday.

Maria, Alexandrine

Die glückliche Geburt eines gesunden Mädchens zeigen hocherfreut an

Willy Sistermann u. Frau
Maria geb. Giefer

Eilendorf, den 13. Februar 1927

The announcement of the birth of Wilhelm and Maria's daughter, Maria Alexandrine.

Wilhelm is out visiting customers, and Maria is working in the kitchen. The baby girl, who they have named Maria, after her mother, is asleep in her crib, fed and clean. Maria tends to her with care and delight. She smiles and softly speaks to the child. Maria treads lightly, handles everything she has to move with care so as not to make a noise, although she does not know yet whether her child can hear.

Every day, friends and relatives come to see the new addition to the family. Everyone is careful not to wake her. Everyone, including Maria, is afraid of discovering the truth. Is it too soon to find out? Maria's mind is restless. Often, when she is alone, she broods over her baby. Is the baby like herself? If the baby can hear, she will be different than her, and live in a different world. Should she, as her mother, not be able to sense it? She wants to know! The baby cries, drinks, and sleeps like any other baby. Where will the child belong in the end? Maria tackles her anxiety bravely. Isn't her baby sweet, even if it should turn out that little Maria can't hear? A moment ago she held her in her arms, washed her tiny soft body in the tub, changed her, and gently brushed her silky hair. Everything looks healthy and normal—the tiny hands and feet, the little nose and mouth—and what cute little ears! Maria can hardly believe that she gave birth to this perfect child! Wilhelm and Maria, made into one—and there she is! Maria's happiness would be complete if only the little ears can hear. There's nothing to be seen. Maria can only wait.

After singing in the choir at High Mass, Josef Hahnengress always comes around on Sundays to say hello. He is always in a good mood; he makes jokes and enjoys seeing Maria's shoulders shaking with laughter. He inquires if everything is all right or if his help is needed with business matters. Today, he wants to have a look at the baby, and Maria is pleased to show her to him. "Sleeping," she says, and puts her finger to her mouth. Gently, she opens the bedroom door and they tiptoe over to the crib. It is cold in the unheated room. The little head is poking out from under the cover. Little Maria is lying on her side, on her left ear. Shining hair peeps out from below the white bonnet. Her little fists are slightly open. Gently breathing, she lies asleep. Maria looks at Wilhelm's friend, and in his smile there is a question, a doubt. Neither of them touches the baby's crib; they are both quite still. Then Josef Hahnengress raises his forefinger, which means "Watch carefully, Maria!" Maria sees him purse his lips and briefly puff out his cheeks. Of course, she has not heard the slightest sound of the whistle. At the same time, she sees her baby start with fright. Her eyes open wide, she screws up her face and begins to cry.

Maria clutches her hands to her heart. "Can hear! Can hear!" she shouts, hugs Josef, and picks up the crying child, holds her tightly, and weeps and weeps. She sobs and sniffs and laughs, and the tears run down her cheeks. "Wilhelm! Wilhelm! Pity, Wilhelm not here! Wilhelm very glad! Very glad!" Maria shouts with joy. She runs out to the landing with her child and calls loudly for Wilhelm's father and mother, and Lisa and Heinrich. They come rushing upstairs, along with Luise and Josef and other friends, too.

"What is matter?" they ask. "Why you shout?" They see her laughing and crying.

She points to her child in utter excitement and keeps saying, "Can hear! Can hear!" She knows for sure! She has seen it! Josef Hahnengress has to tell them about it, and Luise claps her hands and starts crying, too, and they all stare at the crying child as if seeing her for the first time.

Maria can hardly wait for Wilhelm to come home. When he finally walks through the door, he sees a kitchen full of people and a radiant, weeping Maria with the baby in her arms. She rushes over to him. She holds little Maria out to him and, with the forefinger of her free hand, she keeps tapping her own ear and pointing to the child, "Can hear! Can hear!" she repeats. The others nod their heads in confirmation and Maria tells him what has happened. Wilhelm stands openmouthed, reading Maria's lips with questioning, astonished eyes. Maria's face shows absolute certainty. Overwhelmed, Wilhelm takes her and the child in his arms.

Then he pulls out his handkerchief and dries his excited wife's tears. "Glad! Glad! Glad! Glad!" He says it over and over again, and puts his hand on his heart.

Wilhelm's father says that the baby needs a rest now. They all go to the crib with Maria and watch her put her hearing child in the crib and cover her up. In the kitchen, Wilhelm pours a glass of cognac for everyone, and they celebrate as if the child had only just been born. Maria gradually calms down. Wilhelm strokes her head and says, "Don't cry, don't cry."

"Can't help it," she says laughing, and then blows her nose loudly.

The Sunday morning is all in a muddle. The midday meal is not on the table in time. When they all leave, Maria holds Heinrich by the sleeve and says, "Listen! Maria quiet? Not cry anymore?" Heinrich tells her that it is all quiet in the bedroom, and the child must be asleep. How is Maria to know if her child is crying when she is out of sight? Often, in the coming months, somebody will have to come up and tell her that her little daughter is crying. Then, startled, she will run to the crib, pick up her child, and say, "Poor child. Poor child. Your Mama cannot hear when you cry."

Maria writes to her father in Freilingen: *Your grandchild can hear! Wilhelm and I very happy, very happy*! She asks him to tell everyone in the village.

Maria is thirty years old now, a wife and a mother. Her entire being radiates joy from inside. How much happiness has been granted to her! She loves and is loved; motherhood is a wonderful task.

Wilhelm and Maria rarely sense the dark shadows that impose themselves from the outside on their lives. Millions of Germans are out of work, but Wilhelm almost always has something to do. Even if he does not earn much, the family gets by and is content. He has been allowed to carry his title of master craftsman. In 1921, with the help of Josef Hahnengress, he had written the following letter:

To the Trade Corporation, Aachen,

Application by the Painter and Decorator Assistant Wilhelm Sistermann for admission to the Examination for Mastership.

The undersigned (a deaf man) kindly hereby requests admittance to the trade examination for Mastership for the painter and decorator profession and wishes to submit the following documents:

1. *A self-written personal account of my life.*
2. *Proof of the current journeyman's examination taken.*
3. *Record of the activities of employment as a journeyman.*
4. *Record of my work as a self-employed person.*
5. *Official birth certificate.*
6. *Certificate of good conduct.*

As a master piece, a work sample, please accept the redecorating of a house entrance hall (done in oil paints) in Eilendorf, Coelssstrasse 5, right next to the Nirm tram stop. For the costs of any expenses incurred by the examination and for the examination fees, I will of course bear them in person.

> *Since I have two younger siblings who are also deaf, I am the main source of maintenance for my parents, and my father wishes to have my younger brother (now out of school) being apprenticed to me, I am respectfully requesting to be kindly considered for this examination.*

He enclosed his trade license from the Eilendorf authorities. In addition, the mayor certified that Wilhelm had done the redecorating work for the Eilendorf schools independently and to complete satisfaction. The Association of Independent Tradesmen of Eilendorf and Atsch also sent a supporting statement declaring

> *that the applicant has practiced his trade independently, for four years. Grievances over faulty workmanship have to date never been brought to the attention of the Association. Sistermann has been a member of the above mentioned association for one year.*

The application for the Mastership examination was turned down.

In 1925, Wilhelm received a license from the District Committee of Aachen for a fee of 20 Gold Marks, for the storing and selling of the poisons lead, zinc, and chrome-based paints. Wilhelm arranges his workshop according to the regulations. In 1929, he applies once more for admission to the Mastership examination, along with a request to be exempted from the theoretical portion. He justifies the request due to his "lack of hearing and speech."

This application is also turned down.

Wilhelm has been employing his younger brother Josef as his assistant for years, but he now gets an order from the Trade Chamber to dismiss Josef immediately. As Josef has had no proper training in the painting and decorating trade, he is considered an apprentice. But Wilhelm is not authorized to train apprentices. He is threatened with compulsory discharge by the police authority and with prosecution by the official Bar.

Now his hearing friend, Josef Hahnengress, has to stand up for him yet again. So much trouble and struggle! Just because Wilhelm is deaf!

Wilhelm would have liked to have opportunities for further training, but there aren't any for him. His father had, after much urging and pleading from Wilhelm, enrolled him in the Applied Arts School in Aachen, in 1921. Several times each week, Wilhelm went to the school, in addition to keeping up his own, independent work. But after a year, he gave up. There was no one there to talk to, no one to explain things to him. He could not bear the isolation. As time passes, no one mentions the examination. It becomes habit to call him a master of the trade, and Josef stays with him for good as his journeyman. Josef is easy to train and is an additional help to Wilhelm because he can read the customers' lips and they can easily understand his speech. The two deaf brothers in their white overalls riding their bicycles are a jolly team, well-liked by the Eilendorfers.

Rarely, though, a customer takes advantage of Wilhelm's deafness. Once, he was led to understand that individual floor boards were to be patched up in all of the rooms of a certain house. He drew up the cost estimate, but when he was about to start his work, he saw, to his alarm, that all of the rooms in the house had completely new, unfinished wooden floorboards. For that, of course, he needed many more materials and additional hours for labor. Since he could not communicate with the customer, Wilhelm relied on him to be reasonable when he received Wilhelm's bill. But after the work was done, the customer paid only the amount of the estimate. Wilhelm felt powerless, and Maria's attempt at correcting the situation by talking to the customer was also in vain. So they gave up on it and felt humiliated; they wondered how hearing people could be such scoundrels. This customer was a well-off high-ranking official, and he seemed proud of his "achievement." Another time, a wealthy academic, whose large, luxurious house Wilhelm had completely redecorated, inside and out, defrauded Wilhelm of 400 Marks, a small fortune. Such a thing never happened to him with most of the villagers; they even gave him presents in addition to what they owed for the work done.

53

When Wilhelm's parents die in quick succession, the loss does not affect Wilhelm too painfully. Maria gives him so much emotional and practical support that he feels completely at home and secure. His siblings Lisa, Luise, and Josef marry deaf spouses, and the spacious house has enough room for them all. Maria and Wilhelm move down from the attic to the middle floor. It is a sunny flat, with three nice rooms. The kitchen and living area has a large window facing the street. Here, they can stay for good. Here, their little girl will grow up and learn sign language, the language that her deaf parents and relatives use. She will learn to lipread so as to understand her parents when they speak to her in their deaf voices, and she will also learn to converse in the language of hearing people.

Maria sets her child on the windowsill, holds her by the hands, and smiles at her. "All my litt-le duck-ies are swim-ming in the lake." Maria cannot go any further. She speaks the first line of the song over and over again, heavily, in monotone. Little Maria joins in with her and sways to the rhythm.

Wilhelm also "sings" his song to his daughter every day, carrying her on his arm or letting her ride on his knee. The only song of his life is one he has made up himself and, like Maria's song, it has only one note. Wilhelm is sure that it is a song, and it is called "Tarakapafoto—Tarakapafoto—Tarakapafoto."

Little Maria likes the song, and she sings it with her father while he watches her mouth.

Wilhelm often says to his daughter "Mama deaf—I deaf—you hear. Wonderful! A miracle!"

Wilhelm doesn't mind Maria spending four weeks each midsummer in Freilingen with their child, so that she can help with the harvest. Maria's

Wilhelm and Maria with little Maria in 1929.

sisters Setta and Christina, who both are married and living in Cologne, also come to the farm to help. Father picks Maria up from the railway station in his black, open landau carriage, the first in Freilingen.

On Sunday, 25 August 1929, Wilhelm decides to accompany his wife and child to Freilingen. They want to travel via Cologne, so, early that morning, they get on the Paris–Warsaw Northern Express train in the main station in Aachen. It is the first time they are riding on a fast, luxury train, the fulfillment of a long-held dream of Wilhelm. Maria remembers her father's admonition that he drove into her as a schoolgirl: Always take the last carriage on a train!

Wilhelm, Maria, and little Maria survived the crash of the Paris–Warsaw Northern Express in August 1929. Wilhelm took this photograph.

After a brief dispute with Wilhelm, Maria has her way, and they board the last carriage. Wilhelm finds so much caution unnecessary. Their little girl sits between them in the compartment. During the ride, Wilhelm and Maria put their hands on the child's knee, and the girl playfully turns her parents' golden wedding rings around. The parents sign to their child and the other passengers watch with interest. All of a sudden, there is a terrible jolt. Little Maria is thrown under the opposite bench, suitcases crash down, and one man has blood all over his face. Maria and Wilhelm lie in a tangle with other people, and Wilhelm's leg is injured. Outside the shattered windows it is dark.

The train has derailed and crashed into an embankment just before Buir, near Cologne. It is the worst railway accident of the 1920s, and it shocks the whole of Europe. Thirteen people are dead and forty are critically injured at a time when train accidents are rare events. Maria, Wilhelm, and their child climb out of the wreckage. The carriages are completely wedged into one another; two carriages are smashed together. Trembling, they realize that they have survived. What they see is dreadful. Later, they read in the newspapers that most of the passengers on the luxury train were foreigners. They came from Warsaw, Moscow, London, New York, Paris, Marseilles, and Poitiers. In the midst of the chaos, people come hurrying to help. When Wilhelm's head is clear again, he sets up his camera and photographs the scene. In one photograph, Maria is standing with their daughter in front of the wreckage of the train. Wilhelm enlarges it, frames it behind glass, and hangs it on the wall in their living room.

The new reign of Hitler has begun. A photograph of swastika-emblazoned flags and uniforms now hangs in the Sistermann's flat. Wilhelm also has hung up a photograph of the Führer. Like many other people, he and Maria hope and believe that Hitler will change the hard lot of Germany for the better. Many things will be different from now. There is work again, but there is also re-armament and new laws.

On 14 July 1933, the government passes the Law for the Prevention of Offspring with Hereditary Diseases, and a sense of unease and anxiety now pervades the house on Steinstrasse. The law states that anyone who suffers from certain illnesses or congenital disabilities, including deafness, must be sterilized. It is the duty of medical professionals to report all patients who have these illnesses or disabilities, and the people must appear before the Hereditary Health Court to determine if they will be sterilized. Fearful and upset, Maria, Wilhelm, and their friends talk agitatedly among themselves. They want to resist, but how are they to do it? Anyone who refuses is arrested by the police. Wilhelm's brother Josef has run away and gone into hiding. But the police find him and deliver him straight to the hospital. The district physician for the Aachen area puts in a request for Wilhelm and Maria to be sterilized because of their hereditary deafness.

Maria's father in Freilingen arranges for her case to be reviewed before the Hereditary Health Court. He accompanies her to court and gives her moral support. A teacher for the deaf serves as the interpreter. The court in Aachen affirms Maria's hereditary defect according to the law, even though she has given birth to a hearing child. Wilhelm's sterilization has already been decided, so the court decides

> *by reason of the good personal impression the court has received from Mrs. Sistermann née Giefer, it considers it highly improbable that the same will ever practice extramarital sexual intercourse, so that there will be no prob-*

ability of her having any more children after sterilization of her husband. In acknowledgment of the evidence heard and all the circumstances which have been brought to bear, the court has seen fit to dispense with sterilization and has to that effect turned down the application.

Dr. Hurk, the district physician for the Aachen area and also an observer of the Hereditary Health Court in Aachen, files an objection to the court's decision. Therefore, the case is considered by the Hereditary Health Supreme Court in Cologne, and it rescinds the judgment of the court in Aachen, which means Maria is sentenced to sterilization, just like her husband.

It is terrible for both of them. They have tried everything to avert this fate. So much running around and letter-writing, so much worry, so much well-meaning but useless advice from all sides. Maria is tired of it. She does not want to fight any more.

Why should she go on rebelling like the other deaf people? Why go on feeling unwholesome, inferior, degraded, humiliated, insulted, helpless, and ashamed of her defect? Wasn't it God who made her deaf?!

When Wilhelm comes home a few evenings later, little Maria is there alone. "Where Mama?" he asks gently. His face is always kind.

"Mama dressed well, gone to Aachen with bag. There is note from Mama," she replies.

When Wilhelm reads the note, his face becomes contorted. His daughter has never seen him looking like that. He takes down the picture of the Führer, spits on it, and hurls it against the wall above the stove. The glass shatters. The frame breaks, the picture flutters under the coal box. His daughter becomes frightened watching all this.

Wilhelm sits down on a chair next to the sewing machine, and when little Maria comes to him, he lifts her onto his knees. He puts his arms around her and cries bitterly for a long time.

Soon afterward, a policeman comes to the house. He is from Eilendorf. Wilhelm's youngest brother Heinrich has to interpret to tell Wilhelm that he is to pack a bag and follow the policeman. As quietly as Maria went to the hospital, Wilhelm goes now as well. The policeman walks several paces behind Wilhelm so that it does not look as if he has been arrested. Wilhelm stays in the hospital for sixteen days. As compensation for being sterilized, he gets a social welfare benefit of nine Reichsmarks per week.

Wilhelm and Maria must face the reality that they will only ever have this one child! Maria loves her daughter with the greatest passion and tenderness. She is immensely proud of her child. If she goes shopping with her in Aachen, she tells the assistant with shining eyes, "This my daughter!" Wilhelm spoils his hearing daughter like a princess. He plays and has fun with her, takes her for rides on his bicycle, takes her along to visit the customers, and buys her whatever she wants. She also goes to the Deaf Club with them and is shown off proudly. Wherever they go, Wilhelm and Maria make her speak. Then, when people say in surprise, "She can speak so beautifully!" her parents are overjoyed. They themselves will never be able to hear their child speak.

Maria and Wilhelm value their hearing child higher than themselves; they consider her natural ability to hear as untold riches. Because she can hear, they think, all she can feel must be happiness. And yet a fear grows in Maria. In the depths of her soul lies the unforgotten word *reject*! Will her child reject her? At home she sees the little girl continually moving her lips, singing. Maria asks uneasily, "Why you always sing?"

"I like singing. Singing is lovely!" her daughter replies. Maria is hurt because she has no part in it. She doesn't know what singing is or why it is so nice. She only feels that her child is different from her. When her daughter speaks to hearing people, Maria watches her mouth the whole time. Afterwards, she wants to know everything that was said, and if she thinks little Maria has left out something, she will complain, "but you talked a long time, talked exactly half an hour, you only repeat five minutes to me." And probably more bitterly and reproachfully than Maria intends, her daughter often sees the awful words, "You not tell me everything! You reject me!"

Maria is torn by an inner conflict. If her daughter wants books, she buys her whatever she wants. But she is also afraid of the books that keep her child occupied. Maria herself has not read a book for many years. Nevertheless, she proudly says, "My daughter reads a lot!"

Maria regularly receives a magazine from the Hamelin Life Insurance Company. In it, she sees pictures of the story *The Pied Piper of Hamelin*. They make Maria pensive and worried because the children in the story cannot escape. The Pied Piper's music is so beautiful in their ears that they follow him to their death. Her child seeks out and craves people who know a great deal, speak beautifully, and develop a rich vocabulary. Maria warns her child, "Very much knowledge not necessary. Most important, life in order."

Sometimes, when the family goes out, little Maria pleads with her parents, "Don't talk on the street! All people stare." Maria is alarmed. Is her child ashamed of her parents? She does not know that other children make fun of her daughter, and that there are also grownups who slight her because she has deaf parents and relatives.

Maria and her child were born into different worlds: one of absolute silence, the other full of sounds and voices. What a good thing Maria has Wilhelm. She always watches him from the window when he leaves, and without taking her eyes off him, says to their daughter, "Papa fine man, you must honor Papa."

The happiness, the sense of a common bond, and deep trust of the small family is not without difficulty; there is sorrow, loneliness, and tension. Maria realizes that it must have been hard for her mother to have deaf children. It is hard for Maria to have a hearing child. But no one tells little Maria how hard it is to be the only hearing child of deaf parents. Yet, Maria and Wilhelm have made a good life together. They are a perfect couple; they love and understand each other.